A CHILDREN'S HISTORY OF

Britain

AND IRELAND

Christopher Wright
Illustrated by David Salariya

Kingfisher Books

First published in 1986 by Kingfisher Books Limited
Elsley Court, 20–22 Great Titchfield Street
London W1P 7AD
A Grisewood & Dempsey Company

BRITISH LIBRARY CATALOGUING IN PUBLICATION DATA
Wright, Christopher
    Britain and Ireland: an illustrated history.
    1. Great Britain-History-Juvenile literature
    I. Title   II. Salariya, David   III. Willis, Shirley
    941   DA30
ISBN 0 86272 220 9

Edited by Caroline Royds and Trudi Braun
Designed by Ben White
Phototypeset by Tradespools Ltd, Frome, Somerset
Colour separations by Newsele Litho Ltd, Milan, London
Printed in Hong Kong

A CHILDREN'S HISTORY OF

Britain

AND IRELAND

ACKNOWLEDGEMENTS

My thanks are due to Margaret Bircumshaw, Carol Wright and Richard Wright who have read parts of this history in typescript, and to the boys and girls in their classes who have done the same. The schools are Blean Primary School near Canterbury in Kent, Treadworth Junior School in Gloucester, and Calton Junior School in Gloucester.

I would also like to acknowledge my debt to the authors of the different volumes of Penguin Education's *History of Britain* and the Longman secondary Histories – both of them model histories for the use of junior readers. I have learned particularly from the imaginative way they present their material. Throughout the book, I have constantly referred to the one-volume Oxford *Illustrated History of Britain*, edited by K.O. Morgan, and would like to acknowledge my debt to its contributors.

The author and publishers would like to thank the following institutions, photographers and artists for permission to reproduce illustrations and for supplying photographs:

17 Ronald Sheridan; 19 Michael Holford; 23 top British Museum, bottom Reading Museum and Art Gallery; 25 West Country Tourist Board; 28 Cambridge University Museum of Archaeology and Anthropology; 32, 37, 40 British Museum; 43 National Monuments Record. Air Photographs. Crown Copyright Reserved; 45 left Museum of London; 49–50 Fishbourne Roman Palace; 56 British Museum; 58 Chris Fright; 61 W.T. Jones/Mucking Post-Excavation, Thurrock Museum; 67 ZEFA; 68 Board of Trinity College, Dublin; 71 Irish Tourist Board/Brian Lynch; 72 Board of Trinity College, Dublin; 74 British Museum; 76 Bodleian Library. MS. Digby 20, fol. 194.; 78 C.M. Dixon; 80 National Museum of Ireland, Dublin; 81 British Library; 84 C.M. Dixon; 85 Northern Ireland Tourist Board; 87 top British Library; 90 Dean and Chapter Library, The College, Durham; 92 J & C Bord; 93 National Maritime Museum, London; 98 British Museum; 101 J & C Bord; 102 National Museum of Ireland, Dublin; 106 Giraudon; 109 Universitetets Oldsaksamling, Oslo; 111 Ashmolean Museum; 116 Mike S. Duffy/York Archaeological Trust; 120 left British Library; 121, 122, 123, 124, 127 right Michael Holford; 128 Public Records Office; 129 British Library; 133 Cathedral Gifts Ltd, Canterbury; 143 Picturepoint Ltd; 145 Michael Holford; 147 Ronald Sheridan; 149 Copyright Reserved. Reproduced by Gracious Permission of Her Majesty the Queen; 150 Britain on View; 153 Master and Fellows of Corpus Christi College, Cambridge; 157 Master and Fellows of Trinity College, Cambridge; 158 Britain on View; 159 Mansell Collection; 163 Britain on View; 164–65 Copyright Bibliothèque Royale Albert Ier, Bruxelles. "Manuscrit 13076–77 fol. 24 verso; 169 British Library; 173 British Library; 177, 179 Britain on View; 181 & 183 National Portrait Gallery, London; 182 Reproduced by Gracious Permission of Her Majesty the Queen; 185 Royal Armouries, H. M. Tower of London; 187 Mary Rose Trust; 190 Scala, Firenze, Bibl. Nazionale; 191 right British Museum; 193 Victoria and Albert Museum/A.C. Cooper; 196–197 Society of Antiquaries, London; 199 British Library; 201 National Portrait Gallery, London; 208 Fotomas Index; 210 National Portrait Gallery, London; 215 Reproduced by Gracious Permission of Her Majesty the Queen; 220 Mansell Collection; 224 Fotomas Index; 228 BBC Hulton Picture Library; 230 Mansell Collection; 232 National Portrait Gallery, London; 237 Mansell Collection; 241 & 246 National Trust; 247 The Tate Gallery, London; 248 ZEFA; 251 & 252 Mansell Collection; 259 Picturepoint Ltd; 261 top Mansell Collection, bottom Aberdeen Art Gallery; 264 Mansell Collection; 266 The Fotomas Index; 269 Mansell Collection; 270 Sir John Soane's Museum; 276 Royal Geographical Society/Fotomas Index; 278 The Bridgeman Art Library; 283, 284, 287 BBC Hulton Picture Library; 291, 295 Popperfoto; 297, 298 BBC Hulton Picture Library; 305, 306 Popperfoto; 308 BBC Hulton Picture Library; 311 Reflex Picture Agency; 314 top ZEFA; 314 bottom A. Ogden & Sons (Demolitions) Ltd.
Picture research by Jackie Cookson
Maps by Ralph Orme
Additional illustrations by Shirley Willis, Tony Richards and Nick Harris

CONTENTS

Chapter 1
page 8   The First People

Chapter 2
page 16   Farmers and Traders

Chapter 3
page 29   The Roman Conquest

Chapter 4
page 38   Life in Roman Britain

Chapter 5
page 49   Building A Colony

Chapter 6
page 57   Decline and Fall

Chapter 7
page 61   The German Invaders

Chapter 8
page 67   The Early Christians

Chapter 9
page 86   Anglo-Saxon Life

Chapter 10
page 100   Celtic Britain and Ireland
              (500–1066)

Chapter 11
page 106   People from the North

Chapter 12
page 111   Alfred the Great

Chapter 13
page 116   Wessex and the Danelaw

Chapter 14
page 124   The Norman Conquest

Chapter 15
page 129   The First Norman Kings

Chapter 16
page 134   The Feudal System

Chapter 17
page 142   Crusades and Councils

Chapter 18
page 148   Rebellion over the borders

Chapter 19
page 154   The Medieval Church

Chapter 20
page 158   Town Life in Medieval
              England

Chapter 21
page 166   Kings, Barons and Peasants

Chapter 22
page 171   In Quick Succession

Chapter 23
page 174   The Growth of Trade

Chapter 24
page 178   The Power of the Throne

Chapter 25
page 180   King Henry VIII

Chapter 26
page 188   Great Explorations

Chapter 27
page 195   Catholics and Protestants

Chapter 28
page 200   The Reign of Elizabeth I

Chapter 29
page 209   Plotters and Parliaments

Chapter 30
page 214   The Parting of the Ways

Chapter 31
page 221   Civil War

Chapter 32
page 227   Cromwell's Protectorate

Chapter 33
page 233   Plague and Fire

Chapter 34
page 238   Charles II and the
            Popish Plot

Chapter 35
page 242   The End of the Dictator-Kings

Chapter 36
page 246   England in the 18th Century

Chapter 37
page 254   The American War of
            Independence

Chapter 38
page 260   Roads, Railways and
            Factories

Chapter 39
page 268   Social Reform and Change

Chapter 40
page 276   The British Empire

Chapter 41
page 282   The end of the 19th Century

Chapter 42
page 288   The World at War

Chapter 43
page 293   Ireland and Home Rule

Chapter 44
page 297   Between the Wars

Chapter 45
page 301   The Second World War

Chapter 46
page 307   The ever-changing present

The First People

The first men and women settled in Britain in about 250,000 BC, but the story of the human race begins in Africa about two million years ago. Such lengths of time are almost impossible to imagine. To help us to do so, one expert has suggested that we translate the time-scale into our experience by piling up 2p pieces. If we imagine that one 2p piece stands for 100 years, and we pile the pieces one on top of another, a pile of four pieces will represent time from the reign of Queen Elizabeth I (1558–1603) to the present day. Nine pieces will stand for the years since 1066, when the Normans conquered England, and twenty for the period since Jesus Christ.

Only by building up a pile of 2,500 2p pieces (which would be 4½ metres high if it could be made to stand up) can time since the first human settlement in Britain be represented. And it would take 20,000 coins – a pile 34 metres high – to represent the time that has passed since the first humans emerged in Africa.

Written records of people living in Britain start with Julius Caesar's account of the inhabitants of Kent in 55 BC, about 2000 years ago. The only evidence we have of earlier human life are the few remains which men and women have left behind them. These include their bones, the bones of the animals they killed and ate, the remains of the places where they lived, their burial sites, their weapons and their stone tools. With occasional exceptions, their wooden tools have decayed, as have their clothes and buildings. In the case of the earliest peoples of all, tools are often the only relics which have survived; the evidence is tantalizingly little, but it is all we have.

Pebble tools have been discovered in the Olduvai Gorge in Tanzania, and in other parts of Africa, belonging to the first human beings who lived about two million years ago. These people resembled the apes from which they were descended. They were about one metre tall, and had clumsy hands and limbs. Their brains were small compared with human brains today; but they were different from the apes in that they could walk upright, which meant that their arms were free for work of all sorts.

Unlike many hunting animals – lions and tigers, for instance – humans did not have razor-sharp teeth. But they were able to shape stone tools, and used these to attack their prey and to cut up its flesh after they had killed it. The early tools were large, rough pebbles, which had been chipped away to give them sharp points and edges. Bones have been found which suggest that human beings fought and killed baboons (whose marrow

6,000 years ago	People now put bone handles on their stone axes, used razor-sharp flints, and made mugs and bowls of pottery.
10,000 years ago	People were using bows and arrows. They painted on the walls of their caves. Stone tools were now very sharp.
250,000 years ago	The first Britons used stone hand axes. They hunted, fished and ate berries. They lived in windbreaks and caves.
500,000 years ago	Men and women first discovered how to use fire in China. Now they began to speak, not grunt.
2,000,000 years ago	The first people lived in Africa, and were like apes, with long arms. They used sharp-edged pebble tools which they chipped.

9

In earliest times ice covered Britain north of the Thames estuary. Britain was joined to France across the Channel.

bones they split open with their stone tools so that they could suck out the juice), and the southern apes who resembled themselves. From the beginning, people were using their intelligence to get ahead of their rivals.

Like these rivals they hunted in groups, and travelled about as they hunted. Like the Australian aborigines of today, they had no permanent homes, but erected windbreaks or shelters of leaves and twigs for the night. They liked to live by lakes or rivers because their prey came there to drink. As well as larger animals, they lived on small helpless creatures such as frogs, mice and young birds, and snakes.

As they travelled, hunting their prey, these early people spread out from Africa into Asia. But they never entered Europe, most of which was at that time covered in ice. They would have died if they had done so, for they wore no clothes and had not discovered fire. In their hotter climate, they had no need of it for warmth, and perhaps they baked their meat in the hot ground or fried it on hot stones. (Australian aborigines of today have been observed baking kangaroo meat by burying it in the hot sand.)

Fire seems to have been used first by men and women in Beijing in China, in about 500,000 BC. It was at this time, too, that the precious power of speech was developed. Now people were no longer limited to expressing their emotions of love or grief or terror by grunts, or to warning their fellows of danger by a mixture of sounds and signals. They could exchange thoughts, ideas and plans for the next day.

For long periods during the hundreds and thousands of years when the early people were spreading into India, China, Java and Malaysia, most of Britain remained under thick ice. There were four great ice ages, but they were not continuous. In the years between them the climate reached tropical heat. Elephants and hippopotamuses lived north of the river Thames. At that time, Britain was literally part of Europe, for it was attached to it by a strip of land called the land bridge across what is now the English Channel.

It was during the longest of the warm spells, known as the "Great Interglacial", that human beings settled in Britain, around 250,000 BC. A section of a fossilized skull, thought to have belonged to a young woman who lived at this time, has been found in Swanscombe, near Gravesend in Kent. These are the first human remains found in Britain. The settlers were about 1.5 metres tall, and their brains were twice the size of those of the earliest people. Their hands were less clumsy, and with them they made more advanced stone tools. They are called the people of the

Palaeolithic period or Old Stone Age.

Like the first people in Africa, these first British men and women were nomads or travelling hunters, and they continued to be so for well over 200,000 years. They hunted, but they did not domesticate, or tame, the animals which surrounded them. They killed birds and fished the rivers, ate nuts, berries and roots, gathered limpets from the rocks and shellfish from the streams; but they grew nothing. This is why they have been called hunter-gatherers. Their stone flake tools and hand-axes have been collected in large numbers by archaeologists and are to be seen today in museums all over Britain. The slow improvement in the quality of these tools marks the developing skills of their makers.

At first the tools were flat flakes of stone, knocked off lumps of flint by other stones. They were used to scrape skins and meat, and the pointed ends were for boring holes. Some of these tools have been found at Clacton-on-Sea in Essex, along with the wooden end of a spear, preserved in peaty soil. Later people learned how to make hand-axes from blocks of stone. Flakes were struck off, but now it was the remaining "core" which was used and not the flakes. The axes were held in the palm of the hand and could be used for a variety of jobs. They were not fixed to wooden handles until much later. Slowly the tools improved: they became triangular, sharply pointed at one end, and with two cutting edges. They could be used to cut down small trees, to shape wood and scrape skins, and to carve meat.

Old Stone Age hunter-gatherers by a lake. The man and girl are stripping branches for berries. A hunting party is returning, carrying a carcase slung from a pole.

During the thousands of years of the Great Interglacial, small bands of people roamed the country as far west as Wales and as far north as Yorkshire. There were about fifteen people to a group. At any one time the total number of these earliest inhabitants of Britain was probably about 250.

Eventually the long hot period came to an end. Slowly the ice had been creeping south from the polar regions at a rate of about half a kilometre a year, and by 200,000 BC the north of Britain was covered in ice, in places as much as $1\frac{1}{2}$ kilometres thick. For hundreds of kilometres south of the Thames the land was gaunt and treeless, covered only with a thick undergrowth of moss called "tundra", like modern Lapland.

Most human beings appear to have left Britain and gone to southern Europe. But as people became more skilled at hunting and making tools, it seems that some did settle in ice-bound Britain, alongside the mammoths, reindeer and woolly rhinoceroses who have left their bones behind.

These settlers used their new and efficient tools to scrape animal skins and bore holes in them. Then they sewed them into clothes with animal sinew threaded on bone needles. This helped them survive the cold. They now lived in caves rather than building windbreaks; they made stone knives, and they buried their dead.

During the last part of the fourth and final ice age, about 35,000 years ago, a more developed form of people began living in southern Europe, particularly in southern France and northern Spain. Like all the successive waves of human invaders who enter Europe and make up our human story, these peoples of southern Europe had come from the East.

They stopped in southern France and Spain because they could go no further. Far to the north spread the dreary, frozen wastelands of tundra, and beyond that the ice cap, stretching now from the Thames to the North Pole. But in between the tundra and the deep caves of southern France in which the new people settled lay open grasslands, merging into forests of pine and birch, trees which can withstand bitter cold. This area of central France even enjoyed brief summers. Huge herds of reindeer, wild boar, horses, mammoth and bison were drawn to these lands. On them preyed hyenas, lions – and humans.

Stone tools had now become very efficient. Their edges and points were razor-sharp. From lumps of stone, craftsmen struck flint blades, blunt at the back so that they could be held in the hand or slotted into bone handles, like a modern penknife. A tool called a "burin", resembling a modern chisel, was used to cut not only stone but bone. Now men and women hunted with bows and arrows with flint tips, or hurled spears with tips made from antler or ivory. They stitched skin suits with hoods, like duffle coats, and they made fur boots, like those worn by the Inuits (Eskimos) today. They used antlers to make jagged harpoons, then trailed thongs behind them. The throwers held the thongs tightly in their hands so that the animals, once harpooned, could not escape.

The most dramatic achievements of these people are their works of art. Among their creations are a horse carved out of the ivory tusk of a mammoth; it has a long neck and the most delicately carved back. There is also the carved head of a woman with an elaborate hair style (which has been called the first modern portrait), and a pebble engraved with the figure of a deer with spreading antlers. Most interesting of all are the cave paintings, which have been found on the walls of deep caves at places such as Altamira in Spain and Lascaux in France.

Some of the paintings are hunting scenes. They show people hunting stags with bows and arrows, or a bison with three arrows sticking in its side. The wild horses at Lascaux and the bison at Altamira really look as if they are moving. At the cave of Les Trois Frères, in France, a man wearing the skin and tail of an animal and a mask topped by great antlers dances on the wall. The artists used paint made from crushed or powdered minerals, which they mixed with egg yolk, and painted on the walls with their fingers or with brushes made of animal hair. Their colours were black, brown, orange, yellow and light red.

Nobody is quite sure why these first great works of art were created between 30,000 and 10,000 years ago. But many of the most realistic ones are deep in the rock, at the end of long passages in the hillside, not at the entrance to the caves. In one cave, paintings were found about one kilometre deep into the mountain-side. The artists worked by light from little lamps made of animal fat, and their works could only have been dimly seen by the flickering and guttering flames. Perhaps the paintings were not decora-tions, but were used as magic to help bring success in hunting. People may have acted out the hunt in front of the paintings the night before they set off on an expedition.

Around 10,000 BC the ice gradually disappeared, until it was only left in high places, such as the Alps, and in the north. With it disappeared most of the animals which prefer cold climates, such as rein-deer, which are now only to be found in northern countries like Norway. Trees began to grow over the tundra. As the ice went, some of the cave-dwellers of southern France moved north and west, and it was these people who now settled in Britain.

The new British settlers discovered how to fit their sharp axeheads into long wooden handles. And with their new axes they began clearing the forest. Modern experiments have been made with their axeheads which show just how efficient the new settlers must have been. Three men using stone axeheads set in wood and antler hafts started clearing an area of thickets and bushes of 500 square metres. It took them only

four hours to complete the job. For the first time, then, men and women were not just living off the earth and its creatures. They were making their own mark. And ever since then, people have gone on clearing British woods and forests, so that today there are not enough trees left in Britain.

The new arrivals made boats from the tree trunks they felled. They hollowed them out, using fire and stone tools such as the burin, and "adzes" as well as axes. They also used wood to make paddles. They became skilful fishermen. They constructed traps for fish and made nets out of bark, which they weighted with stones and floated with bark floats.

Our knowledge of these ancestors comes from the discoveries made by archaeologists. They have shown, for

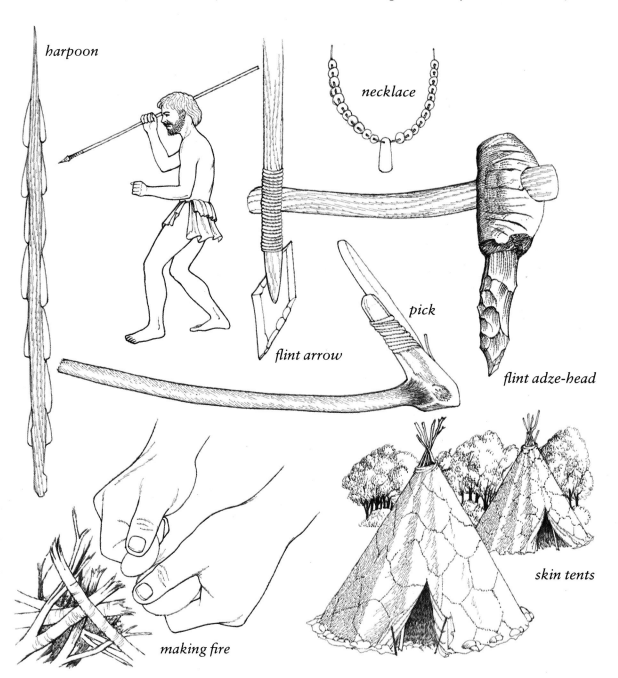

harpoon

necklace

flint arrow

pick

flint adze-head

making fire

skin tents

instance, how the people at Star Carr in North Yorkshire, who lived around 7500 BC, cut down large birch trees to make a platform by the lakeside. They left behind them flint barbs, which would have been mounted in wooden shafts and secured with wood resin to make arrows; barbed spearheads, made from splinters of red-deer antlers; and a wooden paddle. These people seem to have kept a dog, the first sign of a domesticated animal in Britain. And, like the cave-dwellers of southern France, they wore animal head-dresses, for they left behind them two head-dresses made from antlers.

In the room in the British Museum called "Men Before Metals", there is a life-size model showing how a hunter from Star Carr may have looked. The man is dressed in two deer skins, skilfully sewn together. His bearded face looks out from a deerskin hood, and from his forehead branch two antlers. The hunter would have used the dress for tracking game, like the North American Indians, who dressed themselves in wolf skins to hunt bison.

About 1500 years later Britain became an island. As the ice thawed, the level of the sea rose, and in about 6000 BC the marshy land bridge which connected Dover and Calais was swept away. The change, far from decreasing contact with Europe, increased it: the age of invaders was about to begin in Britain.

The people of Starr Carr lived in skin tents on a platform by the lake. Their boats were made from hollowed-out tree trunks and they knew how to build traps for fish. When hunting they wore animal head-dresses.

Farmers and Traders

One of the greatest changes in human life came when people began to stay in one place and farm. They exchanged the exciting life of the hunter and gatherer for the life of the peasant farmer. Instead of windbreaks and caves, they began to live in huts and villages. This did not happen suddenly. Like all such changes, it took a very long time. Over much of the world today – in most of Africa, India, China and South America, for instance – such a life is still the life of most people.

The first village farmers began to appear in Britain about 5000 years ago. The development of farming had begun earlier in what is now the Middle East, particularly Israel and Iraq. People there were sowing and harvesting wheat and barley crops and herding sheep and goats before 7000 BC. The earliest British far-

Farming – sowing crops and herding animals – started in the Middle East and by 6000 BC had spread over the area coloured pale green on the map below. By 5000 BC it had spread over the dark green area and by 3500 BC the area coloured orange.

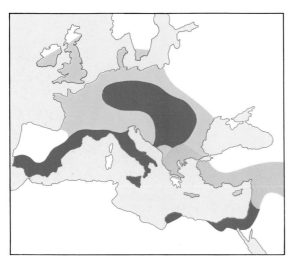

mers came into southern England by boat – perhaps by raft in summer – from northern France. They brought with them seed-corn and animals, particularly sheep and cattle. They used a wooden plough, and with their excellent wooden-handled axes they cleared the chalky high ground of southern and eastern England of trees and undergrowth. One of their settlements at Windmill Hill in north Wiltshire has been carefully excavated, so we can begin to build up a much more accurate picture of human life in Britain than we were able to before.

The Windmill Hill people probably built their hilltop camp for their cattle, not for themselves. The ditches around the site, which can be clearly seen in aerial photographs, do not seem to have been built to keep out attackers, and there are no signs of huts or houses inside. However, quantities of cattle bones have been unearthed. The tribes probably drove their cattle across the flattened earth which interrupts the ditches into the enclosure in the autumn. There would not have been enough food to feed the whole herd through the winter, and so the late autumn would have been the time for a great slaughter. The tribe would camp in the enclosure, feast on the meat, and sew the hides to make their clothes.

A dozen sites of similar date, 3500–3000 BC, have been investigated. The finds there show that these men and women of the Neolithic period, or New Stone Age, used much more advanced techniques than their predecessors. They harvested their crops of wheat and barley with flint sickles. They used red-deer antlers to make picks for breaking up the soil, and the shoulder-blades of cattle and deer to make shovels. They kept pigs, goats and dogs, as well as sheep and cattle. Pierced skulls from which the brains had been extracted and the bones of slaughtered humans have been found, which suggest that they were sometimes cannibals. Two other characteristic remains of these people are their flint mines and their burial mounds.

With farming and settlement in villages came specialization. Some members of the tribe must have spent much of their time making the plain and rather clumsy round-bottomed pottery bowls which have been discovered. Others became flint-miners. The flint mines excavated at Grimes Graves in Norfolk show that the miners sank shafts about

seven metres deep, and then dug galleries along the seams of flint. They worked by the light from hollowed cups of chalk filled with animal grease and a wick.

Among the people of the New Stone Age were skilled craftsmen who shaped the stone for making axes, which were afterwards polished. Archaeologists have discovered the exact mines, or quarries, from which the stone came. These are often hundreds of kilometres away from the places where the axeheads themselves were found. For example, an axehead has been dug up at Bakewell in Derbyshire which was made at Graig Llwyd, in Gwynedd, in North Wales (where axes, adzes and chisels in all stages of manufacture have been found on a site 1.5 kilometres round). This shows that a large amount of trade or barter must have existed between peoples all over Britain. Quarries have also been found in the Lake District, Cornwall, the Prescelly mountains of South Wales and Northern Ireland.

This pick made from a red deer's antler was found at Windmill Hill. New Stone Age men and women used antler picks for breaking up the soil. Then they would sow their crops of wheat and barley.

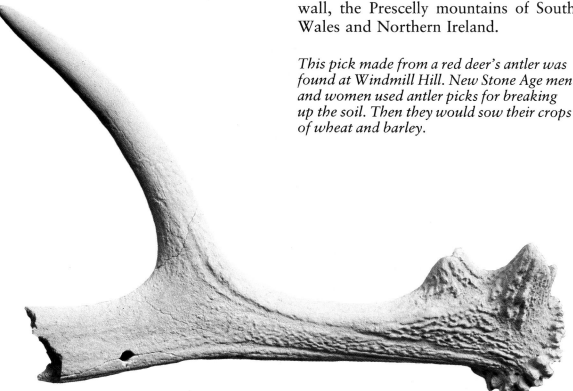

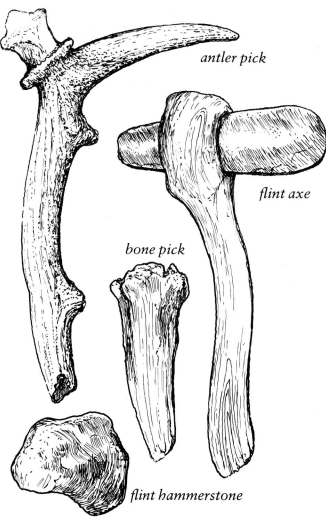

antler pick

flint axe

bone pick

flint hammerstone

At Skara Brae in the Orkney Islands, off the north of Scotland, a whole stone village, built about 2000 BC, has been discovered. It can still clearly be seen, for stone survives where wood, thatch and

At Grimes Graves in Norfolk flint mines of the New Stone Age have been excavated. The shafts were about 7 metres deep. Galleries were dug along the seams of flint. On the left is a collection of miners' tools. In the foreground of the picture are a chalk goddess and a chalk cup used as a lamp.

There are signs that the cave-dwellers who lived before the farmers sometimes carefully buried their dead in the very caves in which they lived. The British village farmers, however, have left behind them long burial "barrows", or mounds. These covered grave "houses" where numbers of people, either from a family or perhaps even from a whole tribe, were buried. There is one at Pimperne, in Dorset. Today turf has grown over the chalk of which the long barrows were built. But originally their dazzling white must have stood out in the sun, or loomed out at night from the downs, to astound and impress passers-by.

18

other building materials do not. The huts are grouped together and linked by covered passages, as in a rabbit warren. Their floors were made of clay, and their walls were built like the dry stone walls which run all over the moors and hills of Wales and Scotland today. The huts contain built-in beds of stone, with niches in the wall to act as cupboards, hearths for peat fires in the floor and stone dressers two storeys high.

The people who lived at Skara Brae buried their dead under the huts, wore beads of teeth and bone, and painted their bodies red, yellow and blue. They do not appear to have grown crops – the windswept, treeless soil would hardly have encouraged them to do so – but kept sheep and cattle, and gathered shellfish. There are open paved areas in

The Long Burial Barrow at West Kennet. Barrows (mounds) of earth covered the great stones. In these burial chambers the people of the New Stone Age were buried together. Some barrows may have been for one family; some for the whole tribe.

At Skara Brae (see next page) the soil was too poor for crops, so the people kept herds of sheep and cattle. One man returns from hunting, while two others are cutting up a deer. Some of the other inhabitants are collecting driftwood on the beach.

front of the village leading down to the sea, and small cells opening out from the huts, some with covered drains in the floor, which must have been storehouses. In this bleak place, the stone houses must have made warm, comfortable shelters for their builders and their builders' families.

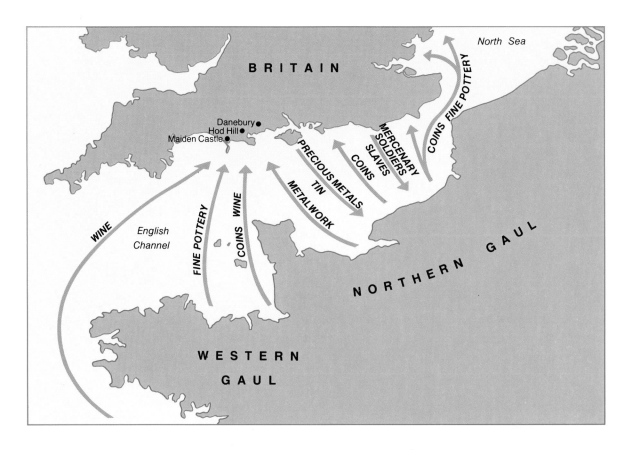

The map shows the thriving trade which was going on between Gaul and Britain from about 1500 BC. The precious metals exported from Britain were copper, bronze, tin and gold. The slaves were probably criminals or prisoners captured in wars between the tribes.

The name of the room in the British Museum mentioned in Chapter I, "Men Before Metals", shows the importance of the next great step in human development. This was the use of metals – first copper, then bronze, which was easier to shape (bronze is a mixture of ninety per cent copper and ten per cent tin). It was the "Beaker" people – so called from the pottery mugs discovered in their round burial mounds – who introduced metal-working into Britain about 2000 years ago. They came originally from Spain, but the remains of their way of life have been found as far east as Poland, as far south as Sicily, as far north as Scotland, and as far west as Ireland. They were skilled sailors, navigating the stormy Bay of Biscay and the North Sea, as well as the shorter English Channel and Irish Sea.

Britain had plentiful supplies of metal – copper, tin (in Cornwall), and gold (in Ireland and Wales). The men and women who lived in these areas during the Bronze Age, which began about 1500 BC, were skilled organizers of trade as well as delicate craftsmen. Their goods of bronze and gold have been discovered as far away as central and eastern Europe. Many have been found in Britain too, often in burial mounds in southern England. They are beautifully made. One of the most famous is a gold cup found at Rillaton in Cornwall, which is now in the British Museum. The gold has been beaten to resemble the waves of the sea, flowing one after another to the thin delicate brim of the cup. Gold earrings in the shape of baskets have been discovered in a grave at Radley in Berkshire, and a superbly decorated cape of sheet gold at Mold in North Wales. Gold bracelets have been found in Ireland, and a massive gold collar at Moulsford in Berkshire. The fact that many beautiful things were found in single graves suggests that these graves belonged to chiefs or rich traders. They have been called "the first rich Englishmen".

Bronze tools have also been dug up in large numbers. The bronze axeheads were hollowed so that wooden handles could be securely fitted into them. Swords were sharp on both sides, so that warriors no longer used the points only. Bronze sickles were now used for reaping corn instead of flint ones. An important archaeological discovery was of some bronze harnesses, which show that people in Britain must have begun to use horses by this time. Even musical instruments, in the shape of horns, have been found in Ireland. Wheeled carts were being used by about 500 BC in Britain, 3000 years after their first use in what is now the Middle East.

The Rillaton Cup

Perhaps the most impressive things that the Bronze Age people have left behind are their great stone monuments – the stone circles at Avebury in Wiltshire (where an avenue of stones a kilometre long leads to the outer circle) and, best known of all, Stonehenge. The blue stones which formed one of the rings at Stonehenge came from the Prescelly mountains in South Wales. They must have been carried across the Bristol Channel and up the river Avon on rafts and then dragged the last 30 kilometres or so on rollers to the site on Salisbury Plain. The huge sarsen (boulder) stones would have needed a vast army of labourers, with skilled organizers to direct them, to transport them from their quarry 50 kilometres away.

The builders of Stonehenge showed great engineering skill in placing on top of the huge upright stones the curved cross-stones, or "lintels", which joined them together in a circle. The circle was exactly arranged so that the first rays of the sun rising on Midsummer Day would strike a particular stone. Details like this have led experts to wonder whether the

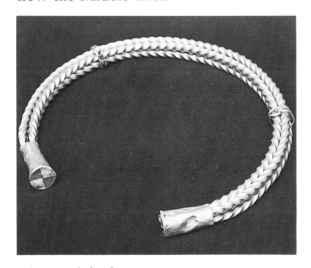

The Moulsford Torque

23

A bronze-smith's workshop of about 700 BC was found in a cave at Heathery Burn in northern England. The smith worked near the entrance where the light was best. The fire was blown to a high temperature by bellows. Then a crucible of scrap metal was held in the fire. When it melted, the smith removed the crucible with tongs and poured the molten metal into moulds. These were shaped in the form of axeheads, spearheads or cauldrons. The goods were finally hammered into shape.

stones have been placed in a particular way to predict the movements of the moon or even the eclipses of the sun and moon. All the evidence from Stonehenge suggests that the people who built it were good organizers and very knowledgeable. They had not yet learned to read and write, but they were observing the seasons, the sun, the moon and stars. People had made a lot of progress since the days of the young woman of Swanscombe.

Iron is stronger than bronze and so is better for making weapons, nails, and carpenters' tools such as saws, axes and adzes. Yet, though iron ore was easy to find in Europe and in Britain, it was a long time before the knowledge of making bronze led to the making of iron goods. It was centuries before people discovered how to heat iron to a high enough temperature, so that it could be cast in a mould and beaten and shaped by blacksmiths. The Hittites, living in the Middle East, were using iron for weapons before 1200 BC. But they kept their secret closely guarded, and it was not until about 600 BC that the first iron-using tribes settled in southern England.

These people came once again from Europe. They were Celts, members of an extraordinary collection of peoples who at one time ruled all the land from Turkey to Ireland; they had sacked Rome and raided Greece. We call the Celtic tribes who settled in Britain and their descendants Britons. The language they spoke is still used today, for Welsh, Gaelic, Irish and Cornish are direct descendants of Celtic. (To about a quarter of the Welsh people today Welsh is as

The people of the New Stone Age built great stone monuments like this stone circle at Avebury in Wiltshire. Within a large circular bank and ditch was an outer ring of about 100 stones. Within were two smaller circles. The circles stood where ancient tracks met. It was probably a sacred place.

much their native language as English.) Many British place names, and the names of rivers and hills, come from Celtic. The Celtic word for river, *avon*, has given its name to many English rivers. Dover, which stands at the mouth of a river, gets its name from a Celtic word similar to the Welsh word *dwfr* and the Cornish *dovr*, meaning water.

The Celts could not write in their own language, but Celtic life in Britain has been described by Greek and Roman writers. They stress the Celts' interest in their appearance. The men wore their hair long. They shaved their beards, but grew long moustaches which covered their mouths. Before battle they washed their hair in lime to stiffen it, then brushed it back so it would flow like a horse's mane. Strabo, a Greek geographer who wrote in the 1st century AD, describes the Celts of Gaul, members of the same people as those in Britain, as follows:

"The whole race is madly fond of war, high-spirited and quick to battle, but otherwise straightforward and not of evil character. And so when they are stirred up, they assemble in their bands for battle ... so that they are easily handled by those who desire to outwit them for ... on whatever pretext you stir them up you will have them ready to face danger even if they have nothing on their side but their own strength and courage. On the other hand, if won over by gentle persuasion, they willingly devote their energies to useful pursuits, and even take to a literary education... To the frankness and high-spiritedness of their temperament may be added the traits of childish boastfulness and love of decoration. They wear ornaments of gold, torques (collars) on their necks and bracelets on their arms and wrists, while people of high rank wear dyed garments besprinkled with gold. It is this vanity which makes them unbearable in victory, and so completely cast down in defeat."[1]

The Britons were led by their chiefs and their priests, the Druids. The chiefs were elected, and were sometimes women, like the famous Boadicea or Boudicca. Julius Caesar praised their horsemanship – praise indeed, coming from so experienced a general. Their light chariots had iron wheels, and their drivers drove them with reckless courage. They built great hill-forts which can

still be seen today, dominating the surrounding countryside from the highest point of the downs in Wiltshire, Hampshire and Dorset.

The best known of them all is Maiden Castle in Dorset. This fort, which held great herds of cattle and sheep, was about 1200 metres long, 600 metres wide, and defended by earthworks 30 metres high. Some of the forts were small towns, with shops, workshops, streets and temples. There were some at Wheathampstead near St Albans in Hertfordshire, built by the Belgae, the last Celts to come to Britain, fifty years before Julius Caesar. They were the first towns in Britain.

Most Britons were farmers, however. They lived in large thatched huts built of wattle and daub – the same mixture of interlaced twigs and branches (wattle) and mud (daub) which was used to build

A Celtic settlement. The picture shows a chariot with basketwork sides, a woman weaving, pottery making, a man chopping wood, and a hut with a fire in its centre. The village is built within a wooden fence. This is how the British were living just before Caesar's raids.

labourers' cottages until about AD 1600. Pytheas, a Greek who visited Britain in the 4th century BC, wrote that their main crop was wheat, which they threshed in barns "because they have so little sunshine and so much rain". They had herds of cattle and flocks of sheep. Their farmsteads were protected with a wooden palisade, or fence, and inside they had barns and storage pits for grain. Their most important tool was their heavy plough. This had an iron blade

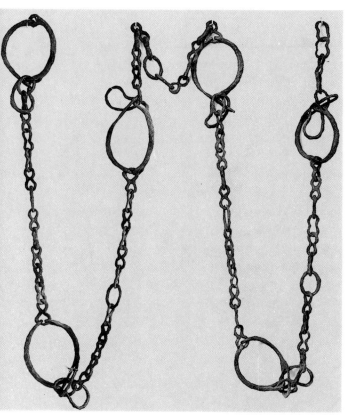

Slave chains (1st century BC) with six collars found at Barton in Cambridgeshire. The slaves were exported for sale in Europe by British chiefs.

which could turn the earth over, and not just furrow it like the light wooden ploughs of earlier farmers. From now on the heavy soil of the valleys in the south-east could be farmed, and people began to settle all over England, not just on the high ground with its light chalky soil.

Unlike the Romans, who regarded illness as a punishment from the gods, and the Germanic tribes, who left their sick to die, the Britons looked after the sick, the wounded and the elderly. They had skilled doctors and seem to have developed remarkably advanced surgery, specializing in operations on the brain. British women had the same right to own property as men, and did not have to hand over their goods when they married. This was a right which British

women living only 100 years before today did not have.

The Greek geographer who wrote about the courage and vanity of the Britons also described their boats with admiration. These were made of oak, with sails of leather, pulled up and down by chains not ropes. The openings between the planks were stuffed with seaweed, which retained its moisture and prevented the wood from drying out when the boat was out of the water. The Britons enjoyed drinking – barley ale and mead made from honey for the ordinary people, and wine for the chief and his court – and they revelled in great banquets. In some ways, with their elected chiefs, their regard for women, and the lack of division between rich and poor, they seem more like ourselves than the military Romans.

British traders were in regular contact with Europe, and trade increased as the Roman Empire spread northwards towards the Channel. Judging from the large numbers of big Roman wine jars that have been found from this time, the Britons imported a lot of wine from Europe. In return they exported woollen cloaks, much prized in Rome, corn, tin, hunting dogs – and slaves. Slave chains, found at camps near Canterbury in Kent and Barton in Cambridgeshire, are the first evidence we have that slaves were traded from Britain. They were probably prisoners of war taken in battle with rival tribes. Large numbers of Celtic coins have been found, first of silver and then of gold. These are our first examples of British coins. The later ones have the heads of British chiefs stamped on them, with abbreviations of their names in the Roman style. The chiefs, it seems, were copying the ways of the great Roman Emperors.

The Roman Conquest

The Roman Empire was one of the great wonders of the world. At first, its central city, Rome, was only the capital of a small "city-state" in Italy. During the centuries before the life of Christ, the Romans, with their powerful armies and efficient government, spread their rule throughout Europe and part of Asia. Their language, Latin, became an international language for the educated.

By the last century BC, when the last of the Celtic tribes, the Belgae, were moving into southern Britain, the Roman Empire stretched to the English Channel. In France, which was then called Gaul, the Roman army legions had reached the river Rhine and were ready to advance eastwards into the Netherlands and Germany. They occupied the Middle East from Turkey to the Red Sea. Spain and Portugal were safely in the Roman net.

The British traders who sold their woollen cloaks in the Roman markets and loaded up Italian wine to take home with them must have felt like modern British businessmen in New York. They stood at the centre of the world.

At first, the Romans could not decide whether to extend their Empire across the Channel and into Britain, about whose wealth and people they knew only what traders had told them. Some Romans saw little point in further conquest. They argued that what the British had to offer – tin, iron ore, cloth, corn, gold and slaves – could easily be obtained by more trade with the different tribes. But others, particularly the army commanders, looked forward to further victories. They imagined themselves leading a column of British captives through the streets of Rome, to the

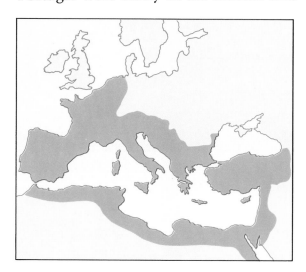

The Roman Empire just before the Roman invasion of Britain in AD 43. They had halted their eastwards expansion in Europe at the Rhine before deciding to go any further.

A British trader visiting Rome (right).

29

applause of their fellow citizens. The captives would be chained together, each column with its sullen chief at the head.

One commander who thought like this was Julius Caesar. His soldiers in Gaul were finding it increasingly difficult to quell revolts by the Celtic tribes there who were supported by the Celts in southern Britain. At the very least, it seemed to the great man, it would be worth landing in Kent, a mere 30 kilometres away from Calais, to see whether an invasion might be possible. He described his plans in an account of his campaign which he wrote for his Roman masters in 55 BC. He referred to himself, as was his custom, in the third person:

"It was now near the end of the summer, and winter sets in early in those parts... Nevertheless Caesar made active preparations for an expedition to Britain, because he knew that in almost all the Gallic campaigns the Gauls had received reinforcements from the Britons. Even if there was not time for a campaign that season, he thought it would be of great advantage to him merely to visit the island, to see what its inhabitants were like, and to make himself acquainted with the lie of the land, the harbours and the landing-places."[2]

Caesar, as he says, left his sailing late, and did not leave Boulogne until the second half of August, 55 BC. He sailed with 10,000 soldiers, infantry and cavalry, and arrived off the white cliffs of Dover at nine o'clock in the morning. He did not like what he saw. The British had their men lined up along the high cliffs. From there they could easily hurl their javelins right on to the narrow beach if the Romans tried to land. So Caesar sailed north-east for about 10 kilometres and ran his ships aground on an evenly sloping beach, probably at Deal.

The Roman soldiers still had a desperate fight to get ashore, and their landing very nearly ended in disaster. At one point Caesar's men were given new courage by the example of the standard-bearer of the 10th legion who carried the great eagle, the legion's standard or flag. Caesar describes what happened:

"The Romans were faced with very grave difficulties. The size of the ships made it impossible to run them aground except in fairly deep water, and the soldiers, unfamiliar with the territory, with their hands full and weighed down by their weapons, had to jump down from the ships, get a footing in the waves, and fight the enemy, all at the same time. Their opponents, standing on dry land, fought with all their limbs unencumbered and on perfectly familiar ground, boldly hurling javelins and galloping their horses, which were trained to this kind of work...But as the Romans hesitated, chiefly on account of the depth of the water, the man who carried the eagle of the 10th legion, after praying to the gods that his action might bring good luck to the legion, cried in a loud voice: 'Jump down, comrades, unless you want to surrender our eagle to the enemy; I, at any rate, mean to do my duty to my country and my general.' With these words, he leapt out of the ship and advanced towards the enemy with the eagle in his hands. At this the soldiers, encouraging each other not to submit to such a disgrace, jumped with one accord from the ship, and the men from the next ships, when they saw them, followed them and advanced against the enemy."[2]

After further fierce fighting, the British asked for peace. But the expedition soon faced another disaster. Because they were used to sailing in the Mediterranean, which does not have tides, the Romans beached their ships too close to the sea. When the weather worsened, some of the ships were swept away with the tide. Then they lost some of their men when a party which had gone inland to look for corn – the local crops won Caesar's praise for their quantity and quality – was ambushed by the British. The Romans decided to return to Gaul.

Next year, 54 BC, the Romans returned. This time, they set off earlier in the year, and in greater numbers, and they landed on 7th July, without meeting any opposition. Once again they lost ships through bad weather and their own inexperience, but they advanced inland and stormed the hill fort at Bigbury, near Canterbury. The British now put all their forces under one chief, Cassivellaunus of the Catuvellauni tribe, whose headquarters were north of the Thames. The

The first Roman landing at Deal in 55 BC.

Coins of King Cunobelinus. He ruled most of south-east England from 7 BC to AD 43 and issued his own coins. Some had CUNO on them, others CAMV (short for Camulodunum – Latin for his capital, Colchester).

Romans advanced rapidly with their usual efficiency. They were particularly skilled at crossing rivers. They crossed first the Medway and then the Thames without much difficulty. Then they marched to Cassivellaunus' headquarters at Wheathampstead near modern St Albans in Hertfordshire, and captured it. Cassivellaunus soon surrendered, and with other chiefs of southern Britain, agreed to accept the Romans as overlords. Caesar also made the British agree to pay tribute. However, once he had returned to Gaul, which he did before the autumn storms came, the Romans found it harder and harder to get them to pay it.

Little else came of Caesar's two expeditions. Back in Rome, he pursued his personal ambitions and eventually became the head of the Roman state, but was then assassinated. The Roman troops and governors left Britain alone for the next ninety years.

Caesar's enemies, the Catuvellauni, were unaffected by their defeat, and soon controlled most of south-east England. Colchester, in Essex, became their capital, and it was there that a great chief, Cunobelinus (whose name is altered to Cymbeline in Shakespeare's play of that name), ruled for fifty years, living in splendour rather like a Roman ruler. For the Roman Empire on the other side of the Channel fascinated the Celtic chiefs. Coins were minted during Cunobelinus' reign showing an ear of corn with the letters CAMV standing for Camulodunum, the Latin name for Colchester. Trade between Britain and Europe increased: large quantities of red glazed pottery made in Gaul before the final Roman invasion have been found all over southern England.

When Cunobelinus died, in AD 43, one of his sons quarrelled with his brothers and fled to Gaul, where he appealed to the Romans to take over his country. The king of another southern tribe, whose territory covered Hampshire and Sussex, was thrown out by his own people and he, too, went to Gaul with the same request. The new Roman Emperor, Claudius, saw that if he answered these requests for help, he might increase his own power and reputation. So he assembled a force of 40,000 men, with

A Roman soldier with his shield, spear, short stabbing sword and light armour. On the right, Roman soldiers attack Maiden Castle, advancing on the main gate under cover of their "tortoise" of shields.

Aulus Plautius as their commander, which set sail for Britain. Its landing on the Kent coast in AD 43 was unopposed.

The new invaders had learned from Caesar's experience. They must have had good advance knowledge of the British coastline, for straight away they occupied Richborough, then a little island off the east Kent coast at Thanet. This gave them the sheltered deep-water port that Caesar had so badly missed. Here their warships could lie at anchor, and their storeships could unload the arms and stores the army needed. On the island they constructed a great base, digging ditches and building earthwork defences, before hurrying inland to begin their conquest of Britain.

The Roman army formed a powerful world of its own. The legions contained experienced infantrymen and smaller groups of cavalry. They also had their own skilled craftsmen and their own administrators, who were used to governing conquered peoples all over Europe and the Middle East. All full-time Roman soldiers had to be able to read and write, which was amazing at a time when very few people anywhere could do either. At this stage the soldiers were mainly Romans, but later there were more and more British recruits.

There were good reasons for joining the Roman army. Its soldiers were much admired. They were regularly paid in money, and had excellent chances of promotion. Perhaps the greatest attraction of all was that, after their twenty-five years of service, soldiers were provided with small farms, where they could spend the rest of their lives.

As a fighting force, no British army, however dashing its cavalry or brave its soldier-farmers, could hope to equal the Roman legions. When they fought rival tribes, the Roman catapults and other weapons smashed through the defences of the British hill-forts; and their javelins killed many Britons before they even joined battle. When it came to hand-to-hand fighting, the Romans closed ranks and used their short stabbing swords, which were far more efficient than the long slashing swords of the Britons. And because the Romans had a well-organized system for supplying food and equipment to their army, the soldiers could fight just as long as the weather held; and then start again in the spring as if they had never left off. Most of the British soldiers, however, were farmers who had been called up for battle. When harvest time came, they were eager to stop fighting and return to their small farms to gather the harvest which otherwise would go to waste. Only the British nobles were professional fighters, like the Romans.

Powerful and confident, the Roman forces defeated the British twice before they reached the river Medway. There they found that the Britons had destroyed the bridge. But this did not stop

them. They had plenty of experience when fighting in Europe of crossing much wider rivers, such as the Rhine. Some troops, including the cavalry, swam across the river at Rochester, and the rest forded it lower down.

The most important battle took place in the hills on the other side of Rochester, and lasted two days. Finally the Britons gave in and fled. Two weeks later the Romans crossed the Thames and occupied Colchester itself, the capital of the Catuvellauni, where King Cunobelinus had ruled with such splendour. The Emperor Claudius himself led the victory procession, which included elephants, into Colchester. Eleven British kings surrendered, and others soon followed. Other tribes in Britain were no doubt pleased to see the over-mighty Catuvellauni toppled.

The British mingle with the Roman soldiers. Some of the British have spears and some have pitchforks. In the background is a stockaded British village. There must have been many peaceful if suspicious meetings like these after the Roman conquest. (The model hand on the Roman standard may have been a good luck charm or a token of loyalty.)

Four years later the Roman soldiers had reached the river Severn in the west and the river Trent in the north. In AD 49 Colchester was declared an official "colony", where retired Roman soldiers could settle, draw their pensions and farm the land. The Romans were in Britain to stay, and the thorough system of Roman colonization had begun.

Because the Roman Empire was so large, the Romans did not have enough soldiers to keep their power over conquered peoples by force. So they used other methods. One was to allow local people, particularly the chiefs, to share in governing their own countries. Another was to make the tribes living on the borders of conquered territories into Roman allies. This is what they did in Britain. In the days of the British Empire in the 19th and 20th centuries, the British used similar methods of government to rule their vast territories in India and Africa.

At the beginning of their occupation of Britain, the Romans ruled a large area of southern and central England. On its eastern border, they made the Iceni tribe in Norfolk their allies. In the north, they signed a treaty with Queen Cartimandua of the Brigantes, who controlled most of northern England. She showed her loyalty by handing over to the Romans the unfortunate King Caractacus of the Catuvellauni, when he fled to her for refuge. He was led through the streets of Rome in chains. As he walked along and looked about him at the wealth and grandeur of the great capital, he is said to have asked: "Why is it that you, who have so much, want to take from us, who have so little, even the few possessions we can call our own?"

In southern and central England, where the Romans ruled directly, they allowed British chiefs to act as magis-

trates and serve on local councils of government. No civilian was allowed to carry arms, and the Roman soldiers mostly went off to protect the frontiers, or stayed out of sight in their barracks, such as the great supply base at Richborough.

Only when it came to collecting taxes did the Romans put all the power in the hands of their own officials. They wanted to get as much wealth for Rome out of Britain as possible. The tax officers were responsible not to the local governor but to the Emperor himself. The Romans controlled trading of all the most important goods; they controlled the mines; and they declared that the lands of captured chiefs now belonged to the Emperor: Britain was regarded as a rich province and the Romans were determined to squeeze it for all that it was worth.

As we have seen, the capital of the Catuvellauni tribe had been at Colchester, which the Romans conquered and declared a colony. The land which they gave to retired Roman soldiers there had been taken from British farmers. Corn was taken from the farmers, too, as taxes. Then the Romans named Colchester the centre of their new religion – emperor worship – and built a temple to Claudius, whom many Romans themselves regarded as a half-wit, in the town. Many of the local men were forced to join the Roman armies whether they wanted to or not. All these things made the British angry, particularly the people living around Colchester.

At about this time, Boudicca, the Queen of the Iceni in Norfolk, whom the Romans had at first chosen as allies and then left alone, protested because her lands had been seized in the name of the Emperor. The Romans flogged her and raped her daughters. Such treatment of a British queen caused a revolt which soon spread from Norfolk over south-east England. Not only Colchester but

London and St Albans were destroyed. Captured Romans were killed and mercilessly tortured. At Colchester 15,000 Romans and their British allies were slaughtered, and a number killed as part of a ritual sacrifice in London. At one point the Romans probably considered leaving Britain altogether, but they went on to win a decisive victory, perhaps at Mancetter in Warwickshire.

The Roman writer Tacitus, whose father-in-law was serving in the Roman army in Britain at the time, has left us a highly coloured account of the battle. It is hard to believe all its details – for instance, how could any Roman have heard, let alone understood, what Queen Boudicca was saying during the battle? But its general outline is probably true:

"Boudicca, with her daughters standing in front of her, was borne about in a war-chariot from tribe to tribe. 'We Britons,' she declared, 'are accustomed to female war-leaders, but I do not now come forward as one of noble descent fighting for my kingdom and my wealth; rather I present myself as an ordinary woman, striving to revenge my lost liberty, my lash-tortured body, and the violated honour of my daughters... Consider our numbers and the reasons why we are fighting; then you will either conquer or die in this battle. I, a woman, am resolved to do so – you men, if you like, can live to be Roman slaves.' Suetonius, the Roman general, cried to his men, 'Don't worry about these yelling savages and their empty threats. There are more women than warriors in their ranks. They are untrained and badly armed, and they will break straight away when they recognize the Roman courage and weapons that have defeated them so often...'"[3]

The remains of Roman weapons found in Britain from around 1st century BC.

His men did as Suetonius told them:

"At first the legionaries stood their ground ... Then as soon as the attacking enemy had come close enough for them to be sure of their aim, they all hurled their javelins together and burst forward in a wedge formation. The auxiliaries charged in the same way, and the cavalry, thrusting with their lances, rode down all who stood to oppose them. The rest of the Britons turned and ran."[3]

Boudicca, seeing that she was defeated, killed herself. The terrible revolt lasted two months and in it 70,000 Romans and British "collaborators" were killed. It was the end of any organized resistance from the conquered British tribes to the power of the Romans.

Life in Roman Britain

The land which the Romans now took over and ruled as part of their Empire was very well worth having. Its population seems to have been about two million, double what it was at the time of the conquest of Britain by the Normans a thousand years later. The British, particularly in the 150 years before the Roman invasion, had cleared large areas of forest, so that human settlements were no longer limited to the drier highlands.

In fact, the proportion of forest to open land seems to have been much the same as it was in the Middle Ages, 1200 years later. Farmsteads and villages, generally guarded with a stockade, were surrounded by fields of corn and big expanses of grazing land. The British herded sheep in large numbers and exported corn and cattle.

One of the main reasons for the Roman invasion had been to obtain valuable British minerals – lead, iron ore, gold and tin. By AD 47 the Romans had begun mining silver-bearing lead in the Mendip Hills, in south-west England, and exporting it to Europe. Roman prospectors began looking for, and sometimes finding, gold in the Lake District and in North Wales. As long as they could protect its borders in the south-west and north, and in Scotland and Wales, the Romans believed that their province of Britannia (as they called occupied Britain) would bring them plenty of profit.

A Roman-British farm in the 1st century AD .

ROMAN BRITAIN

ANTONINE
WALL

P I C T S

HADRIAN'S
WALL

B R I G A N T E S

York

Anglesey

Caernarfon

Chester

R.Trent

Lincoln

Ermine Street

Leicester

CATUVELLAUNI

ICENI

Fen
District

R. Severn

Watling Street

Gloucester

Colchester

Caerleon

R.Thames

St Albans

London

Richborough

Fosse Way

Rochester

Thanet

Lullingstone

Canterbury

Deal

R. Medway

Dover

Fishbourne

Exeter

Boulogne

They tried at first to extend the boundaries of their territory. In the south-west they built a town at Exeter, but they never properly colonized the rest of Devon or Cornwall. In Wales they built a ring of forts from Caerleon in the south to Caernarfon in the north, and even established a fort at Holyhead, after conquering the island of Anglesey. In the north, after AD 70, they took advantage of a civil war raging among the Brigantes, which had brought about the expulsion of their ally Queen Cartimandua, to defeat them, and occupied the whole region up to the Scottish border.

to the Romans and to those British who were prepared to accept their rule. Britain had become a permanent part of the Roman Empire.

For 100 years from AD 70 onwards, Roman-British Britain was peaceful and prosperous. Nobody dared challenge the rule of the Romans, and the Romans did not expect anyone to do so. When they built new towns, they often did not bother to build strong defences for them.

This lead ingot dated AD 44 was found at Matlock in Derbyshire. It shows how quickly the Romans mined lead after their invasion.

Nor did they stop there. By AD 83 Roman armies were occupying Scotland as far as the Highlands. Soon they had reached the northernmost tip of the country. The next year their ships sailed round the Orkneys and into the Irish Sea. The Romans talked of invading Ireland, but they never succeeded. They built a line of forts in the Scottish Lowlands to keep out the tribes in the hills to the north. In Wales, the Britons who retreated to the mountains were left alone; but the valleys and the coastline were left

The walls of Canterbury, for instance, were not constructed until 200 years later. They were then built to defend the city, not against possible Celtic rebels, but against Saxon pirates, who had been landing on the coast and raiding inland.

In the countryside, country houses, known as "villas", were built, surrounded by large estates. They were often extensions of existing British farms. From his villa, the owner, who was as likely to be a Briton as a Roman, controlled the local farmers and farm workers in the same way that in more recent times the squire of a village controlled the villagers' lives. Everywhere great roads were built, which made it easier to reach different parts of the country. Traders went along these roads as often as the Roman legionaries. For the first time most of the island was under one rule. The idea of a nation had been planted.

Whenever they conquered a country and settled there, the Romans liked to build towns. In Britain, they built new towns all over England and Wales (most of them in the south and south-east), which must have attracted, amazed and impressed the Britons. Often they turned the headquarters of Celtic tribes into Roman towns. In the more distant parts of the country, particularly in the north where there was still danger from enemy tribes, they built forts, which later turned into towns. There were about 100 such forts in Roman Britain. A town or city's modern name often shows that it was once a Roman fort (the Latin word for camp, *castrum*, appears in names such as Manchester, Chichester and Chester).

Roman towns were all built in the same general pattern. Their straight streets ran at right angles into each other, like streets in modern New York. There

A busy street in Roman Britain. Notice the stone slabs, the farmer's wife in from the country with her basket, the baker and the pottery shop.

A frieze of a Roman butcher's shop. Notice his scales and his chopper – also the side of bacon and the leg of mutton.

were many open spaces, and so no feeling of crush within the town. The wealthier citizens lived in large, comfortable town villas spaced round their own courtyards and often containing gardens. The public buildings, which were paid for by local rich men and officials and not by the Romans, were large and splendid. This encouraged the local people to feel pride in their town, and to feel part of a great Empire which dominated the known world.

The centre of a Roman town was the "forum" or market place. In the middle there would be a statue erected in honour of an Emperor or Governor, or a

A men's bath house. The tepidarium *is in the middle, the very hot room on the left and the* frigidarium *on the right. In the foreground is the crowded exercise yard.*

column commemorating a military victory. For instance, at Richborough, the main port of entry into Britain in the early days, a great marble monument was built to mark the final conquest of Britain in AD 85. Flanked with bronze statues, it stood looking out to sea, as a permanent reminder of the mighty Empire's power.

Round the forum would stand the stalls of traders, and at one end would be the "basilica" or town hall, perhaps with steps leading up to it and great columns in front of it supporting a triangular pediment. Travellers entering London would see the city's basilica standing on top of a hill, overlooking the river and town. It was more than 150 metres long, longer than any other basilica in northern Europe. Inside, as in a modern town hall, would be the council offices, the council chamber and the law courts where the magistrates, most of them local British leaders, would sit.

On the other three sides of the forum there would be covered pavements, with columns, where people would walk and admire the shops, as we do in a shopping precinct today. Shopkeepers, as they had no plate glass, would display their goods in the front rooms of their houses. These were their shops. They stood next to the pavement, and their owners lived behind and above them. Also in the forum were the other main public buildings, such as temples to Roman and British gods, and the famous Roman baths.

In a Roman town the baths were for everyone: Agricola, governor of Britain from AD 77 to AD 83, said that he built baths to civilize the British. Admission charges were low, and children were allowed in free. They were a social centre, rather than just a place in which to wash. Here townspeople would gather

The remains of the Roman theatre at St Albans seen from the air. The Romans built amphitheatres in several British towns. There they held bull-baiting, cock-fighting, gladiator fights and other spectacular events.

to play dice, to gossip, to do business or merely to kill time, as people in Mediterranean countries still meet in town squares or on waterfronts today. The baths were large and contained a variety of rooms, as in modern Turkish baths. Men and women bathed separately.

The bathers would first undress and leave their clothes in a sort of entrance hall. They would then start off in the *tepidarium*, a warm room which prepared the body for the heat to come. The *tepidarium* made you sweat; water was sprinkled on a floor made hot by underfloor heating and by this means the room was full of steam. The hot room, which they would enter next, would also be full of hot steam and have baths full of hot water sunk into the floor. Sometimes there might also be an even hotter room, like a sauna. Then would come the greatest shock of all – the plunge into the cool pool of the *frigidarium*. After the baths, people would stroll about in the large relaxing yard, where you could swing weights, wrestle, do exercises, play games, or be served with drinks and food. After exercising, the bathers would have oil rubbed over them by one of the many slaves who looked after the baths. Then the dirt was scraped off the skin with a curved metal instrument called a *strigilis*. Other slaves would massage the bathers, or pluck hair from their armpits. A visit to the baths could easily last a whole morning.

Outside many towns in Roman Britain stood an amphitheatre, where shows and entertainments (if they can be called that) took place. In the great amphitheatre in Rome, the Colosseum, 50,000 spectators would watch lions, tigers, bulls and even elephants and rhinoceroses fighting each other to the death. They would gamble on the result, and wait excitedly for the end, when condemned criminals were thrown to those animals that survived. Worse still were the fights between the gladiators (swordfighters). Some of these were criminals, others prisoners captured in war, still others professionals. Gladiators were trained to fight in these shows just as men today are trained as professional boxers. There was only one end to a fight between two gladiators – the death of one of them.

In the amphitheatres of Britain the shows were less lavish, for the officials who ran them had less money than those in Rome, and the crowds were smaller. Bull-baiting, bear-baiting and cock-fighting were organized, as were gladiator fights.

The number of people living in a typical Roman-British town was not large – 5000 at the most. Their way of

A Roman kitchen. The cook, a slave, is at the stove. Around him are large pots – one containing olives – and a milk pail. Some of the pots will be made of bronze and some of iron. Only a rich household could afford this sort of kitchen.

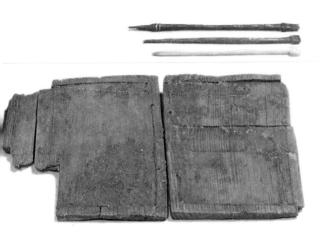

This Roman writing tablet is in the London Museum. The wood was covered with beeswax. You wrote with the sharp end of the stylus and erased with the flat end.

life was thoroughly Roman. Rich and important Britons were made full Roman citizens, and all others who were not farm labourers or slaves were encouraged to wear Roman clothes. Both men and women wore the Roman *toga* on formal occasions. This was a semicircle of white cloth wound round the body. For everyday use, the men wore tunics with short cloaks, and hobnailed boots or sandals, while women wore simple dresses.

The town villas where the well-to-do Celts and Romans lived had plenty of room and their own gardens. They were one-storey houses, built around their own courtyard, and could perhaps be compared to a modern "ranch-type" bungalow with wings extending from the courtyard. There would be about a dozen rooms, joined together by a verandah. The most luxurious of the villas had lavatories that flushed, and were heated by underfloor central heating, fuelled by wood or charcoal furnaces called *hypocausts*. The plaster on the walls would be painted in different colours — a deep red was popular, as was a deep pink — and there would be mosaics on the floor.

Workers and shopkeepers lived in low wooden houses — open in the front, as we have seen, if they were also shops. The roofs were tiled. There were many skilled British craftsmen — blacksmiths and bronzesmiths for instance — who came to the towns for work. There were also cobblers, potters, carpenters and other craftsmen who set up shop in the towns. Many of these learned to read and write, as well as to speak Latin. As we have seen, all soldiers in the Roman army had to learn how to read and write. Since more and more of these soldiers were British and would retire in Britain, literacy now became common for the first time in our history.

After the destruction of London during Queen Boudicca's revolt, a new city was built which became one of the largest towns in Europe north of the Alps. It was the financial centre of the Roman province of Britannia, and possessed its own mint. It was the centre of the road network. The Romans built the first bridge over the Thames at London. Roads from the south, Sussex, Kent and Essex here met Watling Street which took the soldiers to Chester and North Wales. Ermine Street started in London and ran to York and on to Hadrian's Wall. London was probably the headquarters of the Roman Governor of Britannia, and certainly the site of his palace. Along the bank of the Thames where the Embankment runs today, half a mile of quayside was constructed. Here exports were loaded in ships to go to Europe, and imports landed. It is extraordinary to think that in two generations since the Roman invasion a city had been built where before stood a straggling collection of huts. It was more technically advanced than anything to be seen in London for the next 1000 years.

The busy Roman foreshore at Billingsgate in London. Among the goods being unloaded into the warehouse are the large pottery wine vessels (amphorae), remains of which have been found all over the country. Wine drinking was very popular in Britain in Roman times.

The archaeologists discovered that most of the city's houses had had a wooden framework and walls of clay, wattle and daub. The wall plaster was often painted. In one place, for instance, archaeologists were able to piece together a decorative panel which had been painted on a white wall. It has a large rectangular panel with a narrow green border, and a scroll design of green leaves and red flowers had been painted on a blue-green background. The floors were tiled, generally with red tiles. The majority of Londoners, almost all of whom (apart from some immigrants) would have been British, lived like this.

From the archaeologists' finds we have a good idea of the jewellery and make-up worn by women. They include decorated hairpins of bronze and bone, one carved with the head and shoulders of a Roman woman, with her hair piled high with a tiara on top of it. (Roman women wore their hair long.) A gold necklace with emeralds, green glass beads, and bronze, iron and gold rings have been found. The women wore make-up: pottery bottles have been found from which they would have scooped out ointments and powders with a long narrow spoon.

The remains of Roman rubbish dumps tell us a great deal about the diet of the inhabitants of London at this time. From seeds left behind we know that figs, grapes and olives must have been imported in large numbers from the Mediterranean. Apples, blackberries, plums, cherries, damsons, raspberries, strawberries and mulberries were all eaten. A large part of the diet was grain and meat – from cattle, sheep and pigs in particular. The animals were brought to the city alive, then slaughtered in special slaughter houses. The skulls of forty-seven lambs, for instance, have been dug

up in Southwark close to the junction of roads leading from Sussex and Kent. Milk and cheese must also have been important, but they leave no traces behind them. However, bones of herring, mackerel, plaice and eel have all been found, and thousands of oyster shells (oysters were one of the Romans' favourite foods). Traces of cabbages, carrots and cucumbers have been discovered.

London must certainly have had a market which was popular with farmers living around the town, for numbers of agricultural tools have been excavated. They include hoes, sickles, pruning-hooks for fruit trees, rakes with iron spikes and spades with iron edges. The number of bones of oxen that have been found shows that it was they, rather than horses, that dragged the British iron ploughs which had transformed the countryside. Goads used to urge them into action have also been dug up.

The tools found from these years belong to most of the craftsmen you would expect to find in a big and expanding city – builders, carpenters and potters, for instance. Blacksmiths have left some of their hammers, anvils and furnace bars, and the remains of iron slag heaps show where the metal was worked. Fragments of the pottery lamps which lit the houses have been found. But no one would have expected the discovery of a collection of surgical instruments similar to a modern surgeon's, though made of bronze rather than stainless steel. Nor would anyone have expected to dig up two wooden yo-yos, or board games of the racing sort, complete with counters and dice, or to find so much evidence of people keeping dogs as pets (they do not seem to have kept as many cats). London had indeed become part of the so-called civilized world.

Building a Colony

A model of Fishbourne Palace in Sussex. The palace, built about AD 75 by King Cogidubnus, has been called by archaeologists the largest Roman building north of the Alps.

If Britons who lived in the London area must have been amazed to see a great city appearing there, others living on the south coast must have been equally amazed by the construction of the palace at Fishbourne. Its owner was probably King Cogidubnus. He had been a British leader in south-east England when the Romans invaded and had supported them during Queen Boudicca's revolt. As a reward, the Romans allowed him to go on ruling Sussex and Hampshire, so long as he continued to support them. He was given the title of legate (ambassador) to the Emperor and was allowed to sit in the Roman senate. And he was allowed to live in a magnificent palace at Fishbourne, built in AD 75, which modern archaeologists have called the largest Roman building north of the Alps.

The palace was unlike anything else in Britain. It could be compared in size and splendour only to the palaces of the Emperor in Rome. Foreign craftsmen must have worked there in large numbers to build it. The stones came from all over the Empire – marble from Italy, for instance, as well as from Purbeck in Dorset, from the Spanish Pyrenees, and from Greece and Turkey. Fishbourne became the port for the growing town of Chichester nearby, and the sea lapped at the terraced gardens outside the main buildings of the palace.

In the centre of the west wing was a vaulted audience chamber, reached by a flight of steps from the garden. Here the King held court. The main building was entered through a vast hall, at one end of which was a marble-lined pool. More

Part of one of the fine mosaic floors at Fishbourne Palace. It shows a cupid riding on the back of a dolphin.

than sixty mosaics covered the floors of the palace. The rooms had painted ceilings, and the walls were covered with large panels of red, yellow and deep blue. One of them contained a painting showing the corner of a building with the sea in the background. It was painted in brown, blue and white. Doors and windows were framed with marble mouldings and sometimes friezes of stucco (a kind of plaster) ran around the tops of the walls. One of the friezes showed two birds holding fruit in their beaks and facing each other across vases of fruit. Statues and busts would have decorated some of the rooms. A marble head of a child has been found, which probably stood in one of the reception rooms.

The gardens have recently been rebuilt to show how they would have looked and planted with the same trees and shrubs. They are the only formal gardens ever to have been excavated in Britain. They were surrounded with wide colonnaded walks, and across their centre and around their edges there were paths lined with box hedges. Fruit trees, climbing roses and flowering shrubs stood in the middle. Fountains played into marble basins. The beds contained rosemary, lily and acanthus.

Travellers and traders on a Roman road.

Not only had nothing like this palace and its gardens been seen in Britain before, there was nothing like it outside the Mediterranean. One can only wonder what the Roman Governor of Britannia, whose own palace was in London, thought of a British king who could afford to live in such a style.

The most lasting memorial which the Romans left behind them in Britain was their road system. They began building soon after they arrived, and by the time they left had built about 5000 Roman miles of magnificent roads. These were still being used 1300 years later, although the people who came after the Romans had no idea how to repair them. Even today traces of the Roman paving stones, running straight across the countryside, can be seen. I myself came across such stones in a wood near Dover recently and followed the straight track for a mile until it was lost in a farmer's field. Although the Romans built their roads originally in order to move troops quickly across the country, soldiers were

not the only users. Farmers carrying their produce to market, traders from all over the Western world, Roman and British officials going about their duties all travelled by road. They brought British people into closer touch with each other and with the rest of the Empire.

One of the reasons the roads lasted as well as they did was that they were thoroughly drained. The first job of the Roman road engineers was always to dig deep trenches in the soil, into which layers of cobblestones, crushed rubble and concrete would be piled. On top of these deep foundations would be laid a surface of large paving stones, carefully fitted together. The surface would be curved at the edges (cambered), so that water ran off, and drainage ditches would be cut along the sides of the roads. In the towns a kerb separated the road from the footpath. Milestones were placed every Roman mile – about 1400 metres.

In 122 the Roman Emperor Hadrian visited Britain, the first Emperor to do so since Claudius. During the previous few years tribes from Scotland had destroyed the Roman forts built to keep them out and had invaded northern England. The Romans had three choices before them – to move their border back to the river Trent, to conquer the whole of Scotland, or to try to keep the tribes out by a different method. Hadrian chose the last. He built a great wall across England at the point where it is at its narrowest. It stretched from Bowness-on-Solway in the west to Wallsend-on-Tyne in the east, a distance of about 115 kilometres, and was completed in ten years. Hadrian's Wall remained as a "frontier of civilization" for 260 years, and much of it still stands today, attracting thousands of visitors each year, many of them keen to "walk the wall".

Hadrian's Wall had four parts: a ditch to the north, 8 metres wide and 2¾ metres deep; the Wall itself; a second ditch to the south; and a military road south of that. The Wall was a little over 2 metres wide. It was not solid stone, but built of large squarish stones on the outside and packed with broken stones and mortar in the middle. It was 4½ metres high, with a flat top, sometimes turfed, so that sentries could walk along it. On the north side of the sentry walk, there was an extra 2 metres of narrow parapet to protect the sentries from enemy attacks. Every 500 metres a turret was built for the soldiers patrolling the Wall, and every Roman mile a milecastle was built on the south side of the Wall. The milecastle was a barracks for between twenty-five and fifty men. It contained a gateway through the Wall so that soldiers could march out to attack the enemy if necessary.

Winter at Chester's Fort, one of the 16 forts built into Hadrian's Wall. The fort, which housed 500 soldiers, had barracks, a house for the commandant, bath houses, and a strong room for pay.

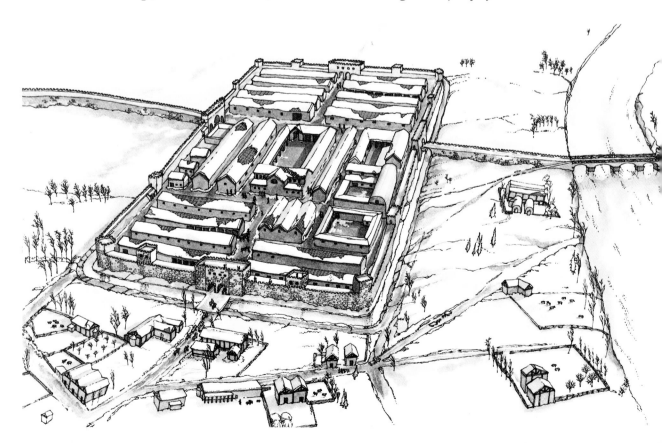

Every 8 kilometres there was a large fort, making a total of sixteen in all. Each of these housed about 500 soldiers, and contained supplies and services. There were granaries, with raised floors so that the corn would not grow damp. There were workshops for blacksmiths and carpenters, a hospital for the sick and, of course, bath houses. The forts had protective walls and turrets. Roads from the south ran into them.

The ditch to the south of the Wall was built for two purposes. If the Brigantes tribesmen of northern England turned against the Romans and attacked the Wall from the south, it would serve as a defence against them. If armies from Scotland did succeed in breaking through the Wall it would serve as an extra barrier against any attempt to return home.

The Wall seems to have given the Romans new confidence. By 140 they had advanced deep into Scotland, and in 142 they built a wall of turf, 60 kilometres long, connecting the river Clyde at what is now Glasgow with the Firth of Forth at Edinburgh. It was called the Antonine Wall, after the Emperor who ruled at the time. Only about 6000 soldiers were needed to patrol it. Twenty years later the Roman army retreated from Scotland to Hadrian's Wall. Then in 196–197 the troops were withdrawn from the Wall, as they were needed to fight in Gaul for the Governor of Britain, who was trying to become Emperor. The Scottish tribes saw their opportunity, and advanced deep into northern England, capturing York. Whole stretches of the Wall were demolished. When a new Emperor, Septimus Severus, visited Britain in 208, he supervised the rebuilding of the Wall. From then on, though badly damaged, the Wall withstood all attacks

A Roman soldier on Hadrian's Wall.

from the north. In 388, the Romans finally abandoned it and the troops left. Roman Britain was to be invaded eventually not from the north, but from the south.

But though the Wall held firm, much of the 3rd century was a time of chaos throughout the Empire. There were civil wars, and at one point Britain joined a separate Empire – "the Empire of the Gallic provinces" – which contained France, Spain and parts of Germany. Many Roman Emperors were assassinated. There was high inflation. By 270 the whole Empire seemed about to collapse. Rich villa owners in Gaul emigrated to live in Britain, to escape attacks

53

by tribes from across the Rhine. In 287 a senior Roman officer, Carausius, rebelled and took over Britain as his own. Many of the troops followed him, but six years later he was murdered. By 296 Britain was back under control of the Roman Emperor. The Emperor Constantius saved London from destruction by rebels and himself led an invasion of Scotland in 306. He died at York, and it was there that the army proclaimed his son the new Emperor Constantine. Constantine the Great, as he was known, regarded Britain as his favourite province. For the next forty-five years Roman Britain was peaceful and prosperous again.

Although some people went to live in the new towns or joined the army, most Britons continued to live and work in the countryside. They usually lived in the same simple timber-framed farmsteads their ancestors had inhabited before the Romans came, and looked after their small farms in the same way, growing just enough to feed themselves and their families. But there were many exceptions. In the south of the country farmers with bigger farms produced a surplus of corn, which they sold to people in the towns or exported to other countries. In the north and west farmers ran large cattle farms and sold the meat and hides. The retired soldiers who were given farms around Colchester, York and Gloucester often used new farming methods to grow more than they needed, in order to sell it, rather than just supporting their family.

There were also big estates belonging to the Emperor made up of the lands which had been seized from the conquered tribal chiefs and from other enemies. These were run by slaves or were divided into tenant farms, whose farmers paid rents to the Emperor.

A country villa in Roman Britain.

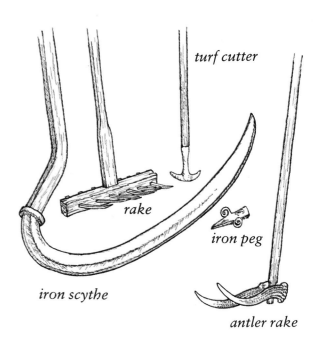

turf cutter

rake

iron peg

iron scythe

antler rake

54

But it was the villa which was the most important Roman introduction to the British countryside. Some of these country houses were small and were really British farmsteads altered after the Romans came. Some were large and luxurious new houses, modelled on villas owned by rich Romans in the Italian countryside. They were surrounded by big estates. Some rich men owned several villas and estates, both in Britain and in Gaul. They would grow one crop on one estate and a different one on another. Most of the villas were lived in by Britons, but some were occupied by Roman civil servants, merchants or high-ranking officers.

Villa life can be studied in detail at the carefully excavated house which stood at Lullingstone, near Kent, 12 kilometres north of modern Sevenoaks. It was lived in for 300 years, and was altered and enlarged during that time. It began as a British farmhouse, of wood and thatch, at the time of the Roman invasion. At the end of the 1st century AD the British owner rebuilt his house to look more like a Roman villa, in flint and mortar and with a thatched roof.

Towards the end of the 2nd century a wealthy Roman lived in the house and he changed it completely. This Roman may have worked in London and travelled to work from his country villa like a commuter does today. It would probably have taken him about the same time to reach his office – two hours!

In about 200, for some reason, the Roman left the area, leaving his treasures behind him. Nobody lived there again for 100 years. Then a rich British farmer came to live in the villa and farm the lands. After about 360, the villa stopped being lived in and about 380 the baths were pulled down and filled in. In the 5th century the buildings were destroyed by fire.

Lullingstone stood on a terrace cut into the hillside overlooking the river Darent. When the rich farmer lived there, in about 330, it must have resembled a very large, spacious modern bungalow, with wings added on to the main building, and with a cluster of farm buildings around the house. The walls were of flint and mortar, built on a wooden framework, and the roof was made of heavy red tiles. The villa was painted inside with brightly coloured designs. In the centre of the villa stood dining and reception rooms, lit by glass windows high up in the walls and with mosaic floors. There was a private bath house, and among the farm buildings there was a large granary, close to the river. There were two temples, one to Roman and the other to British gods.

The farm lands attached to Lullingstone covered many hundreds of acres of downs and woodlands. Corn was grown on the downs, the woods provided oak for building or for the central heating furnace and acorns for the pigs, while cattle and horses could graze along the river banks. The river runs into the Thames, so that produce could be taken easily by water to London or to the Continent. Watling Street, which led to London, was a few kilometres away.

Lullingstone is perhaps best known for the discovery of its Christian chapel. This was built about 365 above a room where the old British or Roman worship still continued. On the plaster of the walls were painted figures of men at prayer and a large painting of the Christian sign. This was the two Greek letters Chi and Rho – CHR – which stands for "Christos", Christ in Greek.

Christians were cruelly persecuted by the Roman authorities for the first 300 years after Jesus' death. The Romans had a number of different religions, while the Britons continued to worship their own gods of nature – of the sun, moon and forest, for instance. Of the few people in Britain who had become Christians by the 3rd century, a number suffered cruelly for their faith.

A change occurred when Constantine became Emperor. He was converted to Christianity and declared it the official religion of the Empire. British bishops were appointed and European bishops came to visit them. Britons worshipping their old gods were even persecuted. British temples were turned into Christian churches, and a number of Britons became Christians. But after the Romans left people soon went back to their old gods and before long there were hardly any signs that Christianity had ever come to Britain.

The Chi-Ro mosaic at Lullingstone.

Decline and Fall

Britain was peaceful during the reign of Emperor Constantine, but for years the Roman Empire had been in trouble. Civil wars were fought, emperors were assassinated, and politicians and generals fought each other to gain control. At the same time, tribes were attacking the borders of the Empire in Europe from the 3rd century onwards. They had come from the Russian steppes and moved into central and eastern Europe. They saw the wealth of the Empire, and believed the Romans were too weak to defend it.

Certainly, the Roman army was not as efficient as it had been in the early days. Many of the soldiers were foreigners, and later officers and even generals were sometimes foreigners too. These foreign soldiers did not always feel as loyal to the Emperor as the Romans themselves did. Sometimes they changed sides in the middle of a battle against an invading tribe. Without strong armies, and with troubles at home, the Romans could no longer defend and control their vast Empire. The fact that they had done so for so many centuries is one of the wonders of history.

By 300, the Romans were very worried about the tribes from Germany who were attacking British shores. These were the Saxons though the Romans tended to call all tribes by the same name, "barbarians" (because their strange languages sounded to them like animal noises – "bar, bar"). The Saxons advanced deep inland looking for wealthy towns and villas to loot. The governors of Britannia had always been reluctant to allow a town to build a circuit of walls, for it could make the

From AD 300 onwards England's south and east coasts were raided by tribes from north Germany and Holland eager for loot. The Romans built coastal forts under their commander the Count of the Saxon Shore, but found it increasingly difficult to defend Britain against such attacks.

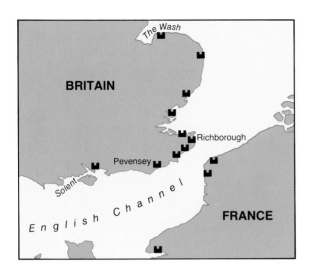

The Saxon Shore forts.

ive walls, from which stone-throwing machines threw balls of stone more than 30 centimetres in diameter. Unlike the forts the Romans built when they invaded, these were to defend the British people; not barracks from which the troops would attack them.

The monument at Richborough which the Romans had originally built to celebrate their victory over the British was now used as a look-out post. Sentries peered anxiously out across the Channel, searching for the dreaded Saxon pirates. From a magnificent monument with shining bronze statues dominating the Channel, Richborough had become a place from which repeated dangers could be spotted.

town difficult to control. Now town governors began to build walls round their towns, particularly those near the coast, to keep out the invaders. A chain of forts was built from the Wash to the Solent, and placed under the command of a man who was known as the Count of the Saxon Shore. The forts had mass-

Richborough in Kent. This massive wall still stands today. Richborough was one of the Saxon Shore forts. Here the Romans first landed in strength and from here they finally left Britain.

In 350 a general of the Roman army in Germany tried to turn the western part of the Roman Empire, including Britain, into a separate empire. This rebellion was defeated, but the British were savagely punished for supporting it. Then in 367 Picts from Scotland and tribes from Ireland invaded the north of England and reached as far south as the Thames. At the same time, the Saxons and the Franks attacked southern England and northern Gaul.

The army was unprepared for attacks from several different directions at once. Like the rest of the Roman army, the army in Britain had become undisciplined and weak. Instead of defending Britain against the invaders, many soldiers deserted. They joined the enemy who roamed the country in small bands; or roamed about themselves, robbing towns and farms. A strong task force under a commander called Theodosius was sent from Rome to re-establish order. He recaptured London and defeated the Saxons at sea. Bands of barbarian soldiers were rounded up. Deserters were pardoned, and the army reorganized. Forts were rebuilt; towns and cities repaired. Villas were still inhabited and farmed. A new system of signal stations was set up on one section of Hadrian's Wall. Everything seemed to have gone back to normal.

At the beginning of the 5th century, the real ruler of the Western Empire was a Vandal who took the Roman name of Flavius Stilicho. He withdrew part of the Roman army out of Britain to fight for him in Europe, for he hoped to take over the whole Empire. Soon the rest of the Roman army left Britain as well. The British were left to fight the Saxon invaders alone. In 440 a group of British leaders asked for help from Rome, but

their request was ignored. The Romans were overwhelmed by troubles of their own, and seemed to have lost interest in Britain. It was no longer part of the Roman Empire.

Once the Roman troops and civil servants had gone, the local chiefs and big landowners were left in charge of the country. A bishop from Gaul who visited St Albans in 429 described the local rich men as being "conspicuous for their riches, brilliant in dress, and surrounded by a fawning multitude". Signs of Roman wealth and organization vanished with extraordinary speed. By 430

Both sides of a coin found at Richborough dated AD 410. One side shows a Briton cowering before a Roman on horseback.

coins were no longer regularly used.

People still went on living in towns for a while – archaeologists have discovered that in Lincoln, for instance, a main street was resurfaced after the legions had gone, while at St Albans a new water main was laid about 450. But soon nobody repaired the roads or kept up the town walls. The forts and Hadrian's Wall were neglected; the villas slowly deserted. People went back to living on their own small farms, and growing just enough for themselves and their families.

It seems extraordinary that a way of life which had existed for nearly 400 years should vanish, leaving so few traces behind. The Romans had tried to get the British to share in their way of life – to help govern the country, to join the army, and to follow Roman methods of trade, industry and farming. In the towns the potters, the jewellers, the blacksmiths were British. Roman engineers may have supervised the building of the great roads, but British workers built and repaired them. The forts and walls were constructed according to Roman designs used all over the Empire, but the work was done by the British.

In the light of all this, how was it that British landowners, accustomed to living the leisurely and comfortable life of the villas, deserted them, leaving thieves to take the bricks and tiles? How could Christian men and women go back to the gods of their ancestors? How could town-dwellers lose interest in the towns in which they had once taken such a pride, let their forum, basilica or theatre fall to pieces, and move to the country again? When you know how to build a road, why let it go and return to using a track? Why give up reading and writing? It is all very strange.

A collapsing Roman villa. After the Romans left, the villas, although most of them had been lived in by British owners, were abandoned. Local farmers took away their wood, tiles and stones.

The German Invaders

Fifty years after the Romans left, the Saxons, Angles and other tribes from north Germany took over England. They settled in much the same areas as those occupied by the Romans. The British were pushed into the north and west of England and into Wales. They became slaves or foreigners in their own country (the Saxon word *walh* or *wealh*, from which the name Wales comes, means both Briton and slave).

Some of the German tribespeople had begun to settle in Britain even before the Romans left. Archaeologists have found the remains of 200 huts, probably Saxon, built around 400 at Mucking on the Thames estuary. Possibly they belonged to Saxon soldiers being paid by the authorities to guard London from other invaders. Later their families may have come to Britain to join them.

The German invaders could neither read nor write. As we have seen, many of the Britons were literate during the Roman period, but none has left us any record of this time. So once again most of our knowledge of this time comes from the findings of archaeologists. But there is also a description of Saxon times written by a Christian monk living in the 8th century called the Venerable Bede. Though Bede was writing 300 years after the events he described, he probably got his information from memories and stories passed on by word of mouth from generation to generation. He drew also on church records. What he wrote may not always be true, but it does seem to fit in with what archaeologists have found. Here is his account of the invaders:

"They came from three very powerful Germanic tribes, the Saxons, Angles and Jutes. The people of Kent, and the inhabitants of the Isle of Wight are of Jutish origin. From the Saxon country came the East Saxons, the South Saxons and the West Saxons. From the country of the Angles, that is the land between the kingdoms of the Jutes and the Saxons, which is called Angulus, came the East Angles, the Middle Angles, the Mercians and all the Northumbrian race (that is the people who dwell north of the river Humber) as well as other Anglian tribes. Angulus is said to have remained deserted from that day to this."[4]

This Saxon cup was found at Mucking on the Thames estuary. Shortly before the Romans left, Saxon soldiers had camped at Mucking. They were being paid to guard Roman London.

Some names of English counties and regions come from the names of these tribes. Essex, Sussex and Northumberland are counties whose names are taken from the peoples Bede describes; Wessex, East Anglia and Mercia are regions.

Bede left out some of the German tribes, and the divisions between the tribal lands was probably not nearly as clear as it seems in his account. He does not mention the many men and women who came from near the river Rhine, such as the Franks, who were great traders, and the Frisians from the northern Netherlands. They sailed from the mouth of the Rhine across the North Sea to Kent. However, we know that what Bede said about tribes deserting their homelands is true because of archaeological excavations near the mouth of the river Weser in north Germany. An abandoned village of large timber buildings has been found where the city of Bremen now stands. It was left uninhabited

Saxon settlers landing in Britain. When their fighting men reported that it was safe to come, whole families arrived to colonize their new lands. They beached their boats and waded ashore with their sheep and cattle, and their possessions packed in wooden cases.

about 450, apparently because the sea was rising and threatening to destroy it.

Why so many people left their homelands in Europe to come to Britain we do not know for certain, but there are various possible reasons. Perhaps they were becoming overcrowded, because the population was growing too fast. Perhaps there was a shortage of food. The first groups of raiders would have gone back and told their people about the rich, fertile lands of southern Britain. They probably also told them that the country would be easy to attack because of its unprotected coastline, and the rivers which ran far inland. It is certainly the case that their own countries were

being attacked by fierce tribes, the Huns and the Goths, moving in from eastern Europe, as the Saxons' own ancestors had done.

There have been many extraordinary migrations in the history of the human race. In the Pacific, the Maori peoples left the Philippines in the 16th century. They travelled in their great outrigger canoes for 6000 kilometres until they reached New Zealand, where they settled down. Earlier, peoples from Java in Indonesia had sailed across the Indian Ocean in primitive boats to Madagascar, where their descendants have lived ever since. Four hundred years after the Anglo-Saxon tribes settled in England, they themselves were overrun by pirates from Scandinavia – the Norsemen or Vikings – who took over eastern England and settled in it as the Saxons had done.

Perhaps all migrating peoples – the Saxons included – were just looking for adventure. The tribes who came to Britain had always been on the move, after all. Their ancestors had come all the way from northern China and north-eastern Russia, across the Russian steppes and into Europe. The Anglo-Saxon poem *Beowulf*, which can claim to be the first English poem, and was written 200 years or so after these migrations, has described one Saxon voyage as follows:

"Time passed on; the ship was on the waves, the boat beneath the cliff. The warriors eagerly embarked. The currents turned the sea against the sand. Men bore bright ornaments, splendid war trappings, to the bosom of the ship. The men, the heroes on their willing venture, shoved out the well-timbered ship. The foamy-necked floater like a bird went over the wave-filled sea, sped by the wind, till after due time on the next day the boat with twisted prow had gone so far that the voyagers saw land, the sea-cliffs shining, the steep headlands, the broad sea-capes. Then the sea was traversed, the journey at an end. The men ... mounted quickly to the land; they made fast the ship. The armour rattled, the garments of battle. They thanked God that the sea voyage had been easy for them."[5]

The biggest invasion of Britain by Angle and Saxon tribes was in about 450. At that time, a Welsh king, Vortigern, ruled much of the country, including the south-east corner of Kent. His people lived along the old border between England and Wales. They had been allies of the Romans, and had adopted many Roman ways. When Saxon raiders kept landing along the south-east coast, Vortigern decided to ask some of those same Saxon people to help defend him from the invaders. He

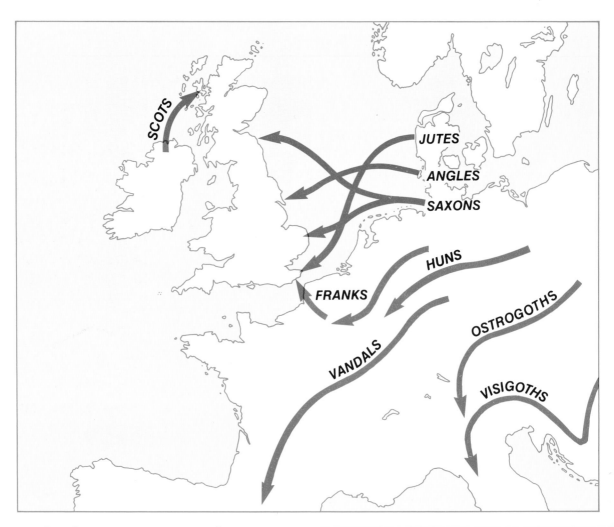

Raiders from Europe were attacking Britain before the Romans left. Once the Roman soldiers had gone there was nothing to stop these Saxons, Angles and Jutes from settling down permanently.

The Anglo-Saxons did more than any previous settlers to clear and plough lands which no one had yet farmed. In the scene on the right an overseer is supervising farm workers who are cutting and carrying corn.

called in Saxon soldiers to defend his people, and offered them lands in east Kent as a reward. Here is how Bede describes what happened:

"At that time the race of the Angles or Saxons, invited by Vortigern, came to Britain in three warships and by his

command were granted a place of settlement in the easternmost part of the island. They pretended they were going to fight on behalf of the country, but their real intention was to conquer it... First they fought against the enemy who attacked from the north, and the Saxons won the victory. A report of this, and of the fertility of the island and the slackness of the Britons, reached their homes, and at once a much larger fleet was sent over, with a stronger band of warriors. This, added to the contingent already there, made an invincible army. The newcomers received from the Britons a grant of land in their midst on condition that they fought against their foes for the peace and safety of the country, and for this the soldiers were also to receive pay."[4]

Soon the new settlers, led by two brothers called Hengist and Horsa, attacked their hosts. This is how *The Anglo-Saxon Chronicle*, the history of their people, written later than Bede's history, tells the next part of the story:

"455. In this year Hengist and Horsa fought againt King Vortigern at the place which is called Aegelesthrep (Aylesford, Kent) and Horsa was killed there.
456. In this year Hengist and his son Aesc fought against the Britons in the place which is called Creaconford (Crayford, Kent) and killed 4000 men; and the Britons then deserted Kent and fled with great fear to London."[6]

For the next 150 years, the Saxons moved farther and farther into England, until by 600 they controlled most of the country. The original tribes were followed by others. Most of Scotland remained under the control of the Picts, though there were settlements of Irish in the west. These Irish were called Scots, and eventually they gave their name to the whole country. The British kept control in north-west England, Somerset, Devon and Cornwall, and Wales. It has been written that the British won a great victory over the Saxons about the year 500, but nobody knows where the battle was fought.

Many stories were later told about a great British leader, Arthur, and his "Knights of the Round Table" who were supposed to have lived at that time. All over Wales and the south-west of England, minstrels used to tell or sing of their deeds around the fires that burned in their lords' halls. In Cornwall and in Brittany in western France, where many British had fled to escape the Saxons, people thought that Arthur was a saint. They waited eagerly for him to return and save Britain. But there is no evidence that such a man, or king, ever existed.

Those Britons who did not flee to the north or south-west of England, or west to Wales, worked as free labourers or slaves of the Saxons. Indeed the Britons formed by far the greatest proportion of the population. During the 6th century, there were only about 100,000 Anglo-Saxons in Britain, one tenth of the population. Some modern place names come from the names of settlements of Britons in forests or marshes: the word Walden in Saffron Walden (in Essex) is old English for "the valley of the Welsh", Walmer (in Kent) means "the lake or marsh of the Welsh".

Life in Anglo-Saxon Britain was very different from that of Roman times. The towns and villas, money and writing, organized armies and law courts had disappeared. The Anglo-Saxons replaced them with their own way of life, which was more like life in Britain before Roman times.

The tribes were farming people, and they lived in the countryside in small groups of about fifty. Each group was made up of the family and relations of one man. The laws were based on loyalty to your family and lord. If you were killed, your family would catch and kill the murderer or one of his family. If someone else in your family was killed, it was up to you to punish the killer. If you failed to do so, you would never be forgiven. Above the family were the lords, and the chiefs. Loyalty to them was as important as loyalty to the family. You would never be forgiven if you broke your oath of loyalty.

The names of some of the Saxon chiefs are to be found in the modern names of places where they settled. The village in which I live is called Adisham, and means the settlement ("ham") of chief Eade. Hastings was inhabited by the people of chief Haesta, whose name means the "violent one". Birmingham means the settlement of Beornmund's people. Sometimes the chief was the original leader of the group which had left Europe for a new life in England.

The Saxons worshipped many gods. Some of their names are remembered today in our days of the week. Tuesday is named after the Saxon god Tiw, Wednesday after Woden. Both were gods of war. Thursday was called after Thunor, god of thunder, and Friday after the goddess Frigg, Woden's wife. Their places of worship were in the countryside – in secluded parts of a wood, in sacred groves, or forest clearings. We know they worshipped trees, springs, stones and rocks because, when England became Christian again, an archbishop specifically ordered them not to.

The Saxons worshipped their gods because they believed they would protect them in battle or during storms; they thought they would cure their children of illness, make their crops fertile and bring them prosperity. As we shall see, many of their beliefs survived for centuries after they became Christians, while others were gradually merged with the new Christian teachings.

The Early Christians

By 500 Christianity had died out in most of England. But it was a different story in Wales and Ireland. In Wales, the Church continued, as in the later Roman time, to live an organized life, complete with bishops and local parish clergy. Some of the most devout Welsh Christians thought that the Church was too involved with day-to-day affairs and the political ambitions of the local kings. So during the 5th and 6th centuries they set up monasteries (called *llans* in Welsh, as in Llandudno or Llandovery). Here small groups of Christians lived dedicated lives of prayer, Bible study, farm work and service to the local poor or sick. Their tiny churches were surrounded by a few simple huts of wood, straw and mud. Other Christians lived as hermits in remote mountain valleys, in forest clearings or on the edges of rocky cliffs overlooking the sea. The monks visited their brother monks in monasteries in other Celtic countries – in Ireland, for instance, or Cornwall, or Brittany in the far west of France. They were in closer touch with people outside their homelands than with their neighbours, the Anglo-Saxons.

Remains of the monastery at Tintagel in Cornwall, the earliest known monastery in Britain, built by Celtic Christian monks about AD 470.

The greatest Christian personality during these years of whom we have knowledge was St Patrick. His letters and a book he wrote called *Declaration* are the only British documents that have survived from the 100 years after the Romans left. From them, and from the history of his life, written by an Irishman called Muirchu 200 years after his death, St Patrick appears to have been a humble man, quietly determined to do what he believed God wanted him to do and surrounded by enemies who campaigned ceaselessly against him.

Patrick was born in about 385. He lived on the west coast of Britain, some say near the Severn estuary. His father was a Roman official, probably of British nationality; his grandfather was a Christian priest. At the age of sixteen Patrick was captured by pirates and taken to Ireland. Here he lived a solitary life as a herdsman, perhaps in Antrim, where he grew to love the Irish people. This is how he himself describes this part of his life:

The opening of St Patrick's Declaration. *Written in Latin, it is now in Trinity College, Dublin. Patrick established Christianity in Ireland more than 100 years before Anglo-Saxon Christianity began.*

"But after I reached Ireland, well, I pastured the flocks every day and I used to pray many times a day; more and more did my love of God and fear of him increase, and my faith grew and my spirit was stirred and as a result I would say up to 100 prayers in one day, and almost as many at night; I would even stay in the forests and on the mountain and would wake to pray before dawn in all weathers, snow, frost and rain; and I felt no harm and there was no tiredness in me — as I now realize, it was because the spirit was busy within me. And it was in fact there that one night while asleep I heard a voice saying to me: 'You do well to fast, since you will soon be going to your home country', and again: 'See your ship is ready.' "[7]

On the instructions of the voice that he

had heard in his sleep, Patrick ran away to the coast and there found a boat as he had been told.

The sailors took him to France. Here he was trained as a priest. Then he returned to his family in Britain. In about 432 he was made Bishop to the Irish and returned to Ireland.

Patrick's family begged him not to go to Ireland, and many other Christians were against it too, and said that he should not have been made bishop. Some said he was not properly educated because he did not read or write fluently in Latin. Patrick felt these criticisms deeply and, in his *Declaration*, kept apologizing for his poor knowledge of languages and of Latin — the international language of the time in which all books in Europe were written.

As for the Irish themselves, they were very suspicious of foreigners. They thought of Patrick as bringing "a strange and troublesome doctrine...from far away...that would overthrow kingdoms and destroy their gods."

Yet in spite of all this opposition, Patrick succeeded in his mission of converting Ireland to Christianity. He set up an organized system of bishops and priests, linked to the European Catholic Church, and encouraged people to build monasteries. After his death in about 461 at the age of seventy-six — a great age for those times — other Christians went out from these monasteries and completed his work. A hundred years after his death, most of Ireland was Christian, when Saxon England had forgotten Christianity.

For thirty years in Ireland, Patrick faced all sorts of difficulties and hardships, including being thrown into prison. He was often anxious and unhappy, as he vividly described in his writings. He wrote of his longing to return to his own people and to his teachers in France:

"I would have been only too glad to part and head for Britain, to see my homeland and family; and not only that, but to go on to Gaul to visit the brethren and to see the face of my Lord's holy men."[7]

But he stayed in Ireland because, as he wrote:

"I am afraid of wasting the labour which I have begun — and not I, but Christ the Lord who commanded me to come to be with them for the rest of my life."[7]

Patrick went all over Ireland baptizing people and ordaining priests. He never asked for any money for his labours, but his enemies accused him of trying to make a profit out of the people. Sometimes women gave him gifts of jewellery. They would throw rings, necklaces and bracelets on the altar, but Patrick would return them at once, so that no one could accuse him of dishonesty. This would make them angry. He defended himself with passion, writing:

"But perhaps when I baptized so many thousands I hoped for even a half penny from any of them? Tell me, and I will give it back. Or when the Lord everywhere ordained clergy through someone as ordinary as me and I conferred on each of them his function free, if I asked any of them so much as the price of my shoe, tell it against me and I shall give it back to you. No, rather I spent money on your behalf so that they would accept me, and I travelled among you and everywhere for your sake, beset by many dangers, even to the remote districts

beyond which there was no one and where no one had ever penetrated to baptize or ordain clergy or confirm the people...”[7]

Often Patrick's life was in danger, but his faith was so strong that he believed that nothing would be too much to suffer in God's name. He wrote:

“Every day I expect to be killed, betrayed, reduced to slavery or whatever ... And if I have ever aimed at any good for my God's sake, whom I love, I beg Him to grant that I may shed my blood for His name along with those exiles and captives, though I should even go without burial or my body be torn most pitiably limb from limb for dogs or savage beasts to share or the birds of the air to devour it. It is my strong conviction that if this should happen to me, I

St Patrick tours Ireland on his mission of conversion. In the distance is a crannog, a village built on water.

would have gained my soul.”[7]

Like their Welsh brothers, the Irish monks who followed St Patrick were in touch with Christians in Europe. They too regarded their monastery as a base from which they would travel, generally by foot and boat, to spread the Christian message. They lived simply, went among the people as humble fellow human beings, and were quite prepared to go among tribes whose languages they did not understand or of whose ways they were ignorant. The monasteries in Ireland became great centres of learning and art. The most famous of all the handwritten and gloriously illustrated manuscripts in Europe is the Book of Kells, an 8th or 9th century manuscript

From Lindisfarne, Aidan and his monks travelled among the Northumbrian people. Aidan was supported by Oswy, the King of Northumbria, and he made many conversions, impressing people with his humility and sincerity. At Lindisfarne he trained English boys for missionary work among their own people. Aidan would not allow the monastery to accumulate wealth – any money left over was to be used to help the poor or to buy slaves their freedom. Bede described Aidan as "a man of remarkable gentleness, goodness and moderation". He went on to say that:

"He rejoiced to hand over at once, to any poor man he met, the gifts which he had received from kings or rich men... He used to travel everywhere, in town and country, not on horseback but on foot...

copy of the New Testament. This may have been written and painted by monks in Iona before being brought to Kells. It is now on show in Dublin in all its glinting beauty.

In about 563, Columba, an Irishman who had been brought up by a priest and wanted to be "a pilgrim for Christ", travelled with twelve companions to the tiny island of Iona, off the south-west corner of Mull in western Scotland. Here, in this wild and lonely spot, he built a monastery and from it travelled widely in Scotland, preaching to the northern Picts, and converting many of them to Christianity. (The southern Picts were already Christian.)

Later Aidan, a monk from the Iona community, built another monastery at Lindisfarne off the coast of Northumberland, north of Newcastle in the northeast of England. This was in about 635.

The remains of the 6th century Skellig monastery, built on 200 metres of sheer rock several kilometres off the coast of southwest Ireland.

The cover of St Matthew's Gospel in the Book Of Kells (left). The monastery at Kells, County Meath, is shown here as it would have been about 1100. The monks lived in the beehive-shaped huts. In the middle of the enclosure stood the stone chapel. The cross was dedicated to St Patrick and St Columba. Round towers were built in many Irish monasteries. The one at Kells was about 30 metres high, with a door about 3 metres above the ground. The tower had five storeys joined by flights of stairs. A bell was rung from the tower to call the monks to prayer. When the monastery was attacked the monks retreated into the tower. Sometimes the raiders were Vikings; sometimes local thieves. The Book Of Kells was stolen in 1007. It was later found, without its gold paint, buried in the ground.

in order that, as he walked along, whenever he saw people whether rich or poor he might at once approach them and, if they were unbelievers, invite them to accept the mystery of faith, urging them by word and deed to practise almsgiving and good works."[4]

Bede told a story which showed how determined Aidan was not to travel on horseback:

"King Oswy had given Bishop Aidan an excellent horse so that, though he was normally accustomed to walk, he could ride if he had to cross a river or if he needed it for some other urgent reason. Soon after Aidan was met by a beggar who asked him for alms. He at once alighted and offered the horse with all its royal trappings to the beggar."[4]

Aidan and Columba both thought of Ireland as being the centre of their Church. Wales, Ireland, Scotland and the north of England all belonged to the Celtic branch of the Christian Church. It was separate from the main branch of the Church, whose head was the Pope in Rome, and had little contact with it despite Patrick's original links with Europe. People like Aidan and his followers thought of themselves as members of their own Celtic Christian Church. Their separation was to cause great problems.

Forty years before Aidan began building his monastery at Lindisfarne, the conversion of southern England to

This casket was made about AD 400. The ivory panel shows Christ's crucifixion. On the right is Judas who betrayed Jesus and then hanged himself.

Christianity had begun. This was also carried out in the first place by monks. But these monks owed obedience to the Roman Catholic Church and to Pope Gregory. Gregory had himself been head of a monastery in Rome, and for several years he had planned to lead a mission to England to convert the people there (France was already Christian).

The King of Kent, Ethelbert, had a Christian wife Bertha, daughter of the King of the Franks in Paris, who was allowed to worship with her court and Christian priest in a little church outside his capital at Canterbury. Gregory thought it was now time to convert the only remaining part of the old Roman Empire in Europe which was not Christian – England.

Gregory had to put off his plan to visit England when he was made Pope, but he did not forget it. He was determined to send a mission to the people whom he described as "placed in the corner of the world and until this time worshipping sticks and stones". In 596 he sent the head of his old monastery in Rome, Augustine, with forty monks to begin the conversion of England. But something went wrong, as Bede described:

"A servant of God named Augustine and several more God-fearing monks were sent to preach the word of God to the English race. In obedience to the Pope's commands they undertook this task and had gone a little way on their journey when they were paralysed with terror. They began to contemplate returning home rather than going to a barbarous, fierce and unbelieving nation whose language they did not understand."[4]

Augustine was sent back to the Pope to ask his permission "to give up so dangerous, wearisome and uncertain a journey". But Gregory sent him back again with a letter dated 23rd July 596, which convinced the monks that they must persevere.

"My dearly beloved sons, it would have been better not to have undertaken a noble task than to turn back deliberately from what you have begun: so it is right that you should carry out with all determination this good work which you have begun with the help of the Lord. Therefore do not let the difficult journey nor the tongues of evil speakers deter you... Be sure that, however great your task may be, the glory of your eternal reward will be still greater. When Augustine your prior returns...humbly obey him in all things."[4]

The area coloured green on the map shows where Celtic Christianity was first practised. It was a long time before all Britain was united in the Roman Catholic Church.

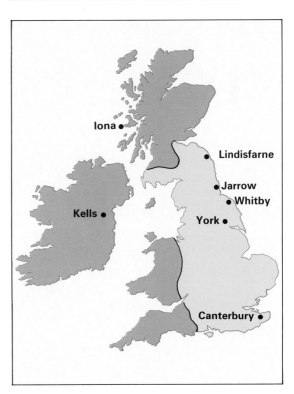

So the group of monks continued on their journey. Before they left France, they recruited some Franks to act as interpreters in England. Then they crossed the Channel and landed in Kent at Thanet.

After they had been there a while, King Ethelbert came to see for himself what the visitors were like, and to hear what they had to say. He insisted that everyone sit in the open air, because he thought that this way the Christians would not be able to get the better of him and his men through any magical arts. Augustine and his monks carried a silver cross and a picture of Christ painted on wood. Although their message did not convince Ethelbert straight away, it had an effect on him. He said to them:

"The words and the promises you bring are fair enough, but because they are new to us and doubtful, I cannot agree to accept them and give up those beliefs which I and the whole English race have held so long. But as you have come on a long pilgrimage and are anxious, I can see, to share with us those things which you believe to be true and good, we do not wish to do you harm, on the contrary, we will receive you hospitably and provide what is necessary for your support; nor do we forbid you to win all you can to your faith and religion by your preaching."[4]

Ethelbert gave them a house in Canterbury and food. So they went on their way to his capital. This is how Bede describes their arrival:

"As they approached the city in accordance with their custom carrying the holy cross and the image of our great King and Lord, Jesus Christ, they sang

This decoration from an early manuscript of Bede's life of St Cuthbert shows Bede writing. Much of our knowledge of early Anglo-Saxon life and Christianity comes from Bede's works.

this litany in unison: 'We beseech thee, O Lord, in Thy great mercy, that Thy wrath and anger may be turned away from this city and from Thy holy house, for we have sinned. Alleluia.' "[4]

Ethelbert allowed Augustine and his monks to use his wife's church, named after St Martin of Tours, for worship. It is still standing today, outside the old Roman walls at Canterbury, the oldest church in England.

After a while, Ethelbert himself became a Christian. Augustine built Canterbury Cathedral on the site of an old Roman church, and a monastery which was named after him, where the King was buried when he died. Other monks from Rome joined Augustine to help him carry on his work. They began to move into other parts of England.

Ethelbert was a useful ally. He claimed to be overlord of the East Saxons and made it possible for Bishop Mellitus to build a church of St Paul in London, which was part of their territory. Redwald, King of the East Angles, was converted to Christianity when he was visiting Ethelbert in Kent. Later he changed his mind and, as Bede says,

"served both Christ and the gods whom he served before; in one and the same temple he had an altar for the sacrifice of Christ and another for the victims of demons."[4]

Augustine and Queen Bertha enter St Martin's Church in Canterbury, followed by some of the first missionary monks. People still worship in St Martin's today.

By about 620 Augustine's missionaries were venturing into the north of England. Once again the Christians were helped by a Christian Queen, Ethelburgh, who came from Kent. When King Edwin of Northumberland married her, he promised to allow her to continue worshipping as a Christian and to consider becoming one himself. Ethelburgh was accompanied on her journey north to join her new husband by Paulinus, one of St Augustine's second band of missionaries, and he baptized the daughter born to the King and Queen at Pentecost (Whitsun) in 626. Soon King Edwin ordered a council of his advisers to be held at York in order to discuss the beliefs of the new religion and the old.

The remains of St Augustine's abbey in Canterbury. "Augustine," wrote Bede, "erected a monastery to the east of Canterbury . . . in which church the body of Augustine himself and those of all the bishops and kings of Canterbury might be laid."

The debate, records Bede, started in a surprising manner. The high priest of the old religion of the Northumbrians, a man called Coifi, said that their religion had neither virtue nor profit in it, and that he no longer believed in it. He was followed by a nobleman who compared human life on earth to the flight of a sparrow who flies into the great hall where the King sits feasting with his chiefs:

"The fire is burning on the hearth, and all inside is warm, while outside the wintry storms of rain and snow are raging. The sparrow flies in at one door, and for a few moments the storm cannot touch it, but after a brief interval it flits out through the other door into the winter again. So this life of man appears but for a moment; what follows or what went before, we know not at all. If this new doctrine brings us more certain information, it seems right that we should accept it."[4]

After others had spoken it was the turn of Paulinus, a tall man, slightly bent. He had black hair, a thin nose shaped like an eagle's beak, and a thin, bony face. He spoke passionately of how God made the world and was the loving father of all. He had sent his son Jesus to show people how to live, but they had cruelly killed him. Yet he had risen from his grave and offered new hope. If we would believe in God, say we're sorry for all we had done wrong, and be baptized, God would help us to live better lives and the world would become a better place.

When Paulinus had finished speaking, Coifi, the high priest, announced that he was deserting the old faith. Although that faith forbade priests to carry weapons and allowed them only to ride a mare, he borrowed a sword, a spear and a stallion from King Edwin. Then he rode to a nearby temple of the old religion, threw his spear at it, and burned it down. Soon King Edwin was baptized at York.

But although Paulinus made several journeys in northern England, people there stopped taking any notice of him after King Edwin had died in battle in 632. Edwin's successor, King Oswald,

The Ruthwell Cross in Dumfrieshire was carved during the 8th century. It is about 6 metres high with scenes from the Gospels on all sides and on its arms. Words from The Dream Of The Rood, *a Saxon poem, are inscribed on it.*

asked for missionaries from the Celtic Church to join him, and, as we have seen, Aidan was sent from Iona to build a monastery at Lindisfarne. For the next thirty years, Christians in Northumberland followed the Celtic Church.

Slowly, with many changes of mind and returns to the old worship of "sticks and stones", the rest of England became Christian. Sussex and the Isle of Wight were two of the last areas to do so. But because Britain was divided into two Christian faiths – with Ireland, Wales, Cornwall, Scotland and the north of England being members of the Celtic Church, and the rest of the Roman Church – there were continual problems. Finally a great "synod", or conference, of Christian leaders from the Celtic and Roman Churches was held at Whitby in Yorkshire in 664. There the Celtic Christians agreed to join the Roman Church and accept the Pope as their head. From then on, for the next 900 years, there was officially only one Christian Church in Britain (though in practice Irish, Scottish and Welsh Christians continued to use many of their own traditional ways).

As they went about, gradually converting the whole of Britain to Christianity, the missionaries set up monasteries – or "minsters" – wherever they could. Once again place names tell us where they were. For example, there was one at Westminster and one at Axminster.

King Edgar's charter for a new monastery at Winchester (right) was granted in 966. The picture shows the King flanked by the Virgin Mary on the left and St Peter, with his key to heaven, on the right. The King is offering his charter to Christ.

The Ardagh Chalice (below). This beautiful cup for Holy Communion wine was made in the 8th century. It is now in the Dublin Museum.

These minsters were simple collections of buildings within an enclosure, and sometimes linked with a farm. The Christians tried to build them in stone, for they regarded wood as "heathen" (or non-Christian). The buildings were designed for only a few monks to live in. They would consist of a church, a dormitory, individual huts for the monks, a guest house and a dining hall (called a refectory). Some of them were double houses – communities of both monks and nuns. These minsters were supervised, perhaps surprisingly, by the head of the nunnery.

The minster formed the local Christian centre. Here babies were baptized, the sick were nursed and the dead were buried. Children would be taught to read and write, and a few clever boys would gain a knowledge of Latin and the Bible. Preachers would go into the countryside round about the minster, preaching the Christian message. In time they set up small churches in the nearby settlements. Later these became the parish churches to be found in every English village.

The people would be as likely to come to the minster – out of curiosity perhaps, or to be cured of their diseases – as to meet a monk travelling past their farm. We can imagine a Saxon peasant peering over the stockade of the minster one Sunday. He might well be tempted to go inside the little church. Here his eyes would be drawn to the altar, where a monk would be holding the service in Latin. The candles would be bright in the gloom, and the air heavy with incense. There would be periods of chanting, in which the monks would bow down so low that their foreheads touched the floor. Gifts not of money but of goods – bread, milk or fruit, for instance – would be collected from the congregation in a basket and carried up to the altar. The

peasant might go away puzzled, but he would probably come back again, perhaps with his family, next Sunday or the Sunday after.

Or his wife might bring their baby to the minster to be cured of an illness. His neighbour might ask for a monk to visit his elderly mother who was dying. The local farmer might seek advice from the monks about his crops, for the monks were known to be the most up-to-date farmers in the land. Parents would ask the monks to teach their children to read and write. One agreement ran that in return for teaching a child to read, the monk would receive a tub of goose grease, two jars of honey, six lambs' skins and six eggs a week. If eggs were not available, goose's quills would do.

The interior of a minster about AD 700.

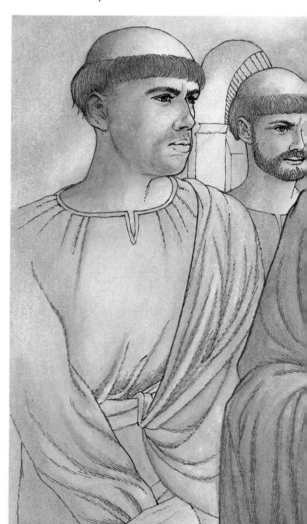

These early monks in the minsters were devoted to their work. According to Bede, they always "practised what they preached" and never gave up because of difficulties or opposition, "even to the point of dying for the truths they proclaimed". Saxon gods and British gods continued to be worshipped secretly for many years. The missionaries followed Pope Gregory's advice and, wherever possible, built their churches in places where the old gods were worshipped, and held their services at the same time of year as the Saxons had held theirs. By doing so, they hoped to make it easier for people to change over to the new religion. The Christian Easter was held at the same time as heathen or "pagan" services held to the goddess of spring, Eostre. Christmas was celebrated at the same time as the heathen festival of Yule. (Men would still dress in animal skins and in the masks of animals at Yuletide. They would dance for eight days in the firelight, and throw fantastic shadows on the wall like their Stone Age ancestors in their caves. By these means they hoped to induce good hunting in the year ahead.)

As the monks had hoped, after a while people thought of the new Christian churches with the same respect that they once had felt for their old places of worship. Many of the Christian carvings – images of the saints, for instance, or statues of Jesus and his mother – must have resembled the old heathen idols. Just as the early Saxons thought that holy wells, magic circles, incantations and charms would protect them from evil which could strike them down at any moment, so later English Christians believed that holy water, the chanting of a prayer, the relics of a saint or the carved figure of Christ on the cross would protect them from evil in the same way.

All the same, the Church fought a bitter battle against many of the old practices. They had to stop people, for example, from burying a widow alive with her husband's body, or from shut-ting a baby girl with fever in an oven to cure her. They tried to stop farmers cutting off their horses' tails. (The farmers believed that unless the tails were cut off, elves would cling to them and drive the horses round and round at night, so that they would be too tired to work in the morning.) Slowly the Church was helping to bring the Saxon settlers into a new world.

This early Christian stone pillar from White Island, Lough Erne, in Northern Ireland, shows a bishop with his symbol of office, the crozier, and a bell to ward off evil spirits.

Anglo-Saxon Life

Despite the slow coming of Christianity, the new world was still like the old one in many ways. Many children died at birth or before their first birthday. Mothers often had miscarriages and rarely had more than two surviving children. Few adults lived past forty. Like their Stone Age predecessors, men and women were surrounded by dangers, some of which came from the violence of the world about them – both natural and man-made – others from the terrors which filled their minds.

Archaeologists have been able to show how short a time the Anglo-Saxons lived by excavating their cemeteries and doing scientific tests on the bones uncovered. In one cemetery, used in the 7th century in Kent, thirty-two bodies of men and women were buried. Twenty-three bodies were of people aged under thirty, eight of men and women between thirty and forty-five, and only one was aged more than forty-five. At another, 6th century cemetery in Suffolk, out of twenty-six people buried there, four had lived past thirty-five (though none had lived past fifty), five died as children, three in their teens and fourteen died between twenty and thirty-five.

The ages at which the later kings of England and Wessex died tell the same story. These kings would have lived far more comfortably than their subjects and received the best medical attention there was available, but they still died quite young. Of the kings who ruled between Alfred the Great (who died in 899) and King Harold (who died in 1066), Alfred was fifty when he died, King Edmund was murdered when he was twenty-five, King Edgar died at thirty-two, and King Edward was also murdered, at the age of seventeen. King Ethelred and King Cnut died in their forties, and King Hardacnut in his twenties. Edward the Confessor lived to his early sixties, but Harold was killed in his forties at the battle of Hastings.

The Bible may talk of the years of a man's life as being three score years and ten, but this was certainly not true of the Anglo-Saxons.

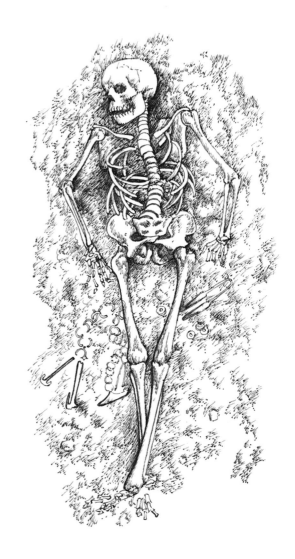

This picture from an Anglo-Saxon calendar (above) is for the month of January. It shows oxen ploughing the heavy soil. Now more land was brought under the plough than ever before. Not for nothing have the Saxons been called the people who colonized England. An Anglo-Saxon settlement (right). The woman is grinding corn with a quern.

A poem written at the time called *The Fates of Men* lists the ways in which people would be likely to die. They might be killed by wolves, starve to death, die in a storm, fall from a tree, or be burned alive (at home in a thatched house or at work in a thatched barn). They might be killed in a feud (a fight between families), or die in battle. They might be hanged for breaking the law or killed in a drunken brawl. Strangely enough, the writer has left out death from cold and, most common of all, from plague.

Anglo-Saxon law was severe. Runaway slaves were killed, as well as certain kinds of thieves, people thought to be witches and those who helped outlaws. The death penalty was inflicted in a number of ways — by hanging, beheading, stoning, burning and drowning. For lesser crimes people could be branded, scalped, scourged or blinded. Their ears could be cut off or their tongue

wrenched out. As the author of *The Fates of Men* describes, it was common for a traveller to see the dead bodies of criminals hanging on "gibbets" or gallows outside city gates.

A journey could be frightening. Most of Britain was still forest, much of it thick, dark and impenetrable. In its heart lived outlaws – people who had been forced to flee from ordinary society, perhaps for committing a crime or because they had made enemies of powerful people. If you stumbled across their forest settlements you were likely to be killed on sight. (In fact, the same thing might very well happen to any stranger arriving at a town or village if he did not immediately show that he was on peaceful business.)

Some of those dense forests of Anglo-Saxon times still survive, but are much smaller now – for instance, the New Forest in Hampshire, the Forest of Dean in Gloucestershire, Epping Forest in Essex, and the Weald of Kent and Sussex. According to *The Anglo-Saxon Chronicle*, in those times the Weald stretched "from east to west 120 miles long or longer and thirty miles broad".[6] It stood as a great barrier between Kent and the rest of England to the west, so that if you landed at Dover and wanted to go to Winchester or as far west as Exeter you would first have to ride north to London.

This Anglo-Saxon town was built within the remains of old Roman walls about AD 700.

In many parts of the country, bogs or marshes also made travelling difficult. The greatest of these were the Fens in East Anglia which were described by the Anglo-Saxon author of a book about St Guthlac, who lived there as a hermit by the banks of the river Welland early in

the 8th century. The writer describes the Fens as "a very long area, now consisting of marshes, now of bogs, sometimes of black waters overhung by fog, sometimes studded with wooded islands and crossed by windings of tortuous streams".[8] When William the Conqueror invaded England, it was here in the Fens that the English resistance lasted longest.

As we have seen, after the Romans left, people soon stopped repairing the roads they had built, and movement from one part of Britain to another became almost as difficult as it had been in early British times. The Roman roads grew to resemble the old long-distance footpaths of earlier days. Travel by river or by sea was the quickest way to move about. We get some idea of how slow travel by road had become when we read

that King Harold's army in 1066 took four or five days to travel the 300 kilometres from York to London. They were not taking their time deliberately. They were on a forced march of the greatest importance to their country, hurrying south to defeat a foreign invasion. And yet they took more than twice as long as the Romans would have taken to cover the distance.

Forests, marshes, moors, crumbling roads – they all helped to make the people of Anglo-Saxon Britain isolated from each other. When the Northumbrian missionary St Cuthbert called one morning at a farmhouse near the border with Scotland, the farmer's wife said that

An Anglo-Saxon settlement.

89

he must stay for a meal. She told him: "You will not find another village on your way, nor even a house, and it will take you to sunset to reach your destination". His experience would have been repeated all over Britain.

We have already seen how the Christian monks tried to stop the Anglo-Saxons from believing in magic and superstitions. But often people's beliefs were so strong that, instead of getting rid of them, the Christians started to mix them up with their own teaching. One Christian monk wrote in *The Anglo-Saxon Chronicle* of how in 793 fiery dragons flew in the skies over Northumberland, foretelling of raids by the terrible Vikings. Another Christian writer described how, when St Guthlac settled in the Fens, his cell was invaded by sprites. They were:

The Pectoral Cross of St Cuthbert in Durham Cathedral is made of gold enamel, gold beads and garnets. St Cuthbert played a great part in converting north-east England to Christianity.

"ferocious in appearance, terrible in shape, with great heads, long necks, thin faces, yellow complexions, filthy beards, shaggy ears, wild foreheads, fierce eyes, foul mouths, horses' teeth, throats vomiting flames, twisted jaws, thick lips, strident voices, singed hair, fat cheeks, pigeon breasts, scabby thighs, knotty knees, crooked legs, swollen ankles, splay feet, spreading mouths and raucous cries."[8]

Most people believed in witches and their male equivalent, warlocks, who were supposed to be in league with the Devil, and to do fearsome things. One writer described how a widow and her son stuck pins into the wax image of an enemy:

"They drove an iron pin into Elfsige... And it was detected and the murderess dragged from her chamber. And the woman was seized and drowned at London Bridge, but her son escaped and became an outlaw."[8]

Against such ever-present dangers, protection was always being sought by charms. The following charm was used to prevent the loss of a swarm of bees:

"Take some earth and throw it up with your right hand, and sow some seed beneath your right foot and recite:
  'I catch it under my foot; I have found it.
  Lo! Earth has power over all creatures,
  And against envy and against forgetfulness
  And against the mighty tongue of man.'

And then, when they swarm, throw sand over them and recite:
  'Settle women of victory, sink to the ground,
  Never fly wild to the wood,
  Be as mindful of my advantage
  As every man is of food and land.' "[8]

The Anglo-Saxon tribes in Britain. Cornwall remained British, and Wales and most of Scotland stayed independent.

(Apart from its supposed magical power, the sand might well prove a practical help in making swarming bees settle.)

Part of another charm, used to improve poor fields, was to put magical potions – such as a mixture of oil, honey, yeast, milk, parts of trees, herbs and holy water – in the plough and then repeat:
  "Erce, Erce, Erce, mother of earth,
  May the almighty eternal lord grant thee
  Fields growing and springing,
  Fruitful and strength-giving."

While the charm was being chanted, the plough cut a furrow. A loaf was then put beneath it and a hymn was chanted. To complete the charm the farmer repeated three times first "Amen" and then the Lord's Prayer.

As we have seen, during the years after the Romans left and before the Vikings invaded (from about 410 to about 850), people in England once again lived not as one nation but in small tribes which often fought one another. There were in the 7th century dozens of men who called themselves kings, but really they were more like tribal chiefs.

As time went by, the smaller tribes were taken over by the larger ones, so that kingdoms such as Kent, Sussex and Wessex in the south, Mercia in the Midlands, and Bernicia and Deira in the north became independent nations, which were often at war with each other. Often a strong king of one of these kingdoms might claim to be a great overlord (the Saxon word was *Bretwalda*) of England, ruling all the peoples who lived outside Cornwall, Wales, Scotland and Ireland. Such kings were Wulfhere of Mercia in the 670s and Raedwald of East Anglia in the 620s. In

fact none succeeded in ruling the whole of England, but they reminded people that they had once been one nation.

It was probably Raedwald who was buried at Sutton Hoo near Ipswich in Suffolk in the 620s. The discovery of the treasures at Sutton Hoo was one of the most sensational archaeological discoveries of modern times. It happened just before the Second World War, when archaeologists examined one of fifteen burial mounds which had been found by the estuary of the river Deben in Suffolk.

The Saxon crypt at Repton Church in Derbyshire (left). The crypt is the cellar of a church and was often used for burials.

The remains of a Viking trading boat found at Graveney in Kent (below). The Viking trading boats were very different from the famous longships used for fighting.

The mound was found to contain a rowing ship 24 metres long as well as an extraordinary store of treasures. The most likely explanation is that the treasure, which has been dated to about the year 620, was buried with the body of King Raedwald.

In the Anglo-Saxon poem *Beowulf* the burial of a great king in a ship with his treasure beside him is described:

"They set down their dear king amidships, close by the mast. A mass of treasure was brought there from distant parts...Then the warriors rode round the barrow...They praised his manhood and the prowess of his hands. They lifted up his name. It is right a man should be lavish in honouring his lord and friend."[5]

The treasures which were buried at Sutton Hoo were amazingly lavish. There were a purse lid and shoulder clasps of glistening gold which glittered with garnets, the red jewels which the Anglo-Saxons particularly loved. There were gold coins from France, silver spoons and bowls from Egypt and the lands of the eastern Mediterranean, and a helmet, shield and sword from Sweden. There were the fragments of a musical instrument, probably a lyre, which had a body of maple wood and strings made of gut or horsehair.

As well as the many kings of Anglo-Saxon England, there were lords who were loyal to them. They fought for the king, spent much of their time in the king's great hall, toasted him at banquets and listened to poets telling tales of his exploits and miraculous courage or minstrels singing songs about him to the accompaniment of the lyre. Such tales would be told round the fire. Swords, shields and helmets would gleam and glitter in the firelight, like the goblets of mead and wine that passed from hand to hand. The greater the king's hospitality, the more he was respected.

In return for their loyalty and friendship, the lords were given estates by the king. But more often than not they were away from home accompanying him on his travels around the kingdom, leaving their lands to be farmed by bailiffs. For the kings were forever on the move; they would descend on some unfortunate lord for a visit and before they left they would eat him out of house and home. No wonder people, from the lord downwards, sometimes took to the woods when they heard their king was coming.

At the centre of each district in the kingdom was the royal manor house or "tun" – the king's tun, as in Kingston-upon-Thames or Kingston-upon-Hull.

The "tun" would be looked after by the king's officials, but it would be regularly visited by the king and his retinue of travelling courtiers. Here were situated the king's law courts, and here all local people would pay their "dues" or taxes. These were in goods and not in money.

At first, both the kings and their lords depended on slaves or serfs to run their estates. Not all the slaves were Britons, for the Anglo-Saxons enslaved their own people too — prisoners-of-war, for instance, taken in battle with other Saxon tribes, people guilty of serious crimes and also "hungry freemen who sold themselves for bread". But certain lords were growing tired of employing slaves. Some argued that rather than pay the full cost of looking after a slave and his family it was cheaper and more efficient to give the slave his own land and some spare time. Others were influenced by Christian teaching, for the Church encouraged the freeing of slaves and tried to prevent them from being sold abroad. As a result, landowners would make arrangements so that, after their deaths, their slaves would be freed. But the ex-slave still had to do virtually anything his lord required of him. By law, even his personal belongings were his lord's.

Below the slave-owning kings and lords came the Anglo-Saxon farmers. Some of these men were *ceorls* or churls, who owned their own land. Others rented their farms from a lord, usually paying rent not in money but in crops or animals. They and the workers on the lords' estates continued the work of clearing the forests and farming the valleys which the Britons and Romans had begun. They too employed slaves or serfs as labourers.

These farmers lived in isolated farms

Inside an Anglo-Saxon hall.

94

or in small groups of farms (the traditional English village, built round a village green, a church and a public house, had not yet developed). Their hard and solitary lives, dominated by the seasons and the weather, can be compared to those of the men and women who colonized North America in the 17th century. The Anglo-Saxon farmers helped to settle England.

It is far easier for us to tell how the palaces, country villas and town villas of Roman Britain must have looked than the kings' halls or farmers' huts of Anglo-Saxon times, because of the materials in which they were built. Whereas the Romans built in bricks or tiles which last, the Saxons built in wood, thatch and wattle, which do not. But as well as what archaeologists tell us from their findings, we can read descriptions of Anglo-Saxon buildings in writings of the time. In *Beowulf*, for example, a magnificent king's hall is described. Its roof is tall; its walls made of long planks held

together with iron. You enter through double doors. Inside, the wooden walls are covered with tapestries which shine with gold. The floor is of stone. Seats or benches line the walls. The king's lords sleep here on beds and mattresses. Their weapons lie beside them in case of attack. But the king and queen and the most important officials sleep away from the hall in separate wooden houses.

A later Anglo-Saxon writer describes building a house as follows:

"First of all the house site is surveyed, then the timber is cut, the ground sills neatly fitted together, the beams laid, the rafters fastened to the ridge-piece and supported with braces, and then the house is elegantly decorated."[8]

Archaeologists investigating one of King Alfred's royal "tuns" at Cheddar in Somerset have given us the following description of what it might have been like: on a 2-acre site surrounded by a

Anglo-Saxon houses. On the left is the chapel followed by the wooden royal hall. In the middle is a thatched longhouse belonging to a rich farmer. On the right is a

ditch and a fence stood the royal hall, 24 metres long and 6 metres wide, with a thatched roof. It was built of posts set closely together. There are signs that the building may have had an upper floor. There was an entrance at the middle of each side leading into a porch. Further inside, an area of scorched clay showed where the open fire must have burned.

Smaller buildings inside the enclosure included a chapel and a weaver's shed. There might also have been a corn mill, with a grain store and bakery attached. Another small building with a pit was the latrine.

Some of the houses and huts which ordinary people lived in have been excavated too. The richer farmers lived in thatched wooden longhouses, built in the shape of a rectangle about 20 metres long and 5 metres wide. Most people's huts, however, were probably more like one, belonging to a farmer of the 6th century, which has been excavated at Dorchester on Thames. It was roughly circular and about 5 metres across. The roof and walls were of thatch, laid on stakes set into the ground. (St Cuthbert described visiting such a house in Chester-le-Street in Durham. His horse entered with him and began pulling the straw from the roof.) The floor of the hut was about three quarters of a metre lower than the outside ground, and for this reason this type of hut is also called a "sunken hut" or pit dwelling. The floor was of earth or gravel, though wooden floorboards may have covered it in places. There were probably seats or lockers round the edge of the hut. The smoke from the open fireplace found its way out through a special hole in the roof or through the entrance. There was no door. Archaeologists believe this hut probably burned down in the end – which is not surprising, considering that it was made entirely of wood and straw.

The whole family would have lived in the one room. The poorer people were, the smaller their huts and the lower the

peasant farmer's house, followed by a serf's hut. The serf and his family lived in one

room. The room was often so low that they could not stand upright.

roofs. Perhaps the low roofs explain the recent report by archaeologists working in Saxon cemeteries which revealed that many of the people's leg bones had been worn away with squatting.

Most of the Anglo-Saxons hardly ever left their own farms or settlements. But there were always pedlars, who visited even the most isolated farms with their medicinal ointments and glass beads, their herbal remedies and newly sharpened knives. They also brought the suspicious settlers news of the outside world. There were merchants carrying wool or cloth to the nearest market town, and then there were the bravest traders of all – those who risked the dangers of attack by robbers on land or by pirates at sea to buy and sell goods in Europe or even in the Middle East. In this way, as in so many others, the life of the Anglo-Saxons resembled that of the Bronze Age and Iron Age peoples who inhabited Britain before them. Like them, they were not completely cut off from the world outside their own valley.

In about the year 1000, an Anglo-Saxon schoolmaster in a monastery in Dorset wrote down a list of different occupations for his pupils. This is how he described the merchant:

"He rows across the seas, returning with silk and other rare cloths, with gems, gold, spices or perfumes, wine, oil, ivory, brass, bronze and tin, sulphur and glass."[8]

Foreign trade was mainly for the rich, though we know that merchants from Rouen in France brought fish to Billingsgate, already a London fish market, in the 11th century. Presumably some of this was food for ordinary Londoners.

We know also that French and Belgian glassmakers worked in the south of England. Other foreign workmen worked as potters in Ipswich, a major centre for producing pottery. People in England traded regularly with Scandinavia (Norway, Sweden and Denmark) as well as with western Europe. Many traders from northern Europe visited York. Their quayside and warehouses there have recently been excavated. Frisian (Dutch) merchants also had a trading area in York, and French merchants regularly brought wine to London and Southampton, where they built warehouses.

Though the schoolmaster's description does not mention it, merchants from England must have been selling English

A helmet found in the Sutton Hoo ship burial. It was buried in the grave along with many other treasures.

wool and cloth in Europe at this time, for in 796 the French Emperor Charles the Great (Charlemagne) complained that the English were sending cloaks which were too small. He demanded that they make them bigger, as they used to do. At St Denis near Paris, where every year an important gathering of traders from all over northern Europe was held, English cloth was said to be in great demand. We have records of English merchants working there and at Marseilles. In the 8th century, English merchants were seen as far away as the mouth of the River Vistula on the Baltic Sea.

The only coins that have been found which were used in Britain between the time the Romans left and about the year 600 are foreign. But after that year, rather rough silver coins were minted. Most of these were only used in the kingdom in which they were made; but King Offa of Mercia (757–796) minted beautiful silver pennies which were used all over England. Money rather than barter (the exchange of goods) was more and more in use.

After about 600, English ports and inland centres of trade also slowly began to grow. As archaeologists have found, sometimes people built new warehouses and shops to carry out their trade among the remains of old Roman buildings within the Roman walls of towns such as York, Canterbury and London. Bede, writing in about the year 730, described London as "an emporium of many peoples coming by land and sea". In other areas trade developed around the royal tun. At Southampton trade grew near such a tun at Hampton. Other traders came to use some of the minsters for their markets – at Winchester, for example. Once again, place names can be useful in telling us where English centres of trade were. Such centres often included the word "wic" as in Norwich, Ipswich, Sandwich or Fordwich.

Wool merchants approaching a Saxon town. Although Britain grew more isolated after the Romans left, the Saxons traded from the time of their earliest settlements, both inland and overseas.

Celtic Britain and Ireland (500–1066)

A Welsh settlement about AD 900. A group of farmers lived within the low walls in thatched beehive huts.

When the Anglo-Saxon tribes first conquered and settled in England, many British people who had lived there fled to Wales. There, for a while, they were left alone by the Saxons.

WALES
Wales, like England, was split into separate kingdoms. Many of them were tiny, a mere 15 kilometres across. Like the English kings, the Welsh kings were always at war with each other. And like them they had lords beneath them and great estates which were worked by serfs or slaves. Often the slaves were young men and women captured from their enemies.

After about 600, Welsh armies started raiding parts of England, not to conquer them but to steal cattle, goods and slaves. Cadwallon, King of Gwynedd in North Wales, for example, led armies to Northumbria in the early 7th century. Afterwards the Welshmen returned to their own country. Such raids were encouraged by Welsh kings, for under the traditional laws of Wales, a king was entitled to one third of the booty seized.

By 800 there were only four main Welsh kingdoms – Gwynedd in the north, Powys in the centre, Deheubarth (Dyfed) in the south-west and Morgannwg (Gwent) in the south-east. Various powerful rulers of these kingdoms tried to take over the whole of Wales. One of these was Hywel Dda (the Good) who ruled Dyfed, Gwynedd and Powys until his death in 950. He put together a code or collection of Welsh customs and laws which were used as the basis of Welsh law for many centuries. He was the first Welsh king to mint coins which were used all over his kingdom, stamped Hywel Rex (King Hywel). During his reign, literature was written in Welsh for the first time.

Another king, Gruffydd ap Llywelyn of Dyfed, killed the king of Gwynedd in 1039 and ruled most of Wales until

1064, when he was killed by his own men. He sent great raiding parties into western England and he employed foreign soldiers to fight his battles. During his rule the English continually plotted with his enemies to overthrow him. After his death they would not let his sons and grandsons rule Wales unless they swore loyalty to the English king.

Like their English enemies, most of the Welsh people were farmers, keeping sheep and cattle in the hills and valleys. There were no towns, apart from the ruins of the old Roman towns. Under Welsh law, the only true Welsh were those who did not have to work for a lord or king. Most of these true Welsh

Part of the remains of Offa's Dyke near Mainstone in Shropshire. The great ditch separated Mercia from Wales, running north-south. King Offa of Mercia built it at the end of the 8th century to stop continual Welsh raids for sheep and cattle.

men lived in the hills. They were independent and quarrelsome, recognizing no authority apart from the king's. There were also craftsmen who smelted iron to make weapons, and others who worked in gold, glass and enamel and made jewellery. Welsh traders, selling such goods, travelled by sea to the far west of France and across the Bay of Biscay, and so into the Mediterranean. They did not go through England at all.

IRELAND

The Anglo-Saxons did not go to Ireland. Most of the people in Ireland at this time were descended from the Celtic settlers who first came in 300 BC and had lived there through Roman times. The Irish composed great sagas (stories sometimes in prose and sometimes in verse) about their past, which were a mixture of fact and fiction. They looked back to the years of the first Celtic settlers with love and awe.

Like England and Wales, Ireland consisted, to begin with, of many kingdoms. By Roman times there were only five, known as the Five Fifths of Ireland – Ulster, Meath, Leinster, Munster and Connaught. But it was not until the 10th century that the descendants of Ulster's Niall of the Nine Hostages, whose court

This outline of a Viking ship was carved on a plank near Dublin in about 1100. The Vikings had been settled there for 300 years.

was at Tara in Meath, claimed to be kings of all Ireland. In the next century Brian Boru of Munster claimed to be the High King of Ireland.

Round the king's power was based that of his lords, who reckoned their wealth mainly in cattle. They in their turn had groups of supporters, who farmed, with the use of serfs and slaves, and looked after the herds of cattle. The life of the tribes was bound by carefully-defined laws, by loyalties to their families, and by duties of revenge against their enemies right down to the most distant cousin.

In Ireland, as in Wales during these years, there were no towns, though there was industry and trade. Most people were farmers. In addition to corn, the Irish grew flax which they wove into fine linen. Their sheep produced good wool from which woollen cloaks (brats) were made, which the lords wore fastened on

An Irish family about 1000. The man's brat and brooch show he may have been a chief. On the left is a currach, a sea-going boat.

their shoulders or breasts with pins or brooches and tied at the waist with a belt. People kept pigs for their meat and, like all early peoples of the British Isles, they fished, hunted, fowled and trapped. They had few wheeled vehicles. By land they carried their goods on packhorses, on the rivers they used dugouts and at sea they travelled by currachs. These were boats made of wicker frames and covered with animal hides. Despite their round shape they could travel long distances in stormy seas. Irish houses, which were of wattle and mud, were built within defended circles. Like other Celtic peoples, their chief musical instrument was the harp.

In 795 pirates from Norway were seen for the first time off the Irish coast. At the same time other Norwegians were settling in Scotland while their cousins the Danes were beginning their massive raids on England. Forty years later Norwegians seized Dublin. From there they advanced inland. In 914 they took Waterford, and in 920 they captured Limerick. They began to settle in Ireland, mixing with the people and taking over Irish trade. For a time it seemed as if they might turn Ireland into a Norwegian kingdom. But in 1014, they and their ally, the King of Dublin, were defeated at the battle of Clontarf by the soldiers of the High King Brian Boru. After that, although the Norwegians continued to control Irish trade, they were content to accept the authority of Irish kings. A century later, their descendants had become Irish men and women.

SCOTLAND

Scotland is divided by mountains into the isolated areas of the Highlands to the north and the low lying Lowland country to the south. Each part of the Highlands is further split into glens and valleys, towered over by mountains and entered only through narrow passes. The people living there were isolated from other parts of Scotland. They knew only their own tribal chiefs and families and did not think of themselves as part of a nation or kingdom of Scotland.

In the 7th century, Scotland was inhabited by four different peoples. In the north and north-east lived the Picts, one of whose languages was Celtic. Their rulers were descended not from the male in the family but the female and they had their court at Scone (pronounced "Scoon") near Perth. By the 8th century they claimed to be rulers of all Scotland. On the west coast were the Scots, who (as we saw in Chapter 7) migrated from Ireland and gave their name to Scotland. They spoke Celtic or Gaelic and they were the first people in Scotland to become Christians.

In the Lowlands to the south were the British tribes who had lived there since Roman times. Although they conquered lands and built up large kingdoms for a while – such as Strathclyde in the west of the country – they were too often fighting amongst themselves to protect these kingdoms from the Picts, or from the fourth people, the Angles. The Angles had advanced into northern England from Deira (Yorkshire) to form the kingdom of Northumbria. At one time they advanced as far as the Firth of Forth at Edinburgh, but they were forced back by armies of Scots and Picts. In 1018 the King of the Scots and Picts reached the modern English frontier.

Scotland was even more influenced than Ireland by settlers from across the North Sea, mostly from Norway. From 780 to 850 many Norwegian peasants, driven from their homelands by poverty, arrived in the islands of Shetland and Orkney, and in the north of Scotland, to start a new life. They fished and farmed and hunted the seals. The population was sparse and scattered, and the settlers faced little opposition. In the west – in the Hebridean islands and Galloway – other Norwegians settled and formed a powerful group based on the Isle of Man.

But it was in the Orkneys that the Norwegians became most powerful. The islands became the centre of a Norwegian empire of the North Sea, which traded with Iceland, Greenland and even perhaps North America. The empire controlled the Orkneys, Shetlands, Caithness and Sutherland. Scottish kings treated the Norwegian kings as equals and were proud to marry into their families. As time went by, these Norwegians, like those in Ireland, had less and less contact with Norway. They became part of the Scottish peoples.

The attacks of the Norwegians, like those of the English from the south, helped create the beginnings of a feeling among the different Scottish peoples that they belonged to one nation – Scotland. Malcolm II (1005 – 1034) claimed to be King of all Scotland, apart from the Norwegian lands in the north. His son inherited a country which seemed to be, at least on the surface, united.

An early Norwegian settlement in the Shetland Islands. The buildings (about AD 800) are of local stone, thatched with reeds tied down with weighted ropes. To the settlers, the land must have seemed as bleak as that which they had left behind them.

People from the North

We have already seen that after the Roman armies left England at the beginning of the 5th century the country was once again divided into tribal kingdoms. People thought of themselves as Northumbrians or Mercians, or as subjects of the kings of Wessex – not as English.

During the 8th century there were two powerful kings of Mercia who claimed, as earlier kings had sometimes done, to be *bretwaldas*, or overlords, of a large part of England. The first of them was Ethelbald, who ruled from 716 to 757. He was called "King not only of the Mercians but of all the provinces called-...southern English", though the people of Wessex never accepted him as king. His successor, Offa, extended the Mercian empire. He took over Kent, Surrey, Sussex and East Anglia, after having the king of East Anglia beheaded. Even Wessex accepted his overlordship for a while. Bede wrote that Offa "held sway over all provinces south of the river Humber". His silver pennies were used all over his kingdom.

The king of the Franks at that time was Charlemagne (meaning "Charles the Great"). In 800 he was crowned Holy Roman Emperor by the Pope, who wanted to create a second Roman Empire in western Europe. Charlemagne, who was a powerful king, wrote to Offa as if he were his equal. He called him "my dearest brother". He also wrote as if Offa and King Ethelred of Northumbria were the only kings in England.

Shortly before Offa died in 796, an incident occurred on the coast of Wessex which probably aroused little notice at the time, but on which the writer of *The Anglo-Saxon Chronicle* laid great stress. He described how:

"While the most pious King Brihtric of Wessex was reigning over the western parts of the English in the year 789, a small fleet of Northmen, numbering three fast ships, came unexpectedly to the coast, and this was their first coming. Hearing of this, the king's official, then staying at the town called Dorchester, leapt on his horse and with a few men made haste to the port, thinking they were merchants rather than enemies, and

A bronze statue of Emperor Charlemagne. As well as being King of the Franks, Charlemagne was crowned Holy Roman Emperor by the Pope in 800. He then claimed to rule over as much land as the Romans had done before him.

commanding them imperiously he ordered them to be sent to the royal palace, but he and his companions were straightaway killed by them."[6]

The murderous Northmen were soon followed by others. Four years later the great monastery of Lindisfarne, from which St Aidan and his monks had set out to convert the people of Northumbria, was looted and destroyed. The nearby monastery at Jarrow suffered the same fate the next year. In 795, the monastery at Iona in Scotland, which St Columba and his missionaries had made their base, was cruelly attacked by the "men from the north". Britain faced a new race of invaders. The descendants of the Saxons, against whom the Romans had constructed their forts of the Saxon Shore, now faced similar enemies from across the sea.

These "men from the north" were members of a people who rank among the great explorers and adventurers of history. Their homes were in Scandinavia – the modern countries of Norway, Denmark and Sweden. They left their homelands for a combination of reasons.

The Norwegians were short of farmland. Because of the shape of their country, they had to live and work hemmed in between the mountains and the sea. Their population was rising, and the land could not feed all the people. There was only enough land for each family's eldest son. The rest had to find some other way of getting their living. So for many years the chiefs of tribes living near the coast had lain in wait at the entrance to the *viks*, the inlets or "fjords" which run along Norway's Atlantic coast, and robbed passing ships. This was how the Northmen got another name – Vikings. By the 8th century Viking sailors (Norwegians) had begun to venture far out into the North Sea, sailing due west to settle in the Faeroes, the Shetlands and the Orkneys. From there, as we have seen, they sailed north of Scotland to settle off its western coast and in Ireland.

In Denmark, during thè 9th century, there were constant wars among the different tribal chiefs. Many of these people sought new lands in which to

A Norwegian fjord in winter. The land was too poor to support its people.

settle. It was they who invaded eastern England. For every Dane who landed along the eastern English coastline looking for plunder, there were two or three who arrived looking for farmland and bringing with them the equipment they needed to build houses and settle there. Other Danes settled, in the 10th century, in part of northern France, which became known as Normandy, the land of the Northmen.

The longboats in which the Norwegians and Danes sailed were a great improvement on the rowing galleys which had carried the first Anglo-Saxon settlers to England. The keel, or backbone, of the longboat was a single length of oak. This made it strong enough to carry a mast and a large square sail. It was steered by a rudder shaped like the blade of an oar, fixed on the right-hand side of the boat near the stern. We still call this side of a ship the starboard side after the Viking "steer-board". Each longboat had a crew of about fifty men. Their captains sailed by the sun or the pole-star. Their voyages were among the most extraordinary in early history.

In the north, Norwegians settled in Iceland and Greenland. Shortly after 1000 they explored the north-east coast of North America, as far south as present-day New York, and attempted to settle in Newfoundland. (All this was 500 years before Christopher Columbus "discovered" America.) In the south, Danes sailed across the Bay of Biscay, entered the Mediterranean through the Straits of Gibraltar and established a settlement in Sicily.

Thanks to the Viking practice of burying their chiefs with their ships, we have a great deal of information about the latter. At Gokstad, near Oslo, a ship was discovered in 1880 which had been buried in blue clay. This had preserved it. A few years later, an exact copy of the Gokstad ship was sailed across the North Sea from Norway to Newfoundland. Its captain, Magnus Andersen, made the crossing in twenty-eight days and reached speeds of 10 or 11 knots (about 20 kilometres an hour). He said it steered excellently, while its springy sides gave flexibly in high seas. It stood 2 metres in the water, was 5 metres broad at its broadest middle point and 24 metres long. The prow of a Viking ship would often be carved in the shape of a dragon's head.

The shallowness of the longboats meant that they were easy to beach and to sail away. They could also be taken far up rivers, as the oarsmen rowed softly and the warriors armed themselves for the fight. The Gokstad ship had sixteen oars on each side, fitted into holes in the oak hull. The oars were 5 metres long. The ship had only four fitted bunks in which four off-duty men could sleep. The rest spread their leather sleeping bags between the sea chests, which were used as seats, and the lockers containing food and vital water. There, permanently soaked and frozen, they would take what rest they could.

Danish raids on the English coast, using similar ships, were frequent during the first half of the 9th century. It was said that by 865 not a single English church within a day's ride of the sea was left standing. Monasteries, with their collections of jewelled crosses, silver chalices, ivory crosses and other objects of great beauty and value, suffered terribly from the Danish attacks, for the monks were not only rich but defenceless. In 865 the Danish Grand Army landed on the east coast of England, and it soon became obvious that the English were faced not just with fearsome raids but with powerful and determined invaders. Since Offa's death, the country had gone back to being ruled by kings who were constantly fighting one another. As a result, they were too weak to resist the invaders.

The Grand Army first went north. Within two years they had captured York, and had chosen a puppet king who would support them to rule Northumbria. In 869 they attacked East Anglia and murdered King Edmund. (He became a saint – St Edmund the Martyr – and the place of his burial has been named after him: Bury St Edmunds in Suffolk). In 870 the Danes captured Reading and prepared to invade Wessex, but the king of Wessex, Ethelred, and his brother Alfred defeated them at Ash-

down on the Berkshire Downs.

The next year a new Danish army landed. Ethelred died suddenly. His brother Alfred decided to try to buy peace. He gave the Danes money to stay away from Wessex, which was called Dane Tax or "Danegeld", and for five years the Danes kept the agreement. During that time they conquered Mercia, and began to colonize it. In 878 the Grand Army split. One group began to divide Yorkshire up into Danish colonies. Another group, led by the Danish king Guthrum, attacked Wessex. Wilt-

A reconstruction of a Viking ship found at Oseberg in Norway. The keel was made from a single oak trunk, with oak ribs, crossbeams and planks. Tarred animal hair stuffed between the planks made the ship waterproof.

shire and Hampshire were quickly conquered. In March, King Alfred fled with 200 lords to take refuge in Athelney, in Somerset, where the Danes left them alone.

However, Alfred did not stay long in the Athelney marshes. In May, according to *The Anglo-Saxon Chronicle* (which, it should be remembered, was written at the time and is therefore particularly reliable):

"Alfred rode to Egbert's stone [thought to be a spot on the Somerset-Wiltshire border]. There came to meet him there all the men of Somerset and Wiltshire and part of Hampshire and they rejoiced to see him."[6]

From this account it looks as if the Danes could not have conquered Wiltshire and Hampshire particularly thoroughly. Alfred and his followers marched northwest towards Chippenham where Guthrum had made his headquarters at a Saxon royal "tun". The Danes met them near the village of Edington, by Salisbury Plain. Fighting started at dawn.

Alfred's men outnumbered the Danes, and after a fierce battle they proved victorious. The Danes retreated to Chippenham, where they were besieged for ten days before they asked for peace. Guthrum, with thirty of his chiefs, agreed to be baptized into the Christian Church before returning to his lands in eastern England. Alfred escorted them to Athelney, where the ceremony was performed with Alfred acting as Guthrum's godfather.

Shortly afterwards, the party travelled north to Wedmore, near the Bristol Channel. Here a frontier line between Wessex and the Danish territory was agreed following the line of Watling Street, the old Roman road that ran from London to Chester. By the treaty of Wedmore (878) Alfred recognized the land to the east of Watling Street as Danish, the territory of King Guthrum. It had taken the Danes just thirteen years to conquer one third of England, a territory from which they were never to be removed, and which was now called the "Danelaw".

By the Treaty of Wedmore (878) Alfred agreed to let the Danes colonize eastern England, which was then known as the Danelaw. The picture shows Alfred's army drawn up near Salisbury Plain before their decisive victory over the Danes.

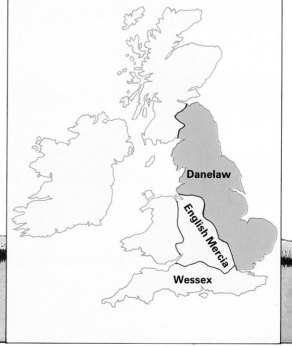

Alfred the Great (849–899)

After the treaty of Wedmore, Wessex became the major English kingdom, and Alfred was accepted as overlord of all England apart from the Danelaw. Because he had defeated the Danes, the people of England thought of him as a king fit to be compared with the earlier King Offa of Mercia. His strong rule after the victory, his wise policies and his encouragement of religion and learning earned him the title "the Great" – a title given to no other king in English history.

As a boy, Alfred probably did not expect ever to be king, as he had three elder brothers, all of whom ruled as king before him. When the last one died, during the Danish invasion, and Alfred became King of Wessex, he was only twenty-two. Although his father had sent him to stay with the Pope when he was four, he does not seem to have had a very good education – something he was always sorry about. He did not learn how to read and write until he was forty. He was brought up to love hunting, a love which remained with him throughout his reign, but he suffered from ill health. The writer of *The Anglo-Saxon Chronicle* does not give any details of Alfred's illness but describes how, although he was often ill until his death, he never complained about it.

After his victory over Guthrum, Alfred treated the Danes without harshness. Both sides seem to have been determined to keep peace, and there was little fighting along the frontier between Wessex and the Danelaw. The part of Mercia which had not been conquered by the Danes was now under Alfred's protection, and he took care not to

The face of a jewel found in the Athelney marshes where the fugitive King Alfred hid from the Danes. Its side (out of sight) is inscribed: "Alfred made me".

provoke the proud people of Mercia into revolting against him. So when London was captured from Danish soldiers, it was handed over to the Mercian ruler, rather than taken as part of the kingdom of Wessex. Alfred also arranged his daughter's marriage to a Mercian noble.

But Alfred knew that he must keep England strongly defended in case of more attacks by the Danes. He was the first English king to build a fleet of fighting ships. They were double the size of the Viking ships and carried sixty oars or more. He organized the Wessex army, the *fyrd*, in which all free men had to serve. There was no professional army, so the fyrd was made up of farmers. At harvest time the soldiers were liable to slip away under cover of darkness to get back to work on their farms. Alfred divided his forces in two. Half the men were on active service. The other half were at home on their farms, ready to be called up at short notice. After a few months the two would change over.

Finally Alfred built fortified towns – *burhs*, or boroughs – from which people could defend the country if it was attacked. They were built according to a careful plan with streets at right angles, like a Roman town, and were sometimes actually built in old Roman towns, such as Winchester, Chichester and Bath, where the old walls could be put to new use. It was the duty of landowners living near the burhs to make sure they were defended. Alfred built more than thirty burhs by the time of his death. They were to become the thriving towns of the 10th century.

Alfred was now the unchallenged ruler of about two-thirds of England. But different laws and customs were still used in different parts of his kingdom. One of the most important things he did was to put together a list of the laws which must be obeyed all over his land. (The laws did not apply to slaves, who seem to have had no rights at all.)

Many of Alfred's laws sound strange today. If someone committed a crime – even as serious a crime as murder – he

A look-out on duty at a Saxon burh. *Alfred established these fortified towns. Within their walls town life began to grow again for the first time since the Romans.*

had to pay compensation to the person he had harmed or, if the person was dead, to his or her family. So long as the money was paid, that was the end of the matter. The amount paid depended on the rank of the person harmed. The *wergild* – life-price – of a nobleman was 1200 shillings – six times that of a churl, which was 200 shillings. Even that was an enormous sum in those days. The less important the victim was, the less the criminal had to pay. Slaves (*thralls*) were worthless. No wergild had to be paid if a slave was killed.

Judges and priests encouraged such peaceful forms of punishment. But if a person accused of a crime could not pay or refused to do so, or if he or she claimed to be not guilty, then the injured person or his family would bring the case to court.

In court, the accused was called on to swear an oath that he or she was innocent. The oath in itself was a solemn test. People believed that anyone who swore a false oath would be punished by eternal torture in hell. If they were found out, they would be cruelly punished by the court as well, so they would be bound to tell the truth. The accused also had to produce "oath-helpers" to testify to his or her innocence. If the accused found enough oath-helpers who were respected in the community, the case collapsed. But if he or she could not do so, or if the evidence was contradictory, then the system of trial by ordeal was used.

One of these was ordeal by water. This was often used in trials for witchcraft. If an accused woman chose ordeal by water, she would be roped to a man on the bank and thrown into a pond or river. If she sank, she would be hauled to land and declared innocent. It was believed that the water had received the innocent woman with open arms, and God who made the water had shown the court the truth. If she floated she was guilty, for her body had been rejected by the water.

If an accused man chose ordeal by fire, he was told to plunge an arm into boiling water and pick up a stone. The arm was then bandaged and left for three days. If, when the bandages were removed, the arm was declared fully healed by the court priest, the man was innocent. Another form of this ordeal was that the accused would be told to carry a very hot rod of iron for a number of paces. If the burns disappeared within three days, it was believed God had proved the man innocent.

If the ordeal proved a man guilty, but he still would not or, more probably, could not pay the wergild, then the family could have their revenge on him. This lawful revenge was called the "blood-feud", and often meant the guilty person was killed.

Pope Stephen V had attacked trials by ordeal as superstitious as early as 816, but many continued to be used in England until the end of the 12th century. Women thought to be witches were still thrown into ponds to find out if they were guilty on the orders of judges right up to the 17th century.

A few crimes were punished by death. One was witchcraft, and another was disloyalty to your lord. If a man plotted against his lord, he could make up for his wickedness only by losing his life. If an accused man failed to appear in court to answer the charges against him, he was declared an outlaw. After that, anyone was entitled to kill him. One of the advantages of Alfred's system of laws was that there was no need to build a large number of prisons.

So that people would understand them, Alfred had his new system of laws written down in the language of the ordinary people, which was called *Englisc*, or English. Although stories and poems had been told in English and passed from one generation to the next, English had not been written down before. In fact almost the only people in England who could read and write were priests and monks, and their books were in Latin, as were all church services.

Because they were the most educated men in the towns and villages, the priests and monks were important people. They helped the king to govern the country rather like today's civil servants. However, when Alfred became King, the English church was in a desperately poor state. Its priests could sometimes not even read and write. They recited services without understanding the words and their lives were poor examples to their congregations. In a letter to the

The verdict in an ordeal by fire. The accused has removed his bandages. His hand has healed, to his relief; but his accuser is horrified.

Bishop of Worcester, Alfred described how, when he came to the throne,

"There were very few priests on this side Humber who could understand their Latin mass-books [service books] and I ween [believe] that there were not many beyond the Humber ... When I consider all this I remembered also how I saw, before it had all been ravaged and burnt, how the churches throughout England stood filled with treasures and books. But the people could not understand anything of them because they were not written in their language."9

Alfred was determined to do something about this problem. It was true that he could not read or write until he was forty, but he certainly learnt quickly after that time. In the next ten years, up to his death in 899 at the age of fifty, he personally wrote and translated, or arranged to have written and translated, a number of books in English. He believed that such books would help to make the clergy better educated, and so they would help their congregations to lead better lives.

The best known of these books was *The Anglo-Saxon Chronicle*, which was written at Alfred's court under his supervision. By putting together in one history book the accounts of how the different Saxon tribes came to England and how they later developed, and by writing them in English, Alfred helped to make the people of the different areas he ruled over think of themselves as members of one English nation – just as his system of laws had done. He now called his country "Angelcynn, the land of the English folk". The *Chronicle* emphasized the part played by the kings of Wessex in the history of England, so that people would accept Wessex as the most important kingdom in England.

Alfred's lords were expected to see that their sons were brought up to write English, so that they could play a full part in governing the nation. The clergy were expected to be able to read and write in English and Latin, though for centuries many still could not do so.

Alfred was a deeply religious man. As well as wanting to make the clergy better educated, he wanted the English Church to be rich and strong. Foreigners, he hoped, would be drawn to its monasteries by the goodness of the monks' lives and the standard of their learning. At Winchester, where Alfred spent much of his time and which came to be the main city of Wessex, he planned a great monastery. After his reign, England had many monasteries full of hard-working monks.

Parish churches now grew up all over the country. Here the local priest held the services, helped the poor, the old and the sick, and taught people who could neither read nor write the beliefs of Jesus. Alfred himself wrote, "I desired to live worthily ... and to leave after my life ... my memory in good works". He gained his desire.

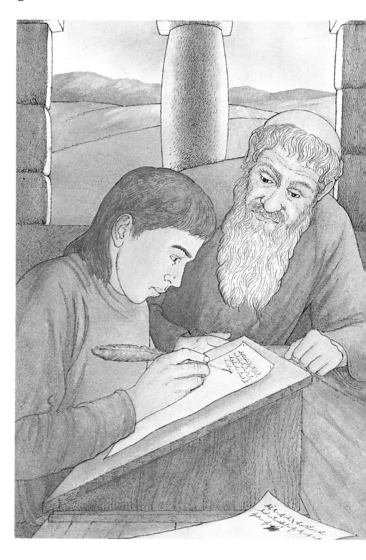

Alfred encouraged the Church to set up schools where clever boys could be taught. Not only did they learn Latin, the international language, but now they learnt to read and write in their own language — "Englisc".

Wessex and The Danelaw

Though the Danes conquered the eastern part of England by force, they settled there quite peacefully. They did not take over the area entirely and enslave or expel the Anglo-Saxon (or English) inhabitants. Indeed they often settled in areas which the English had avoided — on the edge of woodland, for instance, or along small rivers rather than important ones. We know this from their place names. Their word *by*, meaning village, appears in names such as Derby or Grimsby. Another Danish word for village, *thorpe*, and their word for farm-house, *loft*, appear in Scunthorpe and Lowestoft.

The Danes were free people, mainly small farmers, not dependent on their lords like so many of the Saxons. They seem to have looked on the English in the rest of the country with friendly eyes. Indeed they probably preferred them to the other Northmen, the Norwegians, who invaded the north of England in the 10th century from their colonies in Lancashire and Cumberland. It was therefore not difficult for later kings of Wessex, after Alfred, to get the Danes of the Danelaw to accept them as overlords.

Edward the Elder, who was king of Wessex and overlord of all that part of the country Alfred had called England from 899 to 924, extended the frontier of his country to the river Humber, and was at first accepted by the Northumbrians to the north as their overlord. But

Viking women wore pleated linen or wool dresses. They carried the household keys, a needle case and a knife. Men wore woollen trousers and linen or wool shirts. The leather shoes (below) were found at York. They date from the 10th century. The picture on the right shows a Viking smith in his forge hammering rods of wrought iron to make the blade of a sword. His helper pumps the bellows.

Viking children playing Hnefatafl, *a board game like draughts played all over the Viking world. Several 10th century counters have been found in York.*

Norwegians from Dublin invaded northern England, took York, and made it the centre of a Norwegian kingdom.

As we have seen in chapter 9, Norwegian traders had already been at work in York for years. Now York became a thriving trading town, described by *The Anglo-Saxon Chronicle* as "wealthy beyond words ... because of the riches of merchants who gathered there from all quarters". Archaeologists excavating in York recently have discovered how it must have looked in the 10th century – a town of merchants and small craftsmen, living in wooden or wattle and daub houses. Some of the modern street names come from Norwegian words, and we can tell from them how craftsmen doing the same work gathered in certain areas.

For example, the street named Skeldergate was where the shield-makers – *skjaldari* in Norwegian – lived, while the coopers or barrel-makers – the *koppari* – lived in Coppergate.

Many of the goods these craftsmen made were taken by traders to Scandinavia. It was the first time that people in England had had such close links with people living across the North Sea in northern Europe. The north-east of England remained closely linked to Scandinavia by trade and politics until the Norman Conquest in 1066.

King Edward was succeeded by King Athelstan, who ruled from 924 to 939. He actually captured York for a short time, and may have been accepted as an overlord even by Welsh and Scottish rulers. He called himself "King of all Britain" on his coins, and ruled that "one coin shall run throughout the land". If he was really king of Britain, then he was the first such king. He arranged marriage treaties with French and German royal families, so as to be on friendly terms with those countries.

During his reign and the reigns of his successors, particularly King Edgar (who ruled from 959 to 975), most of England became a united, peaceful country. No country in Europe could show such unity and peace. With help from the king, and thanks to the work of a great Archbishop of Canterbury, St Dunstan, many new monasteries were founded. Alfred's dream was fulfilled, and these monasteries became famous as centres of prayer and learning and help to the poor and sick throughout Europe. With peace came prosperity. Towns grew up around the burhs, and the population of London grew to around 10,000.

Then, in the 980s, men from Denmark came to raid England again. These raiders were better organized than the last ones. The Danish King Swein, who had seized the throne from his father King Bluetooth in 988, ruled both Denmark and Norway. He had a strong army of paid soldiers, which was the most organized that had been seen in Britain since the Roman army. King Ethelred, who was king of Wessex from 979 to 1016, and was known as "the Unraed" ("the ill-advised"), knew that he would not be able to defeat such an army. So, as Alfred had done at first, he collected "Danegeld", or protection money, from his people — large sums of money which he paid to the Danish soldiers when they arrived, to persuade them to go elsewhere. From the huge numbers of Ethelred's pennies which have been dug up all over Scandinavia, we know that the Danish soldiers gained large profits from expeditions to England. Ethelred's wife was the daughter of the Duke of Nor-

mandy, and at one time Ethelred was forced to flee to Normandy for help.

When Ethelred and then his son Edmund both died in 1016, the Wessex Grand Council of noblemen, known as the Witan, whose job it was to elect a new king, chose King Swein's younger son, Cnut, to be king of all England. They decided it was better to have a Danish king than to go on paying the Danish armies to stay away or having to fight them.

In the 145 years since Alfred had become king of Wessex, the nation of England had grown out of Wessex. The Danes had made this possible by destroying all English kingdoms other than Wessex. They had cleared the way for union under one king. Now the chosen king of England was a Dane.

Cnut was twenty when he was crowned king in 1016. He promised to preserve English laws, and he married Ethelred's widow in an attempt to show his Englishness, though he killed Ethelred's other son. A writer living at the time described how he "changed from a wild man into a most Christian king". Shortly before he became king, Danish pirates had burned down Canterbury Cathedral and pelted the Archbishop, Alphege, to death with stones and bones, after a drunken feast. Cnut ordered the rebuilding of the cathedral and himself helped to bear the Archbishop's body into the building in a magnificent torchlight ceremony as an act of compensation. He helped to build new churches, and encouraged people to build them in stone rather than wood, so that they would last.

In 1019 Cnut's father died and he became king of Denmark and Norway as well as England. He began to spend less and less time in England. So that there

The map above shows the extent of the territories over which Cnut reigned. On the left is a pen drawing from the Liber Vitae, *an illustrated medieval manuscript. Cnut, now a Christian King, and his wife are placing a cross on the altar of the new minster at Winchester.*

would be strong rulers to look after the country while he was away, he divided England into four separate earldoms – Northumbria and East Anglia, ruled by Danish earls, and Mercia and Wessex, ruled by English earls. At the time this division of the country may have seemed an act of common sense, but as things turned out there was great rivalry between the different earls, and when Cnut died there was fighting for seven years over who would be king.

Then in 1042, the Witan elected a new king, Edward, who was called "the Confessor", which meant "strong believer in the Christian faith". Edward was later made a saint, the only king of England to be so honoured. He was Alfred's great great great grandson, and the last fully English king.

In spite of its recent troubles, England in the reign of Edward the Confessor was the strongest kingdom in Europe at the time. Its towns were growing in size and wealth. In the countryside, there were villages instead of lonely farmhouses. There was a recognized system of raising an army, which Alfred had established, and a collection of ships which could be called on to defend the Channel ports.

Because the kings had needed to collect huge sums of Danegeld, there was

VBI HAROLD:SACRAMENTVM:FECIT:~ HIC HAROL
VVILLELMO DVCI:~

A section from the Bayeux Tapestry showing Harold swearing an oath to William, one hand upon an altar, the other on a chest of holy relics.

now an efficient system of raising taxes. Records were kept of each man's lands and wealth which the later Norman kings of England were to use for making their Domesday Book. Edward rebuilt Westminster Abbey to provide a church and a great hall for the royal palace at Westminster, the village round the bend of the river Thames from London. All the great occasions of the English nation were held there right up to our own times. When Edward died on 5th January 1066 without a son to follow him on the throne, he left the country with the worst of situations — an argument over who would be the next king of England.

There were four men who claimed the right to the title "King of all the English". One of them was William, Duke of Normandy. Edward the Confessor had lived in Normandy during the reign of King Cnut, and William swore that Edward at one time promised him

that he would be king of England when he died, which may well have been true. (He also swore — probably again with truth — that Harold of Wessex had earlier promised him his loyalty on Edward's death.) Then there was Harold Hardrada, from Norway, who claimed the right to follow Cnut as king of England and to unite England with Norway and Denmark again. In addition there were two brothers, Harold of Wessex and Tostig, Earl of Northumbria, who both claimed the right to be king of England.

Harold of Wessex was named king by Edward on his deathbed. The Witan elected him immediately, and he was crowned king. But the other three men would not accept this. The people of

121

Northumbria revolted against Tostig, so he fled across the North Sea to give his support to Harold Hardrada. Now King Harold faced two invasions – one across the North Sea by Harold Hardrada, Tostig and their supporters, and one across the Channel from Normandy by William and his army.

It was William whom King Harold feared the most. Throughout the summer, he stationed his army along the south coast and his navy off the Isle of Wight. Duke William had an invasion army ready in northern France, but found that winds from the north forced his ships to stay in port. By early September, Harold could keep his troops together no longer. They were eager to return to their homes for the harvest. He therefore let them go, and sent his fleet to London. Many ships were lost on their way in storms.

No sooner had Harold let his men and

ships go than dreadful news arrived. The northerly winds which had kept William in port helped Harold Hardrada and Tostig to sail swiftly south from their base in the Orkneys, where the Norwegian army and fleet were gathered. They sailed up the Humber with 200 warships, landed and won a battle near York. But Harold acted with extraordinary speed and firmness. He marched north, gathering an army on the way, and defeated Harold Hardrada and Tostig in battle at Stamford Bridge, near York, on 25th September 1066. Both his rivals were killed and, according to *The Anglo-Saxon Chronicle*, "Few survived and the English remained in command of the field".

But at the height of his success Harold received the very news which he must have been most dreading. William of Normandy, taking advantage of changing winds, had landed at Pevensey Bay

Two more sections from the famous Bayeux Tapestry which tells the story, like a strip cartoon, of William's conquest of England. On the left provisions are being carried for the invasion, and on the right Harold is killed at the Battle of Hastings by a mounted knight.

on the Sussex coast near Hastings on 28th September. There was nothing for it but to march south as quickly as possible. It was 300 kilometres to London, where Harold's men found reinforcements, though not as many as they had hoped. They finally met William's forces at Senlac Hill, 15 kilometres from Hastings. The two sides joined battle on 14th October 1066 at about 9.30 in the morning. The place where they fought was named Battle, and the village there still has that name today.

Harold had more men than William — between 5000 and 6000. But most of them were on foot, and all of them were tired. They occupied the top of the hill, and let William's forces, who were led by trained knights on horseback, advance up the slope. They formed a wall of their shields and kept tightly together. The Norman knights several times rode up Senlac Hill but were forced to retreat. If the English had stayed put, they would almost certainly have won the day. But some of the English charged downhill after a retreating group of Norman soldiers. The Normans rallied their forces, turned and put the English to flight. This made a gap in the English ranks. After this, William ordered his men to make a fake retreat. He did this twice, and each time the English chased the Norman soldiers down the hill. Each time the Normans turned and killed some of them. Finally, towards nightfall, the Normans broke through the shield wall. Harold himself was killed. William's victory was complete.

123

The Norman Conquest

At first the English refused to settle down peacefully under Norman rule. There were fierce rebellions in Kent and Devon, on the Welsh borders, in the north and in the swampy fenland of East Anglia. Here, where rivers flowed far inland among the marshes, the Norwegians sailed to help the English bands. The strongest group of rebels was gathered around Ely, which was then an island, where a great monastery had stood for centuries. The Norwegians camped there after they sailed up the River Ouse.

Local scouts led the Norwegians through the marshes to the rich monastery at Peterborough – so rich that the town was called the Golden Borough – using tracks which only local Fenlanders knew. The Norwegians sacked the monastery on 2nd June 1070, but then lost interest in fighting and returned home with their loot.

The leader of the last English stand against the Normans was Hereward, the son of a Lincolnshire lord. Hereward had been leading a band of outlaws in the area for several years. In the spring of 1070 he made his headquarters at Ely, described by a medieval chronicler – Richard, the author of the *Ely Book* – as an island raised above the surrounding fens "seven miles long, four miles wide, and containing within it twelve villages".

The island was a very good place for rebels to withstand a long siege, as they would always be able to find plenty of food. This is how Richard described it:

"Its soil abounds in fertility, and it is most favoured with pleasant woods, famous for its wild game, no less rich in

Harold's coronation by Archbishop Stigand from the Bayeux Tapestry. Harold holds the sceptre and orb – symbols of monarchy.

pasture and fodder for cattle, and surrounded on all sides by rivers teeming with fish … They call it Ely, that is in English 'eel island', from the vast numbers of eel you can catch in the marshes there."[10]

[The monks received a rent from one of their farms of 172,900 eels a year.]

Most important of all, Ely was surrounded by the rivers, reeds, lakes, marshes and swamps of the fens. Today the fens have been drained, and their black, flat fields form some of the richest soil in Britain. To get some idea of what the fens must have been like in Hereward's time, you must visit the National Trust reserve at Wicken, near Soham, which has been preserved in its old state. A modern author has left this impression of his visit:

"There, especially in ... midwinter ... one can begin to appreciate what the Normans were up against — the impenetrable scrubby undergrowth, the absence of all landmarks, the eerie silence broken only by the derisively laughing calls of unseen water-birds and the ominous bubbling and gurgling of the waterlogged soil. Worst of all is the feeling of total insecurity engendered, while walking along what seems like a firm grassy path, by suddenly ... sinking waist-deep into the mud ..."[11]

For a while the Normans left Hereward and his army alone, but by the summer of 1071 they could do so no longer. King William himself led the attack. This is how the disaster which befell the attackers is described by a monk at Ely in the next century:

"William gathered all his army where the marshes and waters surrounding the island were narrowest. In order to make a causeway over the great river that flowed there he had brought in tools, wood, stone and all kinds of timber piles. Then they placed in the fen whole tree-trunks and beams, fixing them together and laying beneath them complete sheep-skins and tanned hides filled with air, so that they would be better able to carry the load they would have to bear. But as soon as the causeway was finished, so many men rushed over it all together, greedy for the great treasure of gold and silver which they believed to be hidden on the island, that the causeway and the men who had hurried in front sank together into the water. Those in the middle of the column were also sucked down by the deep and liquid swamp, and only a few of those at the back managed to escape the waves that rolled through the mud."[11]

In spite of this disaster, the Normans took their time and returned to the attack. They finally managed to reach the island and defeat the rebels. Hereward was one of those who escaped. A few years later he made peace with the new rulers. After that there were no more English rebellions against the Norman conquerors.

Not long before, in 1069, another powerful rebellion had broken out in the north, where the English were supported by the Danes. York was burned to the ground, and the Norman commander was killed. After William had suppressed the revolt, the Norman army carried out a policy of terror. The soldiers were ordered to destroy every town, village and house between York and Durham.

Norman soldiers like this one were stationed all over England. There were only 10,000 of them, but they subdued one million Englishmen.

They were to burn every barn and hay-stack and kill every animal and human being they found. As the destruction was done in winter, thousands died of cold and hunger, as well as those killed by the soldiers. The terrible lesson was learned. It did not pay to revolt.

William and his Norman army of occupation consisted of only about 10,000 men, whereas the English population was about one million. So William knew that he would have to rule with force if he wanted to stay in Britain. That was why he had treated the English rebels so brutally.

Everywhere the Normans went, starting with Dover, they built castles. At first, these were used as barracks for the occupying troops – including more and more English soldiers, sometimes paid to serve in the Norman army, sometimes conscripted (forced to join up) for a short time. Later, as the castles grew more complicated and fearsome, they became signs of military might with which to terrify the local people. The stone "keep" (tower) of a Norman castle looks like a clenched fist. The fist was a warning to the local people, reminding them of the price of rebellion.

At first, the army built "motte and bailey" castles. The mottes were mounds of earth, like Iron Age camps or Wessex burhs, with deep ditches around them. Connected to them by wooden bridges were the baileys, enclosures of up to 2 hectares in size, where the garrison would live in normal times, ready to retreat to the motte in time of war. A wooden keep, surrounded with a wooden stockade, was built on top of the mound. The baileys were also protected by ditches and stockades.

The moment the Normans moved into an area they would build motte and bailey castles. The site of the castle was carefully chosen. No castle could be built without the king's permission. The king kept the most important castles under his own control. Local lords were given permission to build others under licence from the Crown.

After a few years the Normans began building castles which would last. Stone keeps, with walls 5 metres thick, now stood on the old earth mounds or on new sites. In time they were to be seen all over England. The most impressive was the

The first castles the Normans built were motte and bailey castles like this one. A wooden fort was built on the motte (mound) and the garrison lived in the bailey (enclosure). The Tower of London (right) and Rochester Castle (far right) both dominate important rivers.

White Tower which forms the centre of the present-day Tower of London. This was built at London's most easterly point to guard the capital city from any enemies who sailed up the River Thames.

Over the years, Norman builders worked steadily to improve and enlarge the defences of the castles. The keeps were surrounded first with one stone wall and a ditch, and then two. Towers were built at regular intervals in the walls. At first these towers were square like the keeps. Then it was found that square corners could be chipped by rocks and stones slung from catapults. Square walls were not as secure as rounded ones: they could be made to crumble if attackers built tunnels underneath them at night and dug away their foundations. Or they might split and splinter under attack by battering-rams. So the Normans made the towers round, and rounded the corners of the outer, protecting walls.

A special gatehouse was built through which the soldiers entered the castle. A special bridge was constructed over the surrounding ditch, which was now usually filled with water and called a moat.

The bridge was drawn up at night and in times of trouble. (It was called the drawbridge.) Entry into the gatehouse could also be stopped by lowering a portcullis. This was a special door with spikes which dropped from the roof.

The biggest and strongest Norman castles were built in north Wales against the Welsh. Caernarfon Castle, home of the Prince of Wales, and Conway Castle are two examples. They were built at the end of the 13th century, and were strong enough to withstand any direct attack. The soldiers inside could be starved out by a long siege, but it would have to be a very long siege. Inside the walls there was grass for sheep and cattle, a poultry yard, an orchard and even a herb garden. There were storehouses which could store a year's food supply or more, mews for hawks, stables for horses and forges for blacksmiths. The soldiers' nightmare was that an intruder or traitor in the garrison might poison the castle's well. Then they would have to surrrender. The invention of gunpowder finally ended the power of the castles, but that was not until the 15th century.

The heart of the castle keep was its great hall on the second floor. This could measure up to 25 metres square, with high ceilings. Here the men of the garrison lived all day and sometimes slept at night by the fires. After a while dormitories were built for the soldiers. Their lives resembled those of the Saxons in their great halls. The lord of the castle and his wife ate at a high table on a raised platform at the head of the hall. The men ate at long wooden tables and benches. Rushes covered the floor. They were changed daily in peaceful times. The hall was full of wood smoke, for there were no chimneys, just an outlet above the fireplace to take the smoke through the wall into the open air outside. There was no glass. When the shutters were closed over the windows, the hall was dark.

William I was a very thorough ruler. He was determined to know in as much detail as possible who owned the land in his new kingdom, and how much it was worth. In about 1084, when the Danes were threatening to invade again, he decided to organize a careful survey of England. From it his officials would be able to work out how much tax each of his people could afford to pay towards the cost of a new army. The survey took two years to complete; it was finished in 1086 and became known as the *Domesday Book*. Domesday meant Judgement Day. Just as no argument with God would be possible at the Last Judgement, so it was no use arguing with William's officials when they came to your village.

Most of the *Domesday Book* has survived, and it is kept today in the Public Record Office in London. William's officials seem to have left large areas of northern England out of their survey, and some of their records of towns, such as London and Winchester, have been lost, but enough has been preserved for us to be able to build up an accurate picture of England twenty years after the Norman Conquest.

The difference between rich and poor at that time was staggering. As we have seen, the English population was about one million. Yet three-quarters of the country's wealth – land, oxen, cattle and pigs – was owned by the king and about 300 landowners. Two hundred of these were lords – dukes, counts, earls – and 100 were leading churchmen – archbishops, bishops and heads of great monasteries.

The rest of the land was farmed by a variety of small farmers. Some of them were free men who owned their own land. But most had to work for part of each week on the local lord's farm. They also had to do extra work for him at harvest time. One tenth of the people were still serfs and owned no land.

The other thing which stands out from the *Domesday Book* is the large number of people who worked on the land – about ninety per cent of the population. Although people had started to build towns and live in them again during later Saxon times, England was still almost entirely an agricultural country.

The Domesday Book was first kept in the Royal Treasury. It was still used until 1900 to settle land disputes.

The First Norman Kings

After the Norman Conquest, England had once again become part of a foreign empire. This time it was less independent than ever before. It was not for nothing that William, Duke of Normandy, became known in English history as William the Conqueror. Under his rule, England and northern France became one nation, with one king and one small group of fantastically wealthy "barons", as the lords and churchmen who owned most of the land on both sides of the Channel were known. They stayed one nation until the 13th century. As the Duke of Normandy owed loyalty to the king of France, England became involved in French quarrels. For many years English troops often had to fight in France for their Norman rulers.

Although England and northern France were one nation, England was much the weaker of the two countries. As we have seen, three-quarters of England was owned by the king and 300 lords. Of those lords, only two were English at the time of the *Domesday Book*. The rest were Normans.

Every aspect of life in England became Norman-French. Norman music was the only music to which the educated English were expected to listen. Romantic Norman stories about the love affairs of lords and ladies were the only tales thought to be worth hearing. The law courts carried out their business in Norman-French, so English lawyers had to be able to speak French, as well as read and write Latin.

Just as the English, after the Anglo-Saxon conquest, despised the Celts and looked down on their language, so the Normans now despised the English and everything about their way of life. When the cathedral at Canterbury was burned down in 1174, the monks asked a master-builder from Normandy, William of Sens, to build their new cathedral. The English had become second-class citizens in their own country.

William the Conqueror was followed on the throne by his sons, William II (1087–1100) and Henry I (1100–1135). Although the rule of these first three Norman kings was harsh, it brought some advantages to England.

The four Norman kings. William I and William II are on the top row and Henry I and Stephen below. The first three kings established Norman rule, but it fell apart under King Stephen.

Manuscripts telling stories of courtly love, the romantic love affairs of the day, were very popular in Norman England.

The Normans were the greatest builders in Europe. Their churches and cathedrals were built not of wood, as earlier ones had been, but of stone. Even today, evidence of the skill of Norman builders can still be seen in small country churches and great cathedrals, such as Rochester, Durham or Ely. England was now linked so closely to Europe that trade greatly increased. As a result, the towns which had begun to grow in the 10th century quickly grew larger and wealthier in the 11th and 12th centuries. And because the Norman kings were powerful, and nobody else in the country dared to challenge them, life in England was fairly peaceful and orderly.

Trouble came after Henry I died in 1135. Henry's son, William, had been drowned at sea, when he was crossing the Channel from Normandy to England, so the crown should have passed to Henry's daughter Matilda. However, powerful men at court believed that a woman ruler would ruin the country, just because she was a woman. So strongly did many of the courtiers feel; that they supported Henry's nephew Stephen to become king instead.

Matilda and her husband, Geoffrey of Anjou, were in France when Henry I died. Stephen took his chance and was crowned King of England in 1135. But Matilda insisted on her right to become Queen of England. She sailed across the Channel and gathered an army to challenge Stephen. Eighteen years of civil war followed, during which neither side proved strong enough to achieve complete victory.

During this time the barons, who were always jealous of royal power and keen to increase their own, took advantage of royal weakness. They built new castles for themselves without permission and avoided paying the taxes they owed the Crown. They often refused to give either Stephen or Matilda the fighting men for their armies which they were meant to provide.

For a while, life in England went back to being as it was before the rule of Alfred the Great, with many different leaders quarrelling among themselves. Those who suffered most were the ordinary people. How could a merchant

trade safely overseas, if nobody knew who controlled the customs offices and if there was no navy to protect his goods from pirates? How could a town grow and prosper if robber bands from the country were breaking down its gates and looting its shops? How could a small farmer survive, when armies fought battles over his crops and stole his pigs and sheep?

By 1153 everyone in England, except perhaps those barons who were taking advantage of the wars to seize more power for themselves, longed for peace. In this year, Stephen's son and heir, Eustace, died, so there was no one to follow him on the throne. Two years earlier, Geoffrey of Anjou had died, and his and Matilda's eldest son, Henry, had become lord of their lands in Normandy. Now Stephen and Henry made an agreement that Stephen would rule England for the rest of his life, but on his death it would be ruled by Henry.

Stephen's death came only one year later, in 1154. Henry now added England to his empire in France, which stretched from Normandy to the Spanish border. He had already doubled its size when he gained the French province of Aquitaine by marrying Queen Eleanor of Aquitaine. Later he added Brittany in western France. It was the strongest empire in Europe. Henry was called Henry Plantagenet, from the Latin names for the yellow broom flower which was his father's emblem. The line of English kings which he started are called the Plantagenet kings.

Henry II was twenty-one when he became King of England. His wife Eleanor was thirty-three. Henry was cruel to her, and kept her in prison for years.

Henry had red hair, cut very short. He was broad-shouldered, stocky and rather bandy-legged. His bloodshot eyes were grey. He adored hunting; his real passions were hawks and hounds. He was madly energetic and loved nothing better than to travel quickly from one part of his empire to another at short notice. He liked to tell his servants to pack up everything he needed immediately, for they were leaving in two hours' time. So the great army of cooks and butlers would be on the move again, along with other royal servants such as the tent-keepers and the bearers of the king's bed.

The king was also accompanied by his ministers – men like the Chancellor, the most important of all the ministers, and the Treasurer, who looked after the king's

A Norman castle with its round and square turrets and nearby village is visited by the king. The lord will entertain the king and his great retinue of followers.

finances. With them rode their clerks and secretaries clutching the rolls of parchment on which the king's decrees and laws were written.

Off the great royal procession would go, riding as fast as it could from one castle to the next, landing suddenly on an astonished Norman baron with its hundreds of greedy mouths demanding to be fed at his expense.

Henry II was determined to show the people of England that the king was in charge once more. The barons had been doing as they liked during the civil wars. Henry ordered that any castle which had not been built under royal licence should be destroyed. Three hundred were burned or pulled down. The barons had private armies which were under the command of their knights. These armies were meant to be ready to fight for the king whenever he wanted them to do so. All over England these gangs of armed young men had grown out of control. They were roaming the country, settling private quarrels, destroying farmers' crops and looting houses. Henry encouraged the barons to pay him a special tax called "scutage" (shield money) instead of providing him with troops. With the money, the king paid his own troops to fight for him, and so developed the system of a professional army. More knights now settled down to live in their castles and farm their lands instead of causing trouble.

Henry II is chiefly remembered for founding our modern system of law. Alfred's system of trials and punishments which were the same throughout the country had been forgotten. In the time of Stephen and Matilda most of the courts which tried offenders or settled disputes were under the control of the local lords. The lord decided what the law was, and often pocketed the fines instead of giving them to the king. Henry developed the system of "common law" – law common (the same) throughout the whole country – which we use today.

Royal judges, appointed by the king and not by the barons, travelled all over England, stopping at the chief towns in each area. They held trials, which were known as "assizes", in royal courts called "assize courts". The royal judges used common law to judge people accused of serious crimes. If the people were found guilty, the judges passed sentences of punishment on them, rather than making them pay compensation to their victims, which was the old system.

However, the royal courts only tried the richer people. Everyone else was still tried in the lords' courts. And if you could afford to pay a lot of compensation, the royal judge would often let you pay instead of punishing you.

Henry disliked the old system of trial by ordeals, but it continued during his reign. It only came to an end in 1215, when Pope Innocent III banned a priest from taking part in an ordeal trial. Since people believed that such trials could not take place without priests, another system of deciding people's guilt had to be worked out. In time the answer was found in the system of trial by jury. Twelve local free men – that is, men who did not owe service to any lord – decided whether the accused person was guilty or innocent. The system is still used today.

The most bitter dispute in which Henry II was involved was with the Archbishop of Canterbury, Thomas Becket. For hundreds of years churchmen had been allowed to be tried in their own church courts. In fact, anyone who could read or write could claim to be a clergyman and so be tried in a church court. Punishment in these courts was much less harsh than it was in the king's courts. Henry disliked the fact that so many people – particularly powerful lords – could avoid being tried in his courts. It meant that he had no control over what they did.

Henry wanted to change the system, but the churchmen refused to allow it. So Henry decided to make his best friend, Thomas Becket, Archbishop of Canterbury, hoping that Becket would do what he wanted. Becket had previously been Chancellor, and had supported Henry in his long quarrel with the Church. But when he became Archbishop, Becket changed his opinions. He supported the church courts as loyally as any previous archbishop had done. At one time, in 1164, he accepted much of Henry's argument in an agreement called the Constitutions of Clarendon. Then, having agreed to it, he changed his mind.

Shortly after Christmas 1170, Henry was in Normandy. He heard that he was once again being defied by the Archbishop. He flew into a furious – and probably drunken – rage, and shouted out in anger: "Will no one rid me of this turbulent priest?" (Some reports say "low-born" priest.)

Four knights took the king at his word. They rode for the Channel ports, spent the night of 28th December at Saltwood Castle, near Hythe, and arrived at Canterbury Cathedral, where the archbishop was saying evening prayers, at nightfall. Becket refused to stay at the altar, as his priests urged him to do. There he would have been safe. Even the knights in their rage would not have killed him in such a holy place. They were in another part of the cathedral, calling him to come down and talk to them. Becket did so, pushing aside his priests who tried to stop him. A fierce argument followed. The knights killed him, and rode off into the night.

Becket's brave death did more for the Church than anything he had done in his life. Almost immediately miracles were reported. People who called on him in their prayers to help them, or who touched his relics (the remains of his murdered body), said they were cured of their illnesses. Within three years the Pope made Becket a saint, and thousands of people came from all over Europe to pray at his shrine in Canterbury Cathedral. The knights fled abroad, though later they returned to England.

Henry took no action against them, but he announced his bitter shame at his part in Becket's murder. He walked barefoot through the snowy streets of Canterbury as penance, while the monks lashed his bare back. As for the quarrel about the church courts, no king dared raise the matter again for centuries.

This stained glass window in Canterbury Cathedral shows Henry II and Thomas Becket as friends.

The Feudal System

The Saxons had known all about local lords. They worked for them, and in return relied on them for protection. Ordinary men and women needed someone powerful to protect them against enemies and criminals. There were no policemen or soldiers whose help could be called upon if the village was threatened by looters, or Danish raiders, or the armies of enemy lords. Therefore, long before William conquered England and introduced a system which we call the feudal system, or feudalism, the English had followed a way of life which resembled it.

The Normans made this way of life more organized and more military. The feudal system lasted in England for more than 400 years, from the Norman Conquest to the Wars of the Roses during the 15th century. These years are often called the Middle Ages or the medieval period. They are so called because they come in the middle of, or between, ancient and modern times.

Feudalism was not only a system which gave ordinary people some sort of protection. It was not only a way in which the lord lived very comfortably as a result of the hard work of his labourers, who had to do exactly as he said. It became a way by which the king raised troops for his never-ending wars in France. For under the feudal system each baron had a number of knights under his command. These knights led the baron's troops into battle or, if the king asked for help, they were sent to fight for the king. (Later, as we saw in the case of Henry II, kings preferred to take taxes from the barons instead of soldiers and pay for

their own armies.) As the king rewarded the baron with a big castle, so the baron rewarded the knight with a smaller one.

The system worked out something like this. At the top stood the king. All England, in theory, belonged to him. He kept much of it for himself, particularly the forests, which covered one-third of the country. Almost all the kings in the Middle Ages liked to hunt wherever they went. Much of the rest of England the king let out to his barons in return for their support, particularly in wartime.

These barons were the dukes, the earls, the counts and the leaders of the church – the bishops and archbishops. They in turn let out land to the knights in return for military service. Beneath them came the largest group of Englishmen, the "villeins". They had a little land of their own which they leased from the lord. In return they were forced to work for two or three days a week on their lord's farm, and to do extra work at special times, such as harvests. They could only become free of their duties by buying their freedom from the lord. Few of them could raise enough money to do so. Under the villeins came the serfs. About a tenth of the people in England were serfs in 1066. They worked for the lords, who gave them food and somewhere to live, but they had no land and no rights under the law. They "could be sold in the market-place with rings round their necks, just as any other brute-beasts". In effect, they were slaves.

There were always plenty of men and women who were outside the feudal system. There were the "yeomen" – small farmers who owned their own lands and had no masters, apart from the king. They liked to call themselves "the backbone of England" and were proud of their independence. If you lived in a town you were free – that is, you owed no services to a lord. Skilled carpenters, jewellers and other craftsmen were free. Merchants and shopkeepers had no lords in charge of them. By law, if a villein or serf ran away from his lord and hid (in a town, for instance) for a year and a day, he had earned his freedom. (If he was caught earlier, he was dragged back to his lord's service.)

The feudal system only covered part of England. It did not exist in much of the west and east, and it soon died out in Kent. But everywhere else it ruled people's lives. After 1500, villeins and serfs no longer existed anywhere in England, but people living in the country areas went on living in a similar way right up to the Second World War. Even today visitors to England are amazed to find how deeply the English are still divided into different classes.

A typical medieval village was built round the house where the lord lived. If he was a great lord, he lived in a massive stone castle, and was rarely at home. While he was away, his lands were looked after by his bailiff. We have seen something of the lord's way of life in Chapter 14. His knights lived in smaller castles, and their lives were similar but less grand. The normal lord of a feudal village lived not in a castle but in a manor house, which was partly fortified in case of emergencies, with a wall, a moat and a drawbridge.

The manor house was built of stone. It was the only stone building in the village apart from the church. The centre of the house was the great hall. At one end stood the kitchen. Next door to it stood

Norman kings loved hunting deer and boar. They preserved large forests where they alone were allowed to hunt.

the pantry for storing the food and the "buttery" ("bottle-ry") for storing the bottles of wine and ale. At the other end of the hall stood a downstairs cellar, and above it was the lord's private room, called the "solar" (sun room). As time went on, the lord added other private rooms for himself. There were no carpets or comfortable chairs, but tapestries covered the walls, and curtains were hung round the box beds, to keep out the draughts. Clothes were kept in carved wooden chests, or hung on wooden frames. If you took a bath, you would do so in a round wooden tub.

This reconstruction is based on the manor of Rayleigh in Essex as it is described in the Domesday Book in 1086. In this early Norman manor the castle (1) is separately fortified. The lord lives in the thatched building (2) within the bailey. On the right are the farm buildings (3), the bailiff's house (4) and the blacksmith's shop (5). There is an orchard (6). Both lord and villeins have strips in the village fields. One grows wheat (7), another barley (8) and the third lies fallow (9). The villeins' houses (10) surround the church (11). There is a deer park (12) and a vineyard (13). Wine growing was common in medieval England.

One of the advantages of working as a member of the lord's full-time staff, whether you worked in the house or on his fields, was the food. The lord and his servants still ate together in the great hall, as they did in Saxon times. The food for the lord and his family, at the high table, may have been better than that eaten by their servants, sitting on benches at long tables below them. There was certainly more of it to be found on the lord's silver or pewter plate. But everyone would start their two meals a day – eaten at around eleven in the morning and five in the evening – with a bowl of vegetable soup (pottage). Boiled beef or mutton would follow, or perhaps some fish, such as bream, from the fishpond or river. Cheese would end the meal, and ale would be drunk throughout it. In the evening there would probably be a fourth course – fruit, for instance, or plum tarts or apple flans.

The great majority of the people in the village were the villeins and their families. Their lives were hard. Their houses, still made of wattle and daub and thatched, contained one or two rooms. The windows were holes in the walls, which could only be closed by wooden shutters. When the shutters were shut, the rooms were very dark. The floors were of beaten earth, covered with straw or reeds. On the walls hung the family's garden tools. From the rafters hung a flitch (side) of bacon or a collection of dried herbs. The family's beds were bags of straw, with blankets of rough wool, spun and woven at home from wool shorn off their own sheep. Chickens and dogs would live in the same room as the family. The pigs would live in a corner, behind a partition.

Meals were simple. Breakfast was eaten before dawn, before the men went to work in the fields. It consisted of a chunk of rye bread and a cup of water from the village well. At midday, the men returned home for dinner, which was bread again, this time with cheese and a cup of watery beer or, in some parts of England, cider. The evening meal at the end of the working day (around five o'clock in winter, but later in summer) included thick vegetable soup and some salted meat or bacon, or fish caught in the local river. Beer was drunk again, for tea and coffee did not come to England for hundreds of years. Plates and cups were made of wood, and cleaned after the meal with grass. Lights were made from rushes soaked in animal fat and held in rough iron tweezers stuck in a wooden base. The family went to bed shortly after the evening meal, tired out by their strenuous day.

A villein's house made of wattle and daub (mud and plaster smeared between crossed sticks). This is put on between the beams. The roof is thatched. The house has no windows.

The men worked on two farms, their own and their lord's. Each village was surrounded by three large fields split into long thin strips of land. Each villein owned a number of strips in each of the village fields. His total of strips normally added up to 12–15 hectares. The strips were in different parts of the field so that each farmer would have his fair share of good and poor soil. The fields had no hedges. If a farmer had a strip on the edge of the field, no one stopped him from making it larger by taking in the waste land on the field's edge, which was where the surrounding countryside began.

Wooden markers, called land marks, divided one strip of land from another. Every now and then men would creep out in the night to move them, and so increase the size of their own strips. The *Book of Common Prayer* contained a list of evil-doers. Second on the list, after "Cursed is he that curseth his father or mother", is placed: "Cursed is he that removeth his neighbour's land mark".

The crops to be grown in the fields were decided at the village meeting. This was held in the autumn, after the harvest had been gathered in. All strip-owners could vote on the crops for next year. The choice was limited – generally it would be wheat, oats, rye or barley. Root-crops, such as potatoes and turnips, were not yet known.

The villagers had discovered from experience that if you grew crops over and over again on the same land, the soil grew dusty and the crops were poor. So one of the three fields was left fallow (unfarmed). The next year it would be used again and a different field would be left. On the fallow field, the villeins

At harvest time, carts bring bags of grain to the water mill for grinding. Others leave with sacks of flour.

139

would graze their animals, particularly their sheep and cattle, whose manure would enrich the land for the next year.

Apart from the three fields there was the village common land, which, as its name states, was for everybody's use. The villagers depended on the common. Their sheep and cattle fed off it and their goats were tethered on it. Everyone gathered firewood from the common, or from the local woods, as well as acorns for their pigs and wild fruit, nuts and berries. They used traps, or snares, to catch all sorts of birds to eat. Larks were thought of as delicacies, while blackbirds were baked in pies, as in the nursery rhyme. So were pigeons.

The villein spent two or three days a week working on his lord's strips in the open fields or on the manor farm. When he was working for the lord, the villein was part of a team working under the manor foreman, the "reeve". He also had to spend extra time working on the lord's estate at harvest time or at hay-making. This extra "boon" (work), just when he was busiest on his own farm, must have made the villein grumble a good deal. But there was one advantage – the lord gave free meals to his villeins at boon time.

There were various things a villein and his family had to do. They had to give the lord some of their produce at certain times of the year, such as eggs, or honey from their own bees. (As there was no sugar people relied on honey for sweetening.) The villein had to grind his corn in the lord's mill, at prices fixed by the lord. No wonder that the records of cases held in the lords' courts during the Middle Ages are full of prosecutions of villeins for hiding "querns" (little hand-mills) in their homes. The villein's wife was supposed to bake her bread only in the lord's ovens and to pay for the service – a law which must surely have been broken again and again.

The manor court, where the villeins' cases were heard, was supervised by the lord's steward, unless the lord himself wished to take part. The villein had to get permission from this court, and pay a fee, if he wanted to sell his livestock at market, or let his daughter get married. When he died, the villein's son had to pay the court for the right to take over his father's land.

Whatever type of land he was farming – open fields or the manor farm – the villein's working life varied very little from year to year. The routine of the farmer's year was set by the weather and the hours of daylight.

In January, hours were short, and work on the frozen land was often impossible in any case. The villein might be employed then by the lord's "hay-ward", whose job it was to see that the hedges and ditches on the manor farm were in a good state of repair, for cattle were always breaking into the manor fields from the common lands. Or he might work at home in the short daylight hours, repairing his tools or making cow-leather boots.

Ploughing might start in late February and would certainly be under way by March. Oxen (bullocks) were used to drag the plough, and on heavy soils as many as eight oxen might be needed. (On lighter soil it was possible to work with two.) No villein would own eight oxen, so they would each contribute an animal and plough the land together.

Sowing by hand would follow. The sower would sling a bag of seed over his shoulder, or pile it in his upturned apron. Then he would scatter the seed in the furrows of the ploughed ground, not stopping to cover it. The birds followed the sower, ready to take most of the seed for themselves, unless the bird-scaring boys with their wooden clappers or scarecrows kept them away.

June and July were the months for haymaking. Hay was cut with a scythe, a tool with a large curved blade on a long handle. The grass had to be dry before cutting could begin. Haymaking, like ploughing, was not done by the villein on his own. All the men who had rights in the hay meadow would start in a line one fine summer morning and cut the field, moving forward together at the same speed. At midday their wives would arrive with their dinners, which they would eat in the shade under the trees or by the river. Then they would start again, and work right through till nightfall. Later, when the grass had lain out long enough so that it was as dry as the sun could make it, it would be raked into haycocks (little heaps), then pitched into carts and carried to where the haystack was to stand.

August and early September were the months of the corn harvest. Then the wheat or rye was cut with sickles (like scythes, but with shorter handles) and bound together into sheaves. The sheaves stood upright, six or eight leaning together in the field to dry. Behind the harvesters walked the gleaners, women and children who picked up every piece of wheat.

When the sheaves were dry they were put into carts and taken to the corn stacks. The last part of the corn harvest was the threshing (or thrashing). The corn was spread out on the barn floor and beaten with wooden flails to separate the grain from the husks. This would be done in front of the big barn door so that the draught from the open door would blow out the light chaff, leaving the heavy grain behind. The grain would then be swept up, put in sacks and taken to the miller's – there might be both water-mills and windmills in the village – to be ground into flour for bread. The straw was used for bedding for the animals or for spreading on the earthen floors of the villeins' homes.

The year's end was marked with a great feast – the twelve days of Christmas, which lasted until 6th January. People still had no way of feeding many of their animals through the winter, so the animals would be slaughtered and their bones burned. (Our word bonfire comes from the bone fire.) Their meat was either eaten straight away or salted in order to preserve it. Salt meat was boring and unpleasant to eat for a whole winter, but the villeins could not afford to buy spices from the East, as the lord could. The cooks in the manors and castles would mix cloves, nutmegs or cinammon with the meat to preserve it and make it taste more interesting. Instead the villein had to eat salt meat from January to March, catch what he could in the woods, or go without meat altogether.

The women in the village worked as hard as the men. Apart from looking after her own house, garden and children, and helping the men in the village fields, the wife had to work for the lord in the same way as her husband. Here are some of the duties she had to perform for the manor house: cutting "withies" (rushes) to make baskets, cradles and fish traps; plucking geese for arrow-feathers; stitching sheepskin for saddle-bags; making candles out of rushes; and churning butter (a luxury which she could never afford in her own home). The life of a medieval villager, whether man or woman, was working, eating and sleeping. It was a tough, relentless existence, and few men or women lived past the age of fifty.

Crusades and Councils

Henry II had four sons, two of whom died before their father, leaving Richard, the elder, and John. Richard I, who was thirty-two when he became king in 1189, had spent most of his life in France. He was known for his courage and skill as a soldier, and in 1190 he left his great empire in France and England to go on crusade.

The crusades – or "wars of the cross" – had been taking place ever since the Turks had captured Jerusalem, and others parts of what is now Israel, at the end of the 11th century. The Turks, like the Arabs, were followers of the Islamic religion. They believed in the teachings of the great religious teacher Muhammad. But whereas the Arabs who had been ruling Jerusalem since the 7th century had been prepared to mix with Christians, and even allow some of them to live in the city where Jesus taught and died, the Turks were not.

In particular, the Turks stopped Christian pilgrims (travellers to places of deep religious importance) from visiting their holy places, such as Jesus' place of birth in Bethlehem, and the spot where he was crucified in Jerusalem. Christians had been going on pilgrimages to Jerusalem and the area round about, which they called the Holy Land, for centuries. But now the Turks said that Christians who tried to continue the old pilgrimages would be killed or captured and sold as slaves.

When Pope Urban II heard of this, he called a great council in France in 1096, and declared a Holy War. He called on Christian barons and knights to drop everything and lead their men into battle against the Turks. "Christ himself will be your leader," he cried. "Wear His cross as your badge. If you are killed your sins will be pardoned." The crusaders who answered the Pope's summons called themselves soldiers of Christ, and sewed big crosses onto their clothes.

The Crusades. Many Crusaders started from France or Italy. They aimed to capture Jerusalem or Bethlehem from the Turks so that Christian pilgrimages could start again. Venice was their main port; Cyprus and Malta were military bases.

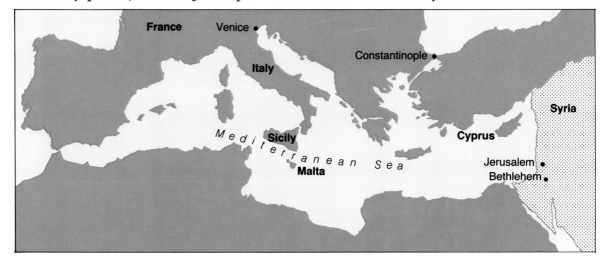

To begin with, many devout Christians from France, Germany and Italy took the Pope at his word. Following the wild leadership of a monk called Peter the Hermit, all kinds of people, including old men, women and children, rushed to join what was called "the People's Crusade". They straggled along the roads of Europe, taking little food or money, mostly travelling on foot and carrying no weapons. When those who had not died of hunger or been killed by bandits on the way finally met a Turkish army, they were easily defeated.

They were followed by a much more professional crusade – the First Crusade. Knights from all over western Europe, but particularly France, made a well-prepared expedition to Jerusalem. They took with them supplies of food, armour and weapons in great creaking wagons. Finally, in 1099, they captured Jerusalem, where they killed the Turkish soldiers mercilessly, looted the shops and slaughtered many innocent inhabitants. Their behaviour seems all the more terrible when it is remembered that they claimed to be fighting under the banner of Christ, the King of Peace and Love.

For nearly 100 years Christian knights, some of them English, many of them French, had control of Jerusalem. The pilgrimages started again. Some of the crusaders formed themselves into full-time regiments of soldiers and lived in Jerusalem to defend it. Soldiers of one such regiment called themselves the Knights of St John. The modern ambulance service, the St John Ambulance Association, is descended from these Christian knights. So is the international Red Cross, which is to be found today treating the sick and caring for the dying whenever a war or natural calamity – such as an earthquake or famine –

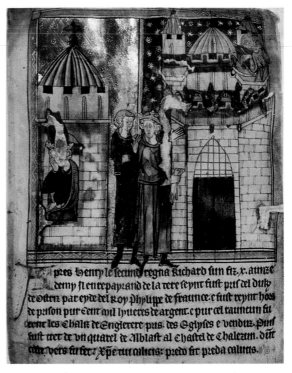

This manuscript drawing shows a sad-looking Richard I in prison in Germany.

occurs. They do truly Christian work.

At last the Turks captured Jerusalem again in 1187. A great new crusade – the Third Crusade – was organized to win it back. The emperor of Germany, Frederick I, and the French king, Philip II, declared that they would lead it. Soon they were joined by Richard I in 1190. The wagon trains were loaded up again, while the blacksmiths and armourers, who shod the crusaders' horses and made their chain mail armour, hammered through the night. The seamstresses worked overtime to sew the linen surcoats which, when worn over the knights' armour, protected them from the glare and heat of the desert sun.

But the Third Crusade, like the others, ended in failure. The ship taking Richard to the Holy Land was blown off course, and he landed not on the coast near Jerusalem but on the island of Cyprus. Then the crusaders advanced to within

20 kilometres of Jerusalem, but could not capture it. Meanwhile Frederick I had drowned in the Mediterranean, and most of the German toops returned home. Philip and Richard quarrelled. Philip went back to France, where he began to plot with Richard's brother John to seize Richard's lands. When, in 1192, Richard heard that there had been a rebellion in England, he decided to make peace with the Turks and go home himself. It was agreed that Jerusalem would remain Turkish, but the Christians would have the right to go on pilgrimages there.

Already the English were having to pay heavy taxes for the Third Crusade, but worse was to come. On his journey back through Italy Richard I was captured and handed over to the German emperor, Henry VI. For thirteen months Richard was imprisoned, while his officials tried to raise the huge ransom demanded as the price of his release. It was 150,000 silver marks. As customs duties, an important part of the English king's income, brought in only about 10,000 marks a year, it was not easy to raise the money. Finally Richard was released, when about 100,000 marks had been paid.

Richard I returned to his empire in France to find that Philip of France had taken important parts of it while he had been away in Jerusalem. He visited England in 1194 to punish those who had backed John's plots against him, but he did not stay there long. He spent his last five years in France, where he managed to regain most of his lands until, in 1199, he was killed in battle.

Although he spent only six months of his reign in England, and despite the heavy taxes which the people had to pay, Richard I does not seem to have been unpopular with the English people. He was remembered as a great warrior king at a time when knights and leading soldiers were treated with great respect. He was called Richard, Cœur de Lion – Richard the Lion Heart.

John, who came to the throne when Richard died, had always been in trouble. When his father, Henry II, had made plans to split up his great empire among his sons, John had complained because his share was too small and had fought a war with him. When Richard was on crusade, John plotted against him with Philip of France, and tried to throw him off the English throne. When finally he became king, at the age of thirty-two, the barons in Anjou and lands to the south decided to choose twelve-year-old Arthur of Brittany, John's nephew, instead. John organized Arthur's murder and took back some lands in France, but he lost most of them in the end.

Unlike Henry II and Richard I, John spent most of his time in England, not France. There too he ran into trouble with the barons. (These wealthy and powerful men were to challenge the power of the king in England for the next 250 years.) Both the barons and the ordinary people had reasons for complaining about the king. The barons, knights and other wealthy men may not have opposed the crusades. But they certainly disliked heavy taxes to pay for them. The barons may themselves have loved hunting, and the ordinary people may have loved to watch the court out hunting when it came their way, but both were furious when John tightened up the forest laws and stopped people straying into the royal forests.

Since Becket's murder, churchmen were not prepared to consider a king's opinions when it came to appointing a

The effigy of Sir John Holcombe on his tomb at Dorchester Abbey in Oxfordshire. Sir John was killed in Israel during the Second Crusade and knighted on the battlefield. His legs are crossed in the crusader fashion.

new Archbishop of Canterbury. But when the Pope appointed Stephen Langton Archbishop of Canterbury, John protested. A quarrel developed which led the Pope to declare an *interdict* on the whole of England. This meant that no church services were allowed. No marriages could be held in churches and no bodies could be buried in the graveyards. John himself was excommunicated (expelled from the Church). It was six years before the interdict was lifted, and the church bells could be rung again.

In 1214 John made one more attempt to recapture his lands in France, but he was defeated by King Philip at the battle of Bouvines. While he was away, a group of English barons, led by Archbishop Langton, rebelled and captured London. John was forced to make peace with them for the time being. The agreement John made with the barons in 1215 was called the Magna Carta – the great charter. For centuries it has been looked on as the agreement which gave freedom to the English people.

At the time, however, the charter was to be nothing of the kind. The barons who had it written thought of it as a list of English customs, which a king should promise to obey. These customs concerned themselves, and other rich and powerful people in England. When they wrote, in the Magna Carta, of "the free men of England" they meant people free of any feudal duties to a lord – the wealthy people. But hundreds of years later, ordinary English men and women, looking back to the Magna Carta, thought it meant everybody and called it a "charter for English liberties".

Archbishop Stephen Langton was in charge of getting the charter written for the barons of England. John signed it on an island in the Thames near Windsor called Runnymede. Four copies survive today. One is at Salisbury Cathedral, and another at Lincoln Cathedral, and two are kept in the British Library in London.

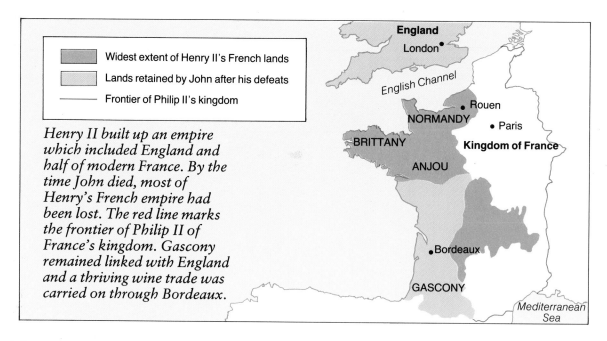

Henry II built up an empire which included England and half of modern France. By the time John died, most of Henry's French empire had been lost. The red line marks the frontier of Philip II of France's kingdom. Gascony remained linked with England and a thriving wine trade was carried on through Bordeaux.

These are some of "the customs of the realm" to which John agreed:

1. Important taxes could not be raised without the agreement of the chief barons.
2. No "freeman" could be punished without a proper trial. [This did not make any difference to most people, who were still tried in the lord's court.]
3. The English Church was right to obey the Pope in Rome as its head.
4. Royal forests should be smaller.
5. Unpopular royal judges and officials should be dismissed.

The agreement did not lead to peace. The two sides started quarrelling again. The barons asked Louis of France, King Philip's son, to become King of England. In 1216 Louis entered London. In the same year John died at Newark, in Nottinghamshire, after attending a banquet. But men and women were to remember the Magna Carta.

Henry III (1216–1272) was only nine when his father John died. Louis soon returned to France. For the next sixteen years, England was ruled by a council of courtiers and barons. During Henry's long reign, people in England protested about the large number of foreign courtiers who were being given large estates of land in England. In 1236, Henry married Eleanor of Provence, in the south of France, and she brought many greedy noblemen and relatives with her, who were rewarded with English lands.

The descendants of the original Norman barons who came to England during the Norman Conquest now thought of themselves as English noblemen. They disliked English land being given to foreigners, and they felt strongly that England should be ruled on its own, quite separate from France. They managed to force the king to agree that the country should be run for the time being by a council of English noblemen.

The king was not prepared to agree to this for long, and in 1264 civil war broke out. The leader of the English barons, Simon de Montfort, led the forces of the English nobles against the king at the battle of Lewes. They defeated Henry and took him prisoner.

Simon then called a Great Council to discuss what should be done about governing the country. In Saxon times kings had often called councils of their earls at important moments in the country's affairs. The earls would give advice if the kings asked for it, and discuss taxes. Norman kings had done the same, calling meetings of their top 300 barons, the tenants-in-chief.

Simon de Montfort's Great Council or *Parleyment* (French for "talking-place") was unusual. To it he invited not only the barons of England. He invited representatives of the knights, two per county, and the burgesses, two for each main town. They had not been invited before. Kings and councillors needed the money which knights and, in particular, wealthy townsmen could provide.

So the English Parliament began to take shape. In time, the Great Council of

The opening lines of the Magna Carta. At first the charter was concerned only with the rights of the wealthy.

the Parliament divided into two houses. Barons and bishops sat, as they still do, in the House of Lords. Knights and burgesses sat in the House of Commons.

As the Commons represented the people with the most money, they became the main source of taxes. The members of the two houses, who began to meet in a permanent place, the Royal Palace of Westminster, were finally to have more say in running the country than the king or queen.

But all this was in the distant future. For the time being the Great Councils met rarely. They were expected to give advice when the king asked for it and not to use the meeting as a time for telling the king of their own grievances. When they were asked for money, they were expected to give it without arguing. A year after the battle of Lewes, Henry's son Edward restored his father's power by defeating Simon de Montfort's men at Evesham, in 1265. But the idea of a Parliament had taken root in the minds of the English and was to grow and grow.

Rebellion over the borders

William the Conqueror decided not to try to occupy Wales in the way that he occupied England. He gave great areas of the country in the south along the English border, and in the river valleys all over Wales, to his barons. Men like the Earl of Hereford in the south and the Earls of Shrewsbury and Chester in the north were given thousands of Welsh hectares, many of them very good farmland. The barons imposed a feudal system on these huge estates: the Welsh were the villeins or slaves, the lords and knights were the Normans and their English allies.

But in the most mountainous parts of the country, particularly in the north, the Welsh were left alone. Here, by the 13th century, the princes of Gwynedd grew powerful. They hoped to rule all Wales. Llywelyn the Great ruled most of the country, outside the area of the Norman lords, until his death in 1240. His grandson, Llywelyn ap Gruffydd, called Llywelyn the Last, married Simon de Montfort's daughter, and was regarded at the English Court as a powerful neighbour. In 1267 Henry III, at the Treaty of Montgomery, recognized Llywelyn the Last as Prince of Wales. In return Llywelyn recognized Henry as his overlord.

When Henry III died in 1272, Edward I became king. Llywelyn the Last failed to attend his coronation and neither side trusted the other. Llywelyn's brother Dafydd, who had plotted against Llywelyn, fled to Edward in 1276 and asked for refuge. Feelings were running high, and that same year Edward launched a campaign on sea and land against Gwynedd.

In the mountains around Snowdon, which even the Romans had never conquered, the Welsh were cornered. Always before, when in trouble, they had retreated to their mountain refuges, and survived, secure in the knowledge that no invader could enter such country for long. This time they met their match.

Edward's soldiers advanced along the coast of north Wales, supported by his fighting ships. As they proceeded, they built great castles at key points such as Conway, Caernarfon and Beaumaris. From these bases they destroyed the corn crops in the surrounding areas — particularly in the fertile island of Anglesey — and killed cattle and sheep. The Welsh in the mountains were starved out.

In 1277 Llywelyn surrendered. The English treated him better than might have been expected: Gwynedd was divided, not destroyed or occupied. Llywelyn's brother Dafydd, however, was dissatisfied with his share. In 1282 he rebelled against his English overlords. Llywelyn was told to suppress the rebellion; instead he joined it. In the next year the English won a complete victory. Llywelyn was killed, and his head stuck on a pike at the entrance to the Tower of London. Dafydd was put on trial as a traitor at Shrewsbury, and tortured to death. By the Statute of Wales (1284), Gwynedd was divided into counties and became an English colony.

The Council of Edward I. The King is shown with Alexander, King of Scotland, and Llywelyn, Prince of Wales. Beneath are lords with their coronets, archbishops with their croziers, bishops with their mitres, and commoners (some of whom were judges).

148

Aussi se ledit collier dor auoit besoing de reparacion il pora
estre mis en la main de louurier iusques a ce quil soit
repare. Lequel collier aussi ne pourra estre enrichy de
pierres ou daultres choses reserue ses ymage qui pourra
estre garny au plaisir du cheualier. Et aussi ne pourra
estre ledit collier vendu engaigie domne ne aliene pour
necessite ou cause quelconque que ce soit

Alexander Rex
Scotor

lewellin
princeps
wallie

Fourteen castles were built with walled towns around them. They became the headquarters of the conquering English in each area. Wherever a garrison town was built, Welsh farmers and their families were evicted. Their lands were given to Englishmen whom the king had recruited from all over England – soldiers, castle builders, and even two cooks of the Earl of Lincoln. The Welsh were moved to mountainous, barren soil, often covered with mist for days on end – a poor exchange for their fertile valley farms.

For a while the English treated the Welsh as badly as they later treated the Irish. They were bitterly resented, though Welsh revolts in 1287 and in 1294–1295 were easily suppressed. In

Harlech Castle in North Wales, one of Edward I's castles. Fourteen castles were built at key points along the coast and garrison towns for English troops grew up around them.

1301 the completion of the conquest was marked when Edward's son was crowned Prince of Wales at Caernarfon Castle in a glittering ceremony.

The last great national Welsh revolt started in 1400. Henry IV had just seen his son Henry crowned Prince of Wales amid rumours of Welsh rebellion. It was said that there were letters going from leading Welshmen to supporters in Scotland asking for their help. The rumours were soon proved true. Owain Glyndŵr, a nobleman who claimed to be descended from one of the old royal families of Wales, raised a rebellion in the north-east, and all over Wales supporters joined his cause.

Glyndŵr was a rather surprising national Welsh leader. He did not come from Gwynedd, the heart of old independent Wales, but from Sycharth, near Llangollen, on the river Dee. He had many contacts with nearby England, had trained as a lawyer at an English law

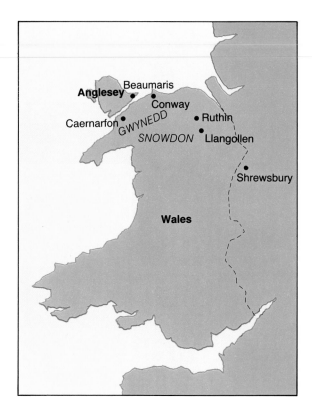

English bases in North Wales. The Welsh were often moved out of an area and given inferior land so that the English could build their castles.

Owain Glyndŵr led a national Welsh revolt against the English in 1400 which nearly succeeded.

school, and had fought in English wars against the Scots. But he quarrelled with an English nobleman over disputed land near his home, and was enraged by the scornful way in which both Henry IV and Parliament dismissed his claim.

For ten years Owain Glyndŵr fought all over Wales. He attacked castles and burned down the hated towns. The English, under Henry IV and Prince Henry, hit back hard. In the winter of 1400–1401, Glyndŵr took to the hills with only seven men, but he reappeared the next spring and conquered most of Wales.

By 1406 it seemed possible that Glyndŵr might be crowned Prince of Wales. He was closely allied to the English barons who were trying to overthrow Henry IV, and had allies in Scotland and in France. French sailors fought for him by sea, and 2000 French soldiers marched with him by land. He drew up an agreement with the Pope for a Welsh Church which would have Welsh-speaking priests and would establish two Welsh universities for the training of future servants of an independent Prince of Wales.

But this dream of an independent Welsh nation soon faded. The Scots, the French and the English barons made their peace with Henry IV. In 1408 Glyndŵr's armies were decisively defeated. The war was over by 1410. Nobody knows what happened to Glyndŵr himself; but his son took a post at the court of Henry V.

From that time Wales and England were united. The accession of a Welsh line of kings – the Tudors – to rule over England in the 16th century further strengthened the union. Welsh law gave way to English law. The official language was English, and all public affairs had to be conducted in it. Welsh continued to be the spoken language in most parts of Wales, but its slow decline had begun.

151

An early Scottish castle in winter. The picture emphasizes the loneliness of many Scottish settlements. The nearly windowless castle would have been difficult to capture.

SCOTLAND

When William I conquered England, Scotland was more united than Wales. Scottish kings ruled over most of the land, apart from the Norwegian colonies in the north, and by the Treaty of Perth in 1266 those lands too came under the King of Scotland's rule.

In Europe, Scotland was now regarded as a nation to be respected. Alexander III (1249–1286) minted silver coins which were accepted all over the kingdom. Import duties were collected by his customs officers at Scottish ports in the same way as at English ports. Children of Scottish kings and queens were married to the children of European rulers. Kings of England still claimed, as they had done in Wales, to be the "overlords" of Scotland. But they claimed no more than that.

In 1286 Alexander III of Scotland fell from his horse and was killed. His only heir was his grand-daughter, Margaret, who was aged two. Edward I proposed to the Scottish lords who ruled the country during Margaret's childhood that she should marry his son Edward. They agreed but unfortunately Margaret died in 1290. If she had lived both England and Scotland might have been spared centuries of wars and bitterness.

After Margaret's death, there were thirteen different claimants. Edward I claimed his right as overlord to choose the new king, and, surprisingly, the Scottish lords agreed with him. He chose John Balliol, who was crowned king on St Andrew's Day, 1292. The English expected Balliol to be their puppet king and when he showed signs of independence Edward marched into Scotland in 1296 and removed him from the throne. He returned to England with the coronation stone from the abbey of Scone. By this dramatic gesture, Edward I showed that there would be no more kings of Scotland. He was King of Scotland now.

But the Scots had other ideas. Sir William Wallace led a national rebellion against the English. In 1297 Scottish forces defeated the English at the battle of Stirling. Edward, deciding to treat the Scots as he had treated the Welsh, marched north. At the battle of Falkirk his archers used their famous 2-metre long bows to fire arrows tipped with iron. The Scots were unable to retaliate and fled. After seven years on the run, William Wallace was captured and taken for trial to London. He was declared a traitor and his head impaled on London Bridge in 1305.

The Scots soon found a new leader: Robert Bruce. He was crowned king at Scone, though without the coronation stone, in 1306. Bruce had few supporters at first, but the French were on his side, and their support started a tradition of Scottish-French friendship (the "auld alliance" as the Scots called it) which was to last for hundreds of years.

At first Bruce's cause seemed hopeless, and he fled from one Highland refuge to another. But his fortunes changed when Edward I, who was travelling north with a strong force, died near Carlisle in 1307. His son Edward II returned to London for his father's funeral.

For the next seven years Bruce won victory after victory. He relied on the speed of his men, whereas the English relied on their horses. So Bruce destroyed not only castles, but the cornfields around them, denying the horses their oats. As one English castle fell after another, more and more Scots joined Bruce's army. He became as much of a hero as the martyred Wallace.

Finally at Bannockburn, just south of Stirling, the decisive battle was fought. The English, though they had many more soldiers than the Scots, were completely defeated. Baggage worth about £200,000 — a staggering sum in those days — fell into Scottish hands. Many English nobles were captured and only released after payment of huge ransoms. Edward II himself, who headed the English army and fought with great courage, only just managed to escape. Finally, in 1328, Edward II's son, Edward III (1327–1377), recognized Robert Bruce as the rightful King of Scotland.

The Battle of Bannockburn.

IRELAND

It was Henry II (1154–1189) who first began the English attempt to conquer Ireland. He went there himself with an army, but succeeded only in capturing Dublin and the area round about called the Pale. There were some attempts to increase English lands in the 13th century, but never any real chance of the English conquering the whole island.

Robert Bruce's brother Edward, knowing how unpopular the English were in Ireland, landed there in 1315. He gained enough support from Irish chiefs to be crowned King of Ireland, but in 1318 his army was defeated by the English and he was killed.

English kings claimed to be overlords of Ireland, but the claim meant little, for the real rulers of most of the country were the great barons, such as the Earls of Ormond and Kildare. Everywhere, except in Dublin and the Pale, the English were forced to leave the Irish alone.

The Medieval Church

Wherever you looked in medieval Britain you found signs of the Christian religion. Every village had its own church – men and women were married there, mothers brought their children to be baptized there, and the dead were buried in the churchyard. Nearly everyone went to church on Sunday, and Christmas, Easter and the birthdays of popular saints were declared rest days. (They were holy days, and we still refer to them as holidays today.)

Medieval churches were built of stone, not of wood. They were used for all sorts of social occasions such as harvest suppers, wedding feasts, funeral meals and parties, which the whole village would attend. In the churchyard stood the stocks, where those who had committed minor offences sat, their ankles and wrists clamped in front of them, while passers-by insulted them or threw bad eggs or mud at them.

The church also contained the only public means of telling the time. (Private clocks and watches were unknown.) In the days before church clocks were built into church towers, sundials were used. The simplest was the finger dial, scratched on the church wall. You stuck your finger into a hole in the middle of the dial. The number on which the shadow fell was the hour.

Each village had its own priest. Before 1200 priests could marry. After that time they could not. The priest, who had a small farm beside the church called the "glebe" land, was a farmer like all the people in his congregation. This meant that he had a great deal in common with them, and this helped him in his work of telling them about the teachings of Jesus.

Everyone in the village had to give one-tenth ("tithe") of their animals and crops each year – the best tenth – to the priest as his wages. The crops were taken to the tithe barn on the glebe land at harvest time. Villagers hated paying tithes, and their collection caused ill-feeling between priests and their congregations which lasted for centuries.

The priest could often barely read or write, and spent much of his life working on his land. Sometimes he did not understand the Latin services he spoke, or the words of the Bible he read. But though he may have seemed ignorant to learned men, he was more educated than anyone else in the village. Sunday after Sunday he spoke to the people about the meaning of life and death, and held the Holy Communion service (the Mass). In this service the people felt joined in spirit to Jesus and to those who had lived before them, particularly their own ancestors.

Inside the church, there were no seats except for stone slabs around the walls, where the old or sick could sit. We are reminded of the churches of those days when we use the saying "The weakest go to the wall". The walls were often painted with murals showing scenes from the Bible, or covered with vivid hangings, and there were statues of Mary, the mother of Jesus, and of Christian saints.

Some of the church windows shone with the colours of stained glass. All this light and colour and decoration impressed people who lived in small cottages without windows, and raised their minds above the daily grind of their heavy work. The pictures in the stained glass, the statues and the painted walls also taught the Christian stories to people who could not read or write.

In every part of medieval Britain there were monasteries and nunneries. These communities owned much of the land, and monks, such as the Cistercian sheep-farming monks in Yorkshire, used the most modern farming methods. They built hospitals for the sick, and gave travellers who came to their doors food and a bed for the night. Their schools were the only places where clever children could be educated, and their libraries were the finest in the country.

Not only did the monks collect and study books; they made them. Before printing was introduced into England in the 15th century, books were written and illustrated by hand on parchment (sheepskin) or vellum (calf-skin).

The monks' manuscripts are magnificent works of art. Their illustrations give us details of everyday life in medieval England, as in the calendar of the farming year on the next page. The capital letters of their Latin sentences are painted in gold and vivid colours with incredible attention to detail. An illustrator might spend a whole year painting one letter.

The greatest of all medieval church buildings were the cathedrals. Many of them were built by monks who, because they were in contact with their fellows all over Europe, learned the latest methods

A medieval hospice (hospital) where monks cared for the sick.

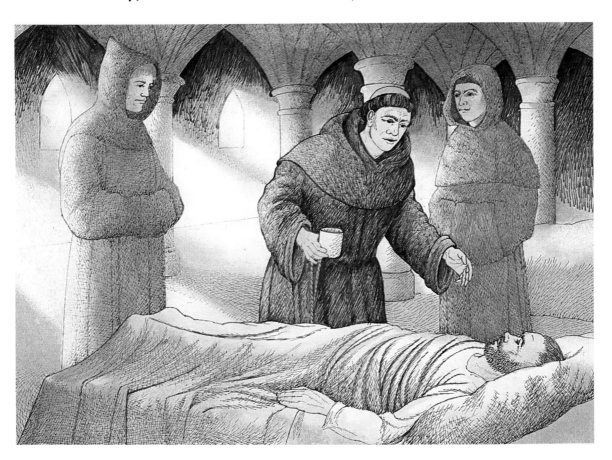

of architecture. They also called in foreign experts to advise them when they planned their new buildings. At Canterbury, the Norman architect William of Sens persuaded the monks to use the new Gothic style of building popular in Europe. This had high pointed arches rather than round ones. Pointed arches soon became popular all over England.

Among the travellers who knocked on the doors of monasteries and nunneries to ask for hospitality were the pilgrims. These were men and women who set out on foot or on horseback to visit a holy shrine. They might go to St Albans Cathedral, built where the first English Christian martyr was killed in the 3rd century, to the tomb of King Edmund in Bury St Edmunds, or to the most popular place of pilgrimage – the shrine of Archbishop Thomas Becket at Canterbury.

People went on pilgrimages for different reasons. Many went because they were holidays, and it was fun to travel in groups of people from all over Britain and beyond, staying in hostels along the way. Geoffrey Chaucer, obviously writing from experience, describes different characters on a pilgrimage in his *Canterbury Tales*, written at the end of the 14th century. Others went to be cured of their illnesses (as people still go to places such as Lourdes in France), believing that if they knelt at a saint's shrine or touched his or her relics they would be cured.

Others went to give thanks to God for particular blessings they had enjoyed. Coming out of the cathedral shadows into a saint's chapel lit by scores of wax tapers, the pilgrims would kneel and pray. And it might be there, for the first time, that they fully experienced the mystery and beauty of their religion.

Though the monks, nuns and priests devoted much of their time to farming or building, and to helping the poor and the sick, the heart of their life lay in prayer. In monasteries and nunneries, prayers were said or sung every four hours throughout the twenty-four. In country churches the priest would say his prayers every day, even if few people were present. By these means the Christians kept in touch with their God.

Fountains Abbey in Yorkshire seen from the hills. The monks were great farmers and used the most modern farming methods of their time. Fountains Abbey was famous for its sheep.

A 14th century calendar of the farming year (right), showing some of the different activities that went on over the twelve months.

January *a time of rest*

February *digging and planting*

March *pruning vines*

April *carrying a flowering branch*

May *Hawking*

June *Mowing hay*

July *Cutting corn*

August *Threshing corn*

September *Picking apples*

October *sowing winter corn*

November *gathering acorns for the pigs*

December *killing a pig*

Town Life in Medieval England

If we were taken back in time to visit a typical medieval town, it would seem to us more like a large village. Five thousand people would live in it at most. (London was the exception; it alone would seem like a city to us.) Towns were walled for protection, but many people lived in the suburbs outside. They would retreat within the walls only in an emergency.

Many townspeople had strips of land in the town fields outside the walls, and pastured their animals outside on the town common. If animals strayed from the common they were put in the town pound (lock-up) and their owners could only reclaim them by paying a fine. (Pound Lanes or Pound Cottages are to be found today in most old towns.)

People living within the walls went to work in their fields each morning by one of the fortified gates. Each evening they returned before the curfew bell rang at nightfall. Nobody was allowed on the streets after the bell stopped ringing. The gates clanged shut. Night-time travellers

A 13th century fortified bridge at Monnon in Monmouth with its gatehouse. At night the gate was shut and people could only enter the town with the keeper's permission.

were only admitted if they could convince the gatekeepers that they were friends and not foes.

Most streets in the town were narrow and the fronts of the houses hung over them. In some narrow lanes it was said that housewives could lean out of their upper windows and shake hands with their friends opposite. Garbage of all sorts and chamber pots were tipped out of upper windows into the streets below. The housewife was meant to give warning before she did so, but she often forgot. In Edinburgh, where many French people lived, the shout was "Gardyloo", a version of the French *Gardez l'eau* (beware of the water). It was customary for a young man, when he went walking with his girlfriend, to walk on the outside so that he would face the dangers of being soaked from above. This is still considered good manners.

Medieval town houses were generally small, for it was rare to have more than two children. They were made of wood and wattle and daub, with thatched roofs. By far the most common danger the nightwatchman looked out for as he patrolled was fire. The only way of fighting a fire once it had taken hold was to pull down the whole house, starting with the roof, using a long hooked fire pole. By 1450, stone and brick houses became more common. Tiled roofs began to replace thatch. Large town houses, built with blackened beams and white plaster, with windows made of leaded panes, began to appear. Such superior houses with their spacious walled gardens would be lived in by wealthy craftsmen or rich merchants.

Medieval towns were mainly lived in by people who manufactured and traded rather than those who farmed the land. They were often skilled craftsmen who,

with their journeymen (workers) and apprentices, made a great variety of goods. Some were sold in the town and surrounding countryside; others much farther away. The cloth woven by weavers, for instance, was the main British export to Europe for hundreds of years.

Other important craftsmen were the goldsmiths. Because their priceless goods required safekeeping, they provided the first "safe houses" in Britain. Soon cash was stored there as well as valuables. So the first British banks developed.

The blacksmiths, who made horseshoes, were often vets as well; the apothecaries (chemists), the doctors of the time, knew everybody's secrets and risked death at the hands of furious

The masterpiece. This picture from a 15th century manuscript shows a stonemason and a carpenter proving their skills by showing their masterpieces to the Warden of the guild.

A town's market day. Shopkeepers live behind their shops and stalls. Food and livestock are being sold, and a juggler and dancing bear provide entertainment.

customers if their confidences were revealed. There were bowyers who made bows and fletchers who made arrows. Houses were built by carpenters, bricklayers, tilers and plasterers, and lit by the chandler who made the candles. Bakers, butchers, grocers and fishmongers provided the townspeople with their food. Brewers brewed their ale and the vintners made their wine.

Crafts were concentrated in streets — Butchery Lane and Bread Street, for instance, and Threadneedle Street, where

The merchants were men of the world and traded their goods by land and sea. Some of the best merchants and bankers were Jews. After 1290, when Edward I, to his shame, expelled them (no Jew could live in Britain till 1655), British trade suffered badly. As in Saxon times, much medieval foreign trade was carried out not by English merchants but by Europeans living in English towns. In London, a whole area of the docks called the Steelyard was owned by members of the Hanseatic League — Dutch and

the tailors sat cross-legged sewing in the shop windows. The craftsmen formed themselves into guilds, which guaranteed the quality of their members' work and kept up their prices. After an apprenticeship, which might last seven years, an apprentice qualified for membership of his craft by presenting his "masterpiece". This, the best example of his work, was carefully examined by officers of the guild. If it reached the required standard, he was allowed to join the craft.

A fourteenth century English port. Much English trade was carried on by Italians and Germans. Goods from the East (like spices and silks) were exchanged for English wool, cloth, boots and silver.

German traders whose ships were well known in all the main ports of northern Europe. At Sandwich in Kent the cloth trade was in the hands of Venetians from Italy. They brought to England such goods as sugar, "comfits" (sweets), preserved fruits, coral beads from the Indian coast, cotton from Malta and saltpetre for gunpowder.

The merchants met together at fairs. Some of these, like St Bartholomew's in London or St Giles's in Oxford, were gatherings of traders from all over Europe. Italians – particularly the Venetians – brought spices, silks, carpets, pearls and ivory from India and China, to exchange for English wool and cloth, English shoes and boots, and English pewter and silver plate. Entertainers of all sorts were always found at fairs – jugglers, dwarfs, grossly fat women and Siamese twins, acrobats, and owners of performing bears or monkeys. Today, when fairs are no longer centres of trade, the entertainment alone survives.

Each medieval town had its local fairs and markets. Indeed we can still tell some of them by their names: selling was called "cheaping", so Chipping Camden and Chipping Norton were market towns, and Cheapside a market street. In one town whose population was a little over 3000, there were two flesh shambles, where slaughterers killed animals to eat, a fish market, a cattle market, a wagon market, a timber market, a butter market and (particularly important) a salt market.

On fair days, the streets – partly cobbled, perhaps, but chiefly made of beaten earth – were crowded. Everywhere there were beggars and cripples, many of them hideously deformed, imploring people for help. The craftsmen's stalls outside their shops blocked the narrow streets, as did the crowds outside the cook-shops. For a penny, the cook would bake your pie or pastry – a popular service since most people had no oven of their own.

Carts and covered wagons were jammed head-on in narrow spaces, their

The market square at Chipping Camden in Gloucestershire ("chipping" means selling). Official business was conducted in the market hall, while traders set up their stalls in the market place round about.

drivers shouting abuse at one another. Servants and delivery boys wove in and out of the crowds, carrying on their heads their wooden boards piled high with fruit tarts, roofing tiles or wooden plates. A man might be put in the pillory for stealing and passers-by would abuse him. Outside the shops and taverns creaked their signs. The barber's white pole with its red spiral stripes always caught the eye.

In the old *English Prayer Book* the priest prays that the people be delivered from "plague, pestilence and famine". The writer was writing from daily experience, particularly if he lived in a medieval town, where every sort of disease was found. There were no drains, and the open sewers running down the middle of the streets, as well as the rotting manure and emptied chamber pots, quickly spread infection. Not only that, but the houses were stuffy and built on top of each other, and most people were underfed.

The importance of cleanliness was not realized. People hardly ever washed; nor did they wash their heavy woollen clothes often enough. In any case there was no public supply of clean water which they could use. When almost all the monks in Christ Church Priory at Canterbury survived the Black Death, while the monks at nearby Rochester did not, people asked why. It was discovered that the Canterbury monks had recently installed a supply of piped fresh water from a spring 3 kilometres away.

The Black Death, the worst outbreak of "plague and pestilence" in England, erupted in 1349. Doctors today would say that the plague was probably a combination of illnesses, all of them likely to prove fatal. The most common version was spread by fleas carried by black rats. (They have now been driven out of Britain by brown rats, which do not carry the deadly fleas.)

The symptoms of the plague were large swellings on the neck, underneath the arms, and between the legs. The sufferer would develop black spots and a high fever, and would appear crazy. About three-quarters of those who caught this plague died of it, generally within about five days.

The plague started in China and India in 1338. By 1347 it had spread to Italy where the trading ports of Genoa and Venice suffered badly. By the beginning of 1349, it had reached England on the backs of the rats which infested foreign cargoes. Within the year about one-third of the people of England had died.

There was no cure. The dead were simply buried in great pits, dug outside the walls, or in damp, disused parts of town. They soon overflowed, so new pits were dug. Though plague was to return again during the next 300 years, no other plague was as terrible as the Black Death.

A nightmarish burial scene during the Black Death from a medieval manuscript. The coffins crowd in for burial. In fact only the wealthy would have been buried in coffins — most plague corpses were thrown into open pits after dark to avoid infection. They were then covered with lime so they burned. On the right is the black rat, the carrier of the deadly plague.

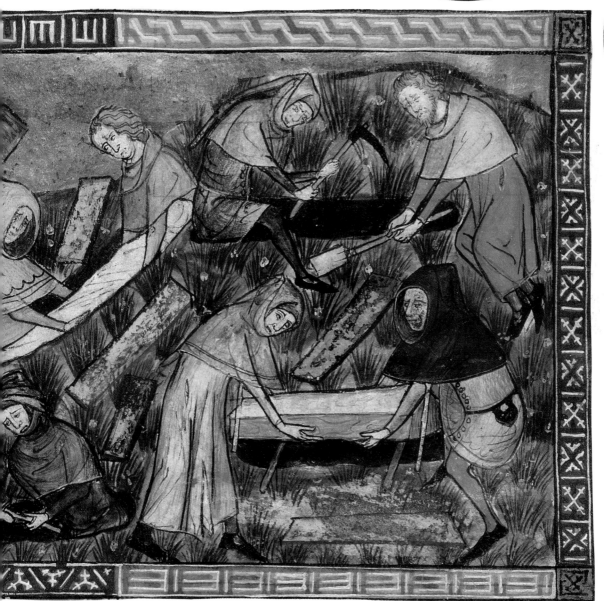

Kings, Barons and Peasants

The feudal system only worked when the king held it together. If he failed to do so, the country split into warring groups led by powerful barons. Troops trampled the crops in the fields, killed animals for meals round their camp-fires, and looted shops in the towns. Traders were afraid to take their goods to market, and merchants trading across the Channel found their ships hijacked and their precious cargoes robbed. Instead of uniting around the king in his troubles, his advisers looked round the court to see who was likely to become the new king.

There was always the threat of trouble when a king was believed to be weak, when he was under age, or spent too much time abroad; when he surrounded himself with unpopular favourites, or when he taxed his people heavily. If things got out of hand, the king might well be deposed and murdered.

The first king to be deposed was Edward II (1307–1327). The courage he showed at the battle of Bannockburn was admired, but many people never forgave him for losing it. He also lost battles in Wales, Ireland and France, and the country suffered a run of disastrous harvests and diseases among cattle and sheep. Edward rewarded his favourites Peter Gaveston and Hugh Despenser with lands taken from barons who had fallen out of favour. Gaveston was murdered by a group of conspirators; Despenser was executed.

After two years of civil war, the king put the barons' leader, Thomas, Earl of Lancaster, on trial as a traitor. He was found guilty, and executed as if he was a common criminal. In the end, Edward's

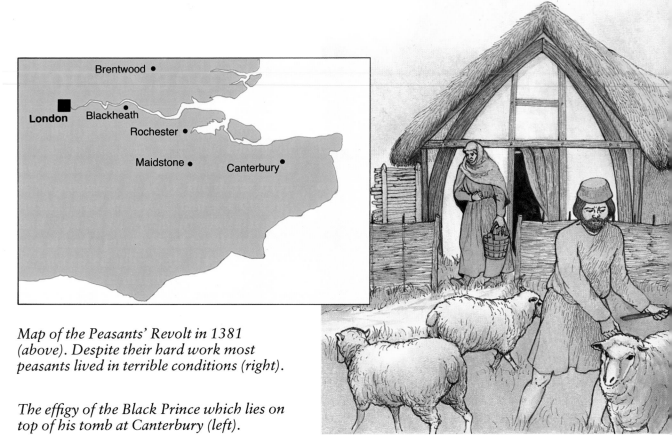

Map of the Peasants' Revolt in 1381 (above). Despite their hard work most peasants lived in terrible conditions (right).

The effigy of the Black Prince which lies on top of his tomb at Canterbury (left).

wife Queen Isabelle took his son Prince Edward and joined the king's enemies. Edward II was taken to Berkeley Castle in Gloucestershire and murdered.

Edward III (1327–1377) became king. Like his grandfather Edward I, he was remembered for centuries as a great warrior king. In 1337, he claimed to be King of France, after the old French ruling family had died out. This claim, repeated by his successors, started a series of wars with France called the Hundred Years War. With his son Edward, called the Black Prince (who died in 1376 before he could become king), Edward III won a number of battles in France.

The English navy's defeat of the French at Sluys in 1340 and the English victory at Crécy in 1346 led to the British occupation of Calais, a port which they held for the next 200 years. At the battle of Poitiers in 1356, the French king was captured and taken to England. His ransom of £500,000 gave some relief to the English taxpayer, but bills for the campaigns in France grew larger every year. At the height of Edward III's campaigns, about 10,000 English troops were fighting in France.

The government was faced with a number of problems. The wars were lasting too long. The barons were no longer prepared to provide the king with fighting men. Horses and armour, bows and arrows cost too much, and soldiers, though they plundered for food wherever they marched, had to be paid.

In 1360 peace was made with the French, but war broke out again nine years later and the fighting went against the English. Soon only Calais and Gascony, in the south-west, remained under English control. The English could no longer afford even to guard their own coasts. In 1360 the port of Winchelsea, which provided the ships for Edward III's navy, was burned and looted. In 1377 Rye suffered the same fate.

The tax collectors grew more and more desperate. They introduced those most unpopular of taxes, poll taxes, which demanded the same amount from both rich and poor. In 1376 Parliament introduced impeachment – a new process by which incompetent or unpopular ministers were put on trial for their lives. In the next year Edward III died. Richard II (1377–1399), who was aged ten when his father the Black Prince died, was soon faced with the greatest crisis of the century – the Peasants' Revolt.

In November 1380, a poll tax was declared at the highest rate yet – a shilling per head, three times the amounts raised in 1377 and 1379. Riots flared up and the tax collectors found that many people were determined not to pay. On 1st June 1381, the king's Chief Justice was sent to deal with trouble at Brentwood in Essex. He was met by a crowd shouting that they would kill all the "lawyers, jurors and royal servants" they could find.

Country people had been boiling with anger ever since the Black Death. There was a shortage of labour after the plague, and those who survived asked for higher wages. They also wanted to pay rent instead of doing the old labour services. The lords refused, and the government supported them. Many villeins ran away; others joined together to force better conditions from their lords.

In Kent, a lord threw one of his villeins, who had been captured fleeing from his estate, into Rochester Castle. A crowd stormed the castle and released him. The rebels marched along the River Medway to Maidstone, where on 7th June they captured the Archbishop of Canterbury's castle and released John Ball, a priest who had been quarrelling with the church authorities for years.

The crowd now moved on under the leadership of Wat (Walter) Tyler to Canterbury. The archbishop was a leading member of the king's government and the rebels held him responsible for the poll tax. They received strong support wherever they went and on 12th June thousands of Kentish men and women camped outside London on Blackheath. People from Essex reached Mile End at the same time. The Mayor of London, William Walworth, ordered the city gates to be shut.

Accounts of the rebel camp at Blackheath tell us how well-disciplined the people were. The rebel leaders, con-

The peasants camp at Blackheath.

cerned for the safety of their country, gave orders that none of their supporters should leave the coast, in case the French took advantage of the revolt to invade. The thousands of people who had risked their lives to march on London listened in rapt silence to the speeches of John Ball, who challenged the very idea of feudalism and the division of human beings into social classes. He called for an end to divisions between rich and poor, asking passionately: "When Adam dalf (dug) and Eve span, who was then a gentleman?" As a later chronicler wrote scornfully of the rebels: "According to their foolish minds there would be no lords thereafter but only kings and commons".

Richard II's meeting with the rebels at Smithfield during the Peasants' Revolt. This picture from Froissart's Chronicles *shows Wat Tyler being killed by the Lord Mayor of London. Only Richard's quick thinking saved his life.*

On the next day, 13th June, London fell to the rebels. The gates were opened to the men and women of Kent and those from Essex, and the crowds surged through them. But now the leaders lost control. The palace of the archbishop at Lambeth was sacked, along with the Savoy Palace of the king's uncle, John of Gaunt. The houses of foreign merchants were set on fire and mobs rampaged through the streets. Soon the peasants ringed the Tower, where the king, archbishop and mayor had taken refuge.

Early the next morning, the boy King Richard II rode out of the Tower to meet the rebels at Mile End. He promised Wat Tyler that labour services would end, that land would be rented at fourpence an acre, and that no man would be compelled to serve another. While Richard and Tyler were talking, men broke into the Tower, seized the Archbishop and Treasurer and beheaded them.

The next day many of the rebels started for home, convinced that their case was won. Tyler and the king met again, this time at Smithfield. Tyler is said to have been insolent to Richard. He called him "brother" and would not kneel in his presence. A scuffle broke out and Mayor Walworth killed Tyler.

But the young king saved the situation. When they heard that Tyler was dead, the rebel archers raised their bows. Richard rode out alone in front of them. "Sirs, will you shoot your king? I will be your captain," he cried. He rode to some nearby fields and the peasants followed him. The mayor took advantage of the lull and sent for support. Soon the peasants were encircled in the fields "like sheep within a pen". They were allowed to return home. Now that Wat Tyler was dead, there was nothing to stop the lords and king's ministers from restoring control.

The peasants had won support in other counties, such as Suffolk and Norfolk, but everywhere their supporters were rounded up and cruelly treated. If the king ever meant to keep his Mile End promises his advisers must have overruled him. On 2nd July the promises were officially withdrawn.

Ball and another peasant leader, Jack Straw, were executed, along with 110 men in Kent and Essex. Many more were killed without trial. In November 1381 Parliament issued a general pardon to the rebels, and the most serious revolt by the common people of England in the history of the country was ended.

The rest of Richard II's reign was filled with tragedy. Parliament attacked his favourites and tried to control him by a council of powerful barons. The king hit back and declared, in 1389, when he was twenty-two: "I am of full age to govern my house, my household and also my realm." But though he made peace with France, an expedition to Ireland proved expensive and led to more taxes.

Richard exiled two great earls, the Earls of Warwick and Nottingham, executed another (the Earl of Arundel) and had the Duke of Gloucester murdered. Finally, while he was in Ireland, the exiled Duke of Lancaster, Henry Bolingbroke, landed at the Humber estuary. The Earl of Northumberland supported him. Richard was forced to abdicate in 1399, and was taken to Pontefract Castle in Yorkshire. He died there a year later, probably murdered.

Henry IV, Duke of Lancaster and son of John of Gaunt, Edward III's third son, was made king in 1399. His rival was the seven-year-old Earl of March, who was descended from Edward III's second son Lionel, Duke of Clarence. Henry IV's seizure of the crown led to nearly 100 years of rivalry between the Lancastrians (supporting Henry IV and his heirs) and the Yorkists, who backed the descendants of the Dukes of Clarence. The wars between the Lancastrians (whose emblem was a red rose) and the Yorkists (whose sign was a white rose) were called the Wars of the Roses.

In Quick Succession

Henry IV had become king by force and only by force could he continue to hold power. For the first nine years he lived in the saddle, rushing from one part of his kingdom to another to suppress challenges to his authority.

Within a few months of becoming king, he overcame an assassination attempt at Windsor. Then in 1403 the Earl of Northumberland, who had been largely responsible for putting Henry on the throne, turned against the king and led a rising in the north. (Northumberland's son Hotspur was killed near Shrewsbury while marching to Wales to join Owain Glyndŵr's revolt.) The Archbishop of York joined the uprising and Henry seemed to be losing control over England north of the Humber. But the archbishop was executed and Northumberland, who had gained Scottish support, was killed at the battle of Bramham Moor in 1408. For the last five years of his reign, Henry IV faced no further serious threats.

His son Henry V was the last of the great warrior kings. He spent much of his reign fighting in northern France, where the English won battle after battle. Henry's victory at Agincourt, not far from Crécy in northern France, in 1415 meant that most of France was now under English control. In 1420 Henry made a treaty with Charles VI, the sick king of France, which marked the height of English power in France. It decreed that Henry was to marry Charles' daughter Catherine and to be Regent of France during the king's illness. After Charles' death he was to become King of France. But Henry V died of dysentery on campaign in France in 1422, shortly after the birth of his son Henry. England returned to the worst of all political situations: the king was a baby.

During the fifteen years of Henry VI's reign, when he was too young to govern, the English were on the retreat in France. A young woman, Joan of Arc, who is still remembered in France as the saviour of her country and who was made a saint by the Catholic Church, led a national war against the English invaders. By 1450 the English were driven out of Normandy. Three years later they lost all of Gascony, and with it the wine and

Joan of Arc was burned at the stake by the English. She led the French war of national liberation.

cloth trade which had brought them great prosperity for 200 years. Only Calais remained in English hands. The Hundred Years War was over. From now on the English and French were separate and competing neighbours.

Henry VI collapsed after the loss of Gascony. He seems to have suffered a nervous breakdown, and to have become incapable of governing. There was much about his policies to admire. He encouraged the development of schools and colleges, and supported the Church, but many of the barons thought he was weak and indecisive. People blamed him for the defeats in France, which were hardly his fault. They said his father had won France and all he had done was lose it.

The government was bankrupt, and the taxpayer had nothing to show for his money. In 1450 John Cade led a rising which can be compared in some ways to the Peasants' Revolt, though it was more

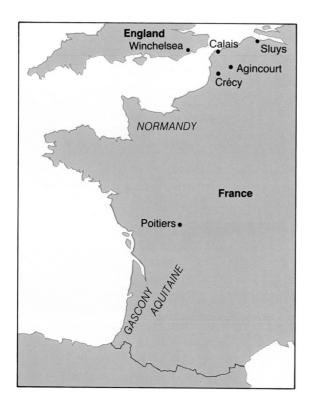

easily suppressed. The rebels attacked the traitors who had lost France, left the south coast undefended, and wasted the King's treasures.

Richard, Duke of York, was made "Protector of the Realm" during the king's illness from 1454 to 1456. He was descended from Edward III's second son, the Duke of Clarence. Protector Richard soon claimed the crown for himself. There was fighting at St Albans in 1455 and Henry VI was wounded. The Wars of the Roses had begun.

Richard submitted to Henry for five years, but in 1460 he rebelled again, and he and the Yorkists claimed that he was the rightful king. He defeated Henry's forces at Northampton and was confirmed in his position as Protector. But in December he was defeated at Wakefield in Yorkshire. His head, crowned with a paper crown, was stuck on one of the gates at York.

Richard's nineteen-year-old son then entered the battle. He became King Edward IV in 1461, after defeating Henry at the battle of Towton (largely thanks to the Earl of Warwick, who became known as "the King-maker").

Like another usurper, Henry IV, before him, Edward knew that his power would last only so long as he proved himself stronger than his enemies. Henry VI, who had fled to Scotland, was receiving support from both the French and the Scots. Warwick and other powerful lords turned against Edward, and in 1470 he fled abroad and Henry VI was made king again.

The next year Edward landed in York-

The main battles of the Hundred Years' War. By 1453 only Calais remained in English hands. The English dream of an empire in France was over.

shire and defeated Warwick at Barnet. Henry VI's only son was killed in battle at Tewkesbury, and Henry himself died in the Tower. (Many believed that he had been murdered.) The direct royal line of the house of Lancaster had ended. The Yorkists were in control.

For the next twelve years, Edward IV's power was unchallenged. He avoided wars in France, and indeed was actually paid by King Louis XI to stay in England. His peaceful policies encouraged trade abroad, and made certain that there were no unpopular demands for taxes. Unfortunately he died in 1483, when his son Edward V was only twelve years old.

The boy was never crowned. His uncle, who was to become Richard III (1483–1485), was appointed Protector until Edward was old enough to rule himself. Like the earlier Protector, the boy's uncle had his own ambitions. He declared himself king, executed the queen, and imprisoned Edward V and his brother in the Tower of London. Here the boys were murdered, probably on their uncle's orders. They are remembered as "the Princes in the Tower".

The seizing of the crown of England by force seemed to have become a habit. Henry Tudor, soon to become Henry VII, challenged Richard III. He claimed the crown through his father the Earl of Richmond, Henry VI's brother. Once again the old Lancastrian group of barons saw its chance of ruling England. Henry landed in south Wales (the Tudors were a Welsh family), and advanced into the Midlands. In 1485, at Bosworth in Leicestershire, Richard III was defeated and killed. Henry VII became king. Though no one realized it, the Wars of the Roses were over.

House of Normandy	
William the Conqueror	1066-1087
William II	1087-1100
Henry I	1100-1135
Stephen	1135-1154
House of Plantagenet	
Henry II	1154-1189
Richard I	1189-1199
John	1199-1216
Henry III	1216-1272
Edward I	1272-1307
Edward II	1307-1327
Edward III	1327-1377
Richard II	1377-1399
House of Lancaster	
Henry IV	1399-1413
Henry V	1413-1422
Henry VI	1422-1461
House of York	
Edward IV	1461-1483
Edward V	1483
Richard III	1483-1485

The Kings of England from 1066 to 1485 (above). Below is the Lancastrian King Henry VI and his strong-willed queen, Margaret of Anjou.

173

The Growth of Trade

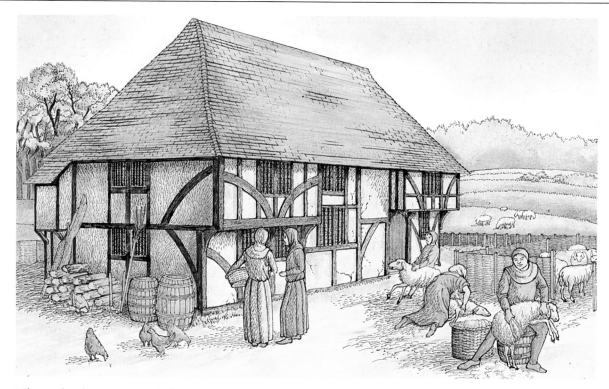

During the 15th century yeomen (free) farmers became increasingly prosperous, particularly if they had flocks of sheep. Such farmhouses are still lived in today.

Though the Wars of the Roses meant a series of violent changes of ruler, the lives of the people were largely unaffected. During thirty years of war, only fifteen months were spent in actual fighting. The armies on both sides were small (Edward IV won the battle of Barnet with 2000 men). Only if the armies entered a village and soldiers fought over the crops or stole sheep and poultry were the people directly affected.

The 15th century saw the end of almost all the feudal labour services. Even before the Black Death killed one labourer in three, lords had been reaching agreements with their labourers. By these agreements, labourers paid for their lands with rents in money and were no longer forced to work on the lord's estate. Some villeins sold their strips and worked for local farmers in return for wages. Others increased their lands,

became prosperous yeomen farmers and turned into employers. The modern system, by which land belongs to a farmer who employs farm labourers to work for him for wages, was now operating all over Britain.

The success of the cloth trade brought about other changes in the English countryside. Since the 12th century, England's main export had been wool — it was now the foundation of the country's wealth. As a sign of this, the Lord Chancellor, head of the country's legal system and Speaker of the House of Lords, sat on a sack of wool when he supervised debates. (He still does.) British wool was exported to Calais, and from there it was carried in heavy sacks by packhorses to Belgian factories to be made into cloth.

But by the 14th century enterprising businessmen were establishing a cloth industry at home. Edward III had enticed Belgian clothiers to Kent, where they set up their craft in villages like Cranbrook. The idea proved popular. Across the country, in East Anglia and Yorkshire, for instance, women were spinning in their kitchens or backyards. Others set up weaving shops, often at home, to weave the wool into cloth; others dyed the cloth.

The demand for wool led to an increase in sheep farming. Lords of the manor and other rich farmers began to take over some of the peasants' strips in the village fields, and some of the village common land. They put fences round the land, or a hedge, and so "enclosed" it to make a sheep farm. The peasants lost land or grazing rights. Some peasants were even given orders to pull down their own houses when the harvest was in and sow their strips with grass seed before they left their employment. The new farms offered fewer jobs, for sheep farming employs few men (one shepherd can look after hundreds of sheep).

Cloth soon took the place of wool as England's chief export. The merchants who exported the cloth, whose company was called the Merchant Adventurers, were some of the richest men in England. Their town houses were among the most splendid in the land, with their leaded glass windows, their intricately plastered ceilings and magnificently carved doors.

Effigies of these merchants still lie on top of tombs in their local churches. Indeed some of the churches, which were built or enlarged by the cloth merchants, stand as memorials to their wealth and support. Those at Burford in Oxfordshire, Lavenham in Suffolk and Thaxted

The farmer and his wife began to live much more comfortably than their ancestors. Separate bedrooms were made upstairs with four-poster beds. Babies' cradles were handed down through the family from generation to generation.

in Essex, for instance, are like small cathedrals.

The ending of labour services changed the position of the feudal lord. The strength of his castle was also weakened by the invention of gunpowder. By the end of the 15th century no castle wall was thick enough to withstand direct cannon fire. The days when a lord was king of an area were over.

During the 15th century, more and more people began to think of themselves as English. While the Scots, Welsh and Irish had felt they were members of nations for centuries, this feeling was held back in England by the connection with France. It was hard to feel part of one English nation while areas of France were combined with England as part of a cross-Channel nation. Now that the Hundred Years War was over and France was separate, national feelings developed. They did so alongside the growth of the English language.

Parliament had been conducting its debates in English and not in French for a long time. English was the main language at court from Edward III's reign onwards. Henry IV was the first king whose native language was English.

"English", however, varied all over the country. Different areas spoke in different dialects. Pronunciation of the words, and even the words themselves, differed so much that people in one county could hardly make themselves understood in another. Even a century later, Elizabeth I complained that she could not understand a word her admiral from Devon, Francis Drake, said.

However, the invention of printing helped to spread the use of a common English language. For William Caxton, who introduced it to England, decided to use the English of the London area as his basic language. Caxton, an English merchant who lived in Belgium, saw the printing presses at work in Germany, where the first printed book was produced in 1450. In 1476 he set up a printing press at Westminster on which he produced more than 100 books. They were printed on paper. Paper, which was made out of linen or rags, was much cheaper than vellum or parchment.

Most of the books Caxton printed were written in English. One of them was Geoffrey Chaucer's *Canterbury Tales*. The way was now open for the full development of a literature written in English. This was to go alongside the further development, during the next century, of the English nation.

Burford Church in Oxfordshire (right) is a 15th century church built with the help of wealthy wool and cloth merchants.

Caxton first saw printing, which was invented by the Chinese, at work in Germany. He set up this press in Westminster in 1476. His books, chiefly written in English, were printed on paper.

The Power of the Throne

England was changing in many ways at the end of the 15th century. The Wars of the Roses had made the barons weaker than at any time since the Norman Conquest. Out of the sixty leading families which dominated England at the beginning of the wars, only about half now had an adult head. Most were bankrupt. Even the leading Yorkists were keen to make peace. When Henry VII married Elizabeth of York, daughter of Edward IV, in 1486, most Yorkist families were prepared to accept his rule. They were exhausted. The king had shrewdly made the possession of gunpowder a royal monopoly, so their castles were at his mercy. Furthermore, their personal armies were costing too much.

From the beginning of his reign, Henry set out to ban private armies. These uniformed gangs of young men, called

Henry VII came from a Welsh family. He reasserted the power of the king over the barons who had threatened to tear England apart during the Wars of the Roses.

retainers, were the curse of the country. They had been recruited by powerful barons to fight for them in the Wars of the Roses. But now that the fighting was over, they had nothing to do but pillage the countryside or pick quarrels with rival gangs. Their suppression was one of Henry's greatest achievements.

Henry also undermined the power of the great barons in another way. Whenever he met with opposition from a noble family, he used every opportunity to declare the lord a traitor. Not only might this mean the lord's execution; it meant that his lands fell into the hands of the king. In this way, Henry took over 138 estates during his reign. His marriage to Elizabeth of York brought him further lands. As he became more powerful, his "overmighty subjects" weakened. He made a number of sound decisions about foreign and financial policies which further increased his power.

Throughout medieval times, English kings had been bankrupted by wars, particularly in France. Despite their huge costs and the unpopularity of the taxes raised to pay for them, the wars had proved popular. Warrior-kings like Richard I, Edward III and Henry V were national heroes. Edward II and Henry VI never lived down their defeats at the hands of the Scots and the French.

The ending of the Hundred Years War had put a stop to ideas of military grandeur. But England still owned Calais, and if Henry had wished he could have used the town as a base from which to renew the fighting. Fortunately he avoided the temptation. Although he was drawn into war with France in

1492, he soon ended it. He spent only £50,000 out of the £100,000 allowed him by Parliament for the campaign. By the peace treaty the French paid Henry money each year to forget about his claim to the French throne.

Peace with France brought peace with their allies, the Scots. Henry VII married his daughter to the Scottish King James IV and the frontier fighting was now confined to cattle raids.

Peace at home and abroad brought a greatly increased royal income. Customs' duties on imports increased by about one quarter. As the amount of royal estates grew, the rents grew with them. Heavy fines were placed on lords who broke the ban on private armies. Henry also tightened his grip on government. He brought

Newark Castle, near Selkirk, a Scottish border house built about 1450. It was fortified against English attack.

back Henry II's system of royal judges who travelled all over the country to administer the common law. The Privy Council used its own courts, such as the Court of Star Chamber, when the government detected barons breaking the law. When the barons tried to influence local juries, the king transferred cases to the Privy Council courts in London which were under his control. Parliament was not called to meet very often and when it was called it voted Henry the taxes he wanted.

By the time of his death, Henry had re-established the power of the throne. For the next 100 years no English subject succeeded in challenging royal power again. By then the danger had swung the other way. Kings and queens were in danger of becoming dictators.

A royal judge travelling around England from town to town.

King Henry VIII (1509–1547)

Henry VIII, who became king at the age of seventeen in 1509, was determined to cut a glamorous figure at his court and in Europe. Whereas his father had been careful – some people said mean – with money, Henry VIII was extravagant. Whereas his father avoided war, Henry VIII welcomed it. Within four years the king was fighting in France. Soon the Scots were over the northern border. It was as if the lessons of the Hundred Years War had been entirely forgotten.

Henry VIII had all the gifts which people then expected of a king. The Venetian ambassador in London at the time reported to his government:

"His majesty is ... extremely handsome ... very accomplished, a good musician, composes well, is a most capital horseman, a fine jouster, speaks French, Latin and Spanish, is very religious ... He is extremely fond of tennis, at which game it is the prettiest thing in the world to see him play."[13]

A short time before his coronation, Henry married a Spanish princess, Catherine of Aragon. She had married Henry's elder brother Arthur in 1502. The marriage had shown how greatly respected England had become in Europe during the reign of Henry VII. For a marriage between members of the royal families was the usual way of creating an alliance between two nations. And Spain was one of the most powerful countries in Europe. Therefore when Arthur died Henry VII proposed that Catherine re-marry his younger son. The marriage of a man to his brother's widow was against the law of the Church and could only be allowed if the Pope gave special permission for it to occur. The permission was eventually granted, but the marriage was to have an important effect on future events.

Henry liked to think of himself as a warrior-king, and the Pope encouraged him by calling him the rightful King of France. When he landed in France in the summer of 1513, to take up the old struggle with the French once more, he was met by the Emperor of Germany, Maximilian. The Emperor offered to serve under Henry's command, so long as Henry paid his troops. The combined force won a battle over the French, captured some important prisoners, and destroyed the garrison town of Thérouanne. To Henry, who had seen the Emperor serve under him, and a small French force flee from the field of battle, it was as if Agincourt had been repeated, 100 years later.

The news from the Scottish border was even better. The Scottish army under King James IV was utterly defeated at the battle of Flodden. Eleven thousand Scotsmen were killed, including the King himself. James IV's bloodstained coat was sent to Henry VIII at Thérouanne, who displayed it proudly to the Emperor Maximilian. The French made peace and doubled the annual payment originally given to Henry's father. The French king married Henry VIII's sister, Mary. Henry was on top of the world.

The young Henry VIII had a romantic image. Flatterers exaggerated his gifts, but he was certainly a good horseman and a skilled linguist.

All this success required a great deal of organization. The mind behind the campaign in France was Cardinal Thomas Wolsey's. Wolsey had become a priest because of his political ambitions rather than his religious beliefs. He was valued by Henry VII because of his organizing skills and his attention to detail and Henry VIII came to rely on him more and more. While Henry hunted or danced or listened to music (his song *Green Sleeves* is still popular today), Wolsey devoted his time and energies to the paperwork.

In 1520 Henry had a meeting with Francis I, the young King of France. Francis lived as extravagantly as Henry, and loved to ride, drink, wrestle and dance. The meeting took place near Calais and became known as the meeting of the Field of the Cloth of Gold.

Henry had given orders that a special palace should be built where he could entertain Francis in an impressive style.

Henry VIII arriving at the Field of the Cloth of Gold with Wolsey riding beside him and 5000 courtiers.

Six thousand men were employed in altering and extending a castle for the purpose. Another 5000 accompanied Henry and Catherine as their travelling court. The emblems of the Tudor family – Tudor roses and royal beasts, lions and unicorns, winged dragons and stags, gryphons and greyhounds – hung in the huge banqueting hall. A pavilion of crimson and cloth of gold (cloth with gold thread woven into it) was specially built.

The exact spot where the kings were to meet was carefully decided. The hills were even levelled and reshaped so that both kings would catch sight of each other at the same time. Wolsey's sharp brain and keen eye were behind each detail of the arrangements. Not for him the embarrassment which overcame Francis I's organizer. He had designed a pavilion to beat all pavilions in which his master could entertain Henry. It proved to be top-heavy and fell in a high wind.

The first meeting went according to plan. The two kings caught sight of each other at the same time. They stopped and the two groups of courtiers stopped with

them. For a while there was silence. Then the trumpets sounded. The two kings rode forward and met where a spear marked the spot. They embraced.

For nearly a fortnight the kings and their courtiers feasted, jousted and danced. One day the two kings wrestled, and Francis threw Henry. It was all Henry's courtiers could do to prevent their master from charging at his royal friend, intent on revenge. The meeting ended with a solemn service sung by Wolsey.

Two years later they were at war with each other again. The fighting dragged on. By 1530 England had nothing to show for all the fighting and flamboyant display. But by that time Henry's mind was concentrated on other matters, and in particular his marriage to Catherine of Aragon. At some time in the 1520s, Henry VIII decided to get rid of his wife.

Holbein's painting of Sir Thomas More and his family. More, once Henry's friend and Chancellor, was later executed for refusing to accept his religious changes. He was canonized by the Catholic Church.

He had started a love affair with a lady at his court, Anne Boleyn, and, moreover, had become convinced that he must have a son to succeed him.

Catherine had given birth to seven children, but six died in childbirth or early in their lives. Only one lived – a girl, Mary – and it was thought that no woman ruler would be able to hold the country together after Henry died. The King convinced himself that his wife's misfortunes had been judgements of God upon them both for their marriage. The Pope, he said, should never have agreed to let him marry his brother's widow in the first place. Now the new Pope, successor to Clement VII, must admit that his predecessor had been mistaken. He must cancel the ruling and declare Henry and Catherine to be no longer man and wife. Then Henry could marry Anne, who would give him the baby boy he wanted.

Even if the Pope had wished to do as Henry said, he was in no position to do so. Emperor Charles V of Spain, Catherine's nephew, had recently occupied Rome and the Pope had become Charles' prisoner. Catherine refused to give up her rights as queen, or her daughter Mary's rights to succeed her father. The Emperor supported his aunt. Nothing that Wolsey could do would make the Pope agree to carry out Henry's wishes.

In 1530 Wolsey fell from Henry's favour. He died before the trial which the King had prepared for him, and so avoided a traitor's death. The new Archbishop of Canterbury, Thomas Cranmer, was no more successful than Wolsey in persuading the Pope to change his mind. By the end of 1532 Anne Boleyn was pregnant. Henry was now forced to decide. Either he would have to stay married to Catherine, which would mean that Anne's baby would be illegitimate and Mary would succeed him, or he could defy the Pope and set up a new Church under his own control. This Church would legally separate Catherine and Henry and marry Henry to Anne. He chose the second.

The Archbishop of Canterbury supported the King. Catherine and Mary were sent to a nunnery. Cranmer secretly married Henry and Anne. In September 1533 Anne gave birth to a baby. It was a girl – Elizabeth, the future Elizabeth I. Then Henry set up a new Church of England and made himself the head of it.

The Pope did not take such an open challenge to the authority of his Roman Catholic Church quietly. Already, for the first time in western Europe for over a thousand years, a Christian leader had set up a rival Christian Church. This was Martin Luther, whose Protestant Church was now the main Church in northern Germany. Protestant Christianity was spreading fast into Holland, France and Switzerland. There were increasing numbers of Lutherans in England. The Pope was determined to act decisively to stop the spread of rival churches. He "excommunicated" Henry (expelled him from the Church), and called on all Catholic Christians to have nothing to do with Henry's separate English Church.

It seems extraordinary that, after a thousand years of membership, England should leave the Roman Catholic Church over a dispute about a royal marriage. But there were a number of reasons why people were prepared to give up their loyalty to the Pope.

First of all, there was the strength of Henry VIII himself. Henry had built on his father's success in establishing a firm control over his kingdom. He used his power ruthlessly. Any man or woman who challenged him faced execution. What had happened to Wolsey made it certain that other ministers and Church leaders would face the same fate if they dared stand up to Henry.

Next, the Church had been unpopular in England for a long time. Though people admired many of the local priests, who lived simply and tried sincerely to follow Jesus' teaching, they resented the Church's great wealth. Nobody liked paying taxes to the Pope. Some monks and friars lived unworthy lives, though no more so in Henry's time than earlier.

Some ate and drank too much. Some were lazy. A few had secret lovers.

Wolsey's career had been a scandal. Though the law forbade a man to be bishop of more than one "diocese" (district), Wolsey was Archbishop of York and a bishop six times over. He did not even visit his dioceses, but merely took the money. As for the Pope, people had asked for generations why English taxes should go to support an Italian Church leader with his court of cardinals and bishops in Rome. Was not the Pope a second Wolsey?

Finally – though Henry VIII himself had done what he could to prevent it – some people were secretly talking of the need for a new Christian start. They taught that the Roman Catholic Church was too corrupt to be changed, and only a new Church could bring back the true worship of Jesus. In Europe, as we have seen, Protestants were sweeping northern Germany and Holland. As long before as the 1380s, John Wycliffe in England had taught that Christians should refuse to obey churchmen who lived in luxury. He translated the Bible into English, and said the Communion services should be simple reminders of Christ's Last Supper with his disciples.

So it came about that only a few brave men, such as Sir Thomas More (who had become Lord Chancellor after Wolsey), John Fisher, Bishop of Rochester, and the heads of some monasteries refused to swear loyalty to the new Church of England. To most ordinary people, it seemed that the old Church continued, except that it was ruled by the King and not by a foreign Pope. It was only the monks and nuns whose lives were completely changed. The destruction of their monasteries was the work of Thomas

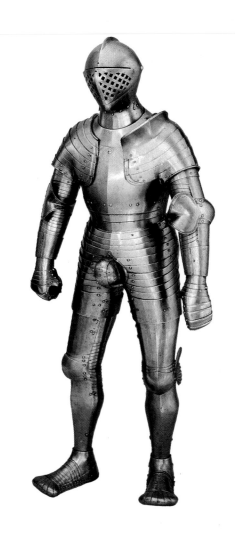

Henry VIII's full armour. No wonder that in his later years the King had to be winched up onto his horse!

Cromwell, who now became Henry's main minister.

As the years had gone by, the monks had gained great estates. By the reign of Henry VIII, they owned about a quarter of English farmland. Henry, who had wasted hundreds of thousands of pounds in the French wars, was very keen to get his hands on their wealth.

The inspectors that Cromwell sent to monasteries and nunneries from 1535 onwards had no difficulty in proving that some of the monks were no longer living the sort of lives which their founders had wanted them to lead. Some had few members, for not nearly as many men and women were joining the orders as had done in medieval times. Their work of teaching and producing books had often been taken over by others. They were not giving as much of their money to the poor or elderly or sick as they should have been.

There was nothing that could not have been put right by reform. The monks had been reforming themselves for hundreds of years. But the King wanted the monasteries closed, and their wealth given to his government. When there was a rising in the North in support of the monks called the Pilgrimage of Grace, it was suppressed. By 1540 it was all over. Christian communities which had been serving their neighbourhoods for up to a thousand years, were wiped away in five.

Henry's government made some attempts to fill the gaps in the country's life brought about by the closure of all the monasteries and nunneries. Their schools were allowed to continue, so long as they took the name of their destroyer: Henry VIII School, Coventry, King's School, Canterbury, and King's School, Ely, are just three of the old monastic schools which still thrive today. The monks were well treated. Those who wanted to become clergy in Henry's Church were welcomed. The rest were given pensions.

The King had had his way, though Thomas Cromwell also fell foul of his master and was executed in 1540. It was not until Victorian times that monasteries and convents were allowed to be refounded.

Nothing could stop Henry now. From 1536 onwards he changed wives four more times. Anne Boleyn, who never gave Henry the son he wanted, was beheaded. She was supposed to have been unfaithful to him, though the evidence was false. Jane Seymour gave Henry his male heir, Edward (who became Edward VI when his father died in 1547), but she died shortly after giving birth. Henry sent away his next wife, Ann of Cleves, soon after he married her. She came from northern Germany, and Henry had never seen her until she came to England for her coronation. He had chosen her from a portrait painted by the great portrait-painter Holbein. Henry said that Holbein had flattered her. (Holbein had the good sense not to visit England again.)

Henry's fifth wife, Katherine Howard, was also executed for being unfaithful to him. His last wife, an intelligent widow, Catherine Parr, survived him. She was the only one of his wives who knew how to handle him and calm his great rages.

In his last years Henry grew fat, even bloated. His little eyes gleam coldly from his portraits, making one glad, even today, not to have suffered their gaze at court. He was so fat that when he was in full armour he had to be winched on to his horse by a special winch. For he went on fighting in France to the end, even though the wars left the country bankrupt. He was in great pain from the ulcers on his leg.

By the beginning of January 1547 it was clear that Henry VIII was very seriously ill. Soon the doctors knew he was dying, but they dared not say so. (Six years earlier a lord had been executed for foretelling the King's death.) On 28th January he died. His huge coffin was buried, on his orders, in the grave of Jane Seymour, the mother of Edward VI, who was now King of England.

The recent raising of the "Mary Rose", Henry VIII's great ship which was sunk off Portsmouth during the French wars, has provided many details of life at the time. Below are a sail maker's brass thimble and two ear-scoops and on the right are three gold "angel" coins. The photograph above shows a barber-surgeon's tools. Among them a bleeding bowl, a chafing dish, and a wooden mallet for knocking patients out during an operation.

Great Explorations

Maps drawn during the Middle Ages show the world as ordinary people in Europe imagined it to be. It was flat. It consisted of Europe, probably with north Africa and the eastern Mediterranean coastline added. Some maps were drawn with Jerusalem as their centre, for this was where Jesus was crucified and rose from the dead. But from the crusades onwards, educated people began to realize that Europe was not the whole world.

For the crusaders had met the Turks. Not only did they come from lands which the crusaders had not known existed. They mixed all the time with the Arabs. From the Arabs Europeans learned many new things — for example, how to sail long distances out of sight of land, often by using the stars as direction-pointers. The Arabs were great traders. Their merchants, sometimes going by ship, sometimes riding on horses or on camels in groups known as "caravans", travelled long distances to trade with the countries of the East.

Italian merchants from Venice were the first to take advantage of the Arab knowledge of a wider world. They began to send traders and explorers to the East. The most famous of these men was Marco Polo.

Marco Polo travelled all over China, India and south-east Asia during the 13th century. At this time the Mongolian empire, with its headquarters in northern China, was at the height of its power. It stretched from Poland in the west to China in the east. Its merchants traded with Indonesia, India and Iran. Its lands were connected by roads which resembled those of Roman times.

Marco Polo was welcomed at the court of the great Mongol emperor, Kublai Khan. He was even made governor of a large Chinese city for a time. When he finally got back to Venice, after twenty years away, he set down what he had experienced in a book. His *Travels* became a bestseller.

Soon the Venetians were carrying out the most profitable of all trade in the

Vasco da Gama's ships rounded Africa and sailed on to India. Trade with the East was opened up again to Europeans — this time by sea.

Middle Ages. Their merchants, or Arabs working for them, travelled the East in search of goods which they knew would sell well in Europe. They brought back cargoes of spices – cinnamon, nutmeg and cloves – from Indonesia, which became known as the Spice Islands. Rich people in Europe came to rely on the spices to preserve their meat in winter, and to make it more tasty when it was salted. They were prepared to pay high prices for them.

Other Venetian merchants bargained for pearls bought from divers working off the coast of Sri Lanka. They bought silk from China, or tapestries and carpets from Iran. They were always on the lookout for opium, which was then almost the only known "anaesthetic", or painkiller. (Often the best way to stop pain was to drink yourself into a stupor!)

As we have seen, Venetian merchants visited the ports of southern England. There they exchanged eastern goods for English ones, particularly English cloth.

This trade between Europe and the East continued for 200 years. But in the 15th century the Turks stopped allowing European traders to cross their empire – which stretched from Istanbul to Egypt – on their way east. Europeans now had to find new ways to reach the silks, the jewels, and above all the spices, to which they had grown so accustomed.

Geographers in Europe were called in by kings and merchants to answer the question: "How can we reach the East without going by the old eastern Mediterranean route?" There were two rival answers. One was: "Sail south." The other was: "Sail west." The answers showed that geographers now knew that the world was round, and that Europe was only a part of it.

The Portuguese decided to try the southern way. Throughout the 15th century they sailed further and further south along the west coast of Africa. Finally Vasco da Gama sailed round the Cape of Good Hope with four ships in 1497. He sailed up the east African coast and found an Arab sailor to guide his ships to Calicut in India. When he came home after two years, he had lost half his men but made a fortune. Within a few years, Portuguese sailors had reached Malaysia, Japan and the precious Spice Islands. For the next hundred years the Portuguese controlled one of the greatest trading empires the world has ever seen.

The Spanish, after many disagreements, decided to explore the second solution. Christopher Columbus, an Italian sailor, had tried unsuccessfully to persuade Henry VII, along with many others, to support a voyage to the west. In 1492, just when he believed that his plan would never be put to the test, the Spanish king and queen gave him three ships and told him to sail west across the Atlantic to reach the East.

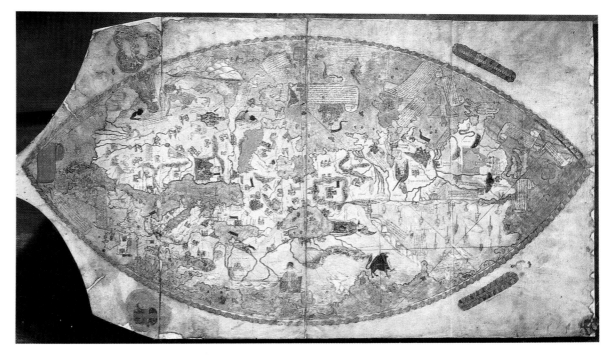

It is important to remember that Christopher Columbus and his backers were wrong. They miscalculated the actual size of the globe and believed that the rich trading lands of the East – what were called the "Indies" – were where North America is. When Columbus saw the islands of the West Indies, he believed that his dreams had come true. That is how they got their name. For the same reason, we still call the original inhabitants of America "Indians". Never till his dying day would Columbus admit that instead of finding a new way to the East he had stumbled on a great new continent – America.

But it was obvious to everyone else that ideas about a western route to the east would have either to be scrapped or at least completely altered. Only by sailing round America to the north or to the south could European sailors find a new route and compete with the Portuguese. Again, geographers were divided into two schools of thought – those who supported the idea of a "south-west

Toscanelli's map of the world which Christopher Columbus used. Because of Toscanelli's miscalculations, Columbus always refused to believe he had discovered a New World.

passage" and those who believed in a "north-west passage".

After Columbus' discovery, the Spanish began to build up a huge empire in south and central America. (Even today Spanish is still the language of South America, though the Spanish empire has long since ended.) They explored both the coasts of South America, and in 1519 a Spaniard called Ferdinand Magellan sailed through the straits which still bear his name today and into the Pacific Ocean. From there, though his sailors were so short of food that they had to eat mice and chew the worms in the ship's supply of biscuits, Magellan sailed across the Pacific and found the Spice Islands. Here he was killed in a fight with some of the inhabitants. Only nineteen out of the original 234 who had set out reached Spain again three years later. But they had the honour of being the first Europeans to sail round the world.

The British had stood aside from all these dangers and adventures. But in 1497 another Italian, John Cabotto (known to the British as John Cabot), persuaded some merchants in Bristol to pay for an expedition to search for a north-west passage round the north of America. Henry VII was one of Cabot's backers. Though Cabot could find no passage to the East, his voyage led to the settlement of the first British colony. This was at Newfoundland, off the eastern Canadian coast. The settlement led to a great trade in fish – particularly cod – which English fishermen caught in vast numbers in the Atlantic there.

The idea of a north-west passage continued to excite the imaginations of English sailors throughout the 16th century. Martin Frobisher, Sir Humphrey Gilbert,

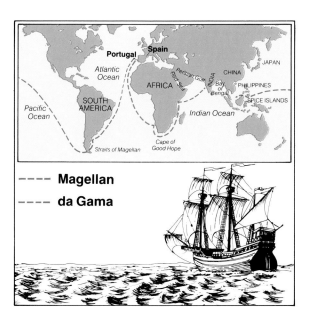

Vasco da Gama's voyage to India gave the Portuguese the monopoly of the route to the East via Africa. For the Spaniards, Magellan tried to reach the East by sailing south of South America – a desperately dangerous route.

An Indian settlement in North Carolina, USA, painted by John White. White led an unsuccessful attempt to found a colony in North America in 1587.

John Davis, William Baffin and John Bylot all believed for a few glorious days that they had discovered the passage and won eternal fame. But their hopes were soon dashed. Some found that the open sea through which they believed they were passing turned out to be the entrance to a great river, such as the St Lawrence or the Hudson.

William Hudson's was the most pathetic case of all. For days, he and his men sailed excitedly across the huge bay which bears his name today. But they found no passage to the Pacific, and were forced to spend the winter in Canada. In the spring the men mutinied. They put

Hudson and his ten-year-old son in an open boat with food and water for a few weeks, and set them adrift in the bay. They were never seen again.

One theory, which was suggested by Sebastian Cabot, John Cabot's son, was that there might be a north-east passage to the East. In 1553 an expedition led by Sir Henry Willoughby, with Richard Chancellor as second in command, left London to sail round northern Russia. Willoughby and all his crew were frozen to death in Lapland, but Chancellor landed at Archangel on the White Sea. He was escorted to Moscow by horse-sleigh over the ice. Here he had an interview with the Russian emperor, Tsar Ivan the Terrible, who showed great interest in trade between England and Russia.

The Russians wanted English cloth and weapons. The English were interested in Russian furs, hemp for ships' ropes, and tallow for making soap and candles. Chancellor was drowned, but the Muscovy Company was later founded in London to begin the first regular trade between the two countries.

England was becoming more and more a trading nation during the 16th century, but the majority of its people remained country people. The population of England and Wales may have more than doubled, from a little over two million in 1500 to about four and a half million 100 years later. But it had only returned to the size it was just before the Black Death. England was changing fast, but if we were taken back to it by time machine today, it would still seem very different from our own country.

As we saw in Chapter 23, some landlords and rich farmers in the 15th century changed from growing crops to farming sheep. Other landlords did the same in the first part of the 16th century, particularly in the Midlands and East Anglia. Wherever this happened, it caused trouble among the people of that area. The landlords' enclosures of common land hurt the poor most. They could no longer keep a cow, some sheep or a goat on the common and so grew even poorer and more underfed. Others lost their work and land.

The Tudor monarchs and their governments disliked enclosures as much as the poor. This was not only because they stirred up rebellion, but because local archers practised on the common land. If the common land disappeared, the archers would have nowhere for shooting arrows at targets from their famous longbows, which were as tall as themselves. The defence of the nation might one day depend on their skill.

The Duke of Somerset, who was Protector of England while Henry VIII's son Edward VI was too young to rule, put a tax on sheep and banned further enclosures. In the summer of 1549, a wealthy tanner, Robert Ket, led a party of men in Norfolk. They pulled down fences which had recently been put up around commons. They believed that they had the government's support. Soon they were joined by others and marched on Norwich.

Protector Somerset's ruling council disagreed with his policies, and his rival, the Duke of Northumberland, led an army to put down the rising. It contained 1500 German mercenaries. People bitterly resented foreign troops being used in a dispute between British farmers and

This 16th century miniature, painted Simon Beninck, gives an idealized picture of country life.

labourers. The labourers, most of whom were unarmed, were no match for the soldiers. Three thousand men were cut down in battle. A further 300 were executed. One more popular rising had been cruelly put down.

As we saw, since the closure of the monasteries, those who were desperate – the homeless, beggars, tramps and many others – could no longer knock on the door of a monastery or nunnery and be given food or a bed for the night. There was always the local church. Clergymen were generally poor and so were their congregations, but the Church in each area would usually build almshouses which the church wardens would give to old people who could no longer support themselves. The local squire often looked after tramps who came to the servants' quarters begging for a meal, as the feudal lord had done before him.

But kindness and Christian charity on their own were not enough. London, in particular, was crowded with beggars who clutched at the sleeves of passers-by and cried for help. Soldiers and sailors who lost a leg or an arm fighting for their country could claim no pension. They could not get work; so they begged because they had no alternative.

Tudor governments were most reluctant to help the poor, but in the end Elizabeth I's government produced a rough and ready system. It was summed up in the Poor Law of 1601. Overseers were appointed in each area to help the poor. They would always include the vicar and the squire. They could make each householder pay a yearly rate (a small local tax) which was to be used for the support of the poor. Each area was responsible only for its own poor. Any beggar not born in an area who asked the overseers for help was sent back to his or her birthplace. The needy were divided into three groups. There were those who were too old or ill to work. They were to be housed and looked after. There were the able-bodied, who could work, and were prepared to do so. The overseers had to find work for them. If they could not afford to live at home, they must live in special workhouses, which were to be built for them. Their children would be apprenticed to local employers.

The third group were to be treated ferociously. They were those who were able to work but refused to – the "sturdy beggars" who, the act said, "licked the sweat from the labourer's brow". No treatment was thought to be too harsh for these people. They must be whipped "until his or her body be bloody" and put in "houses of correction". Such a house had already been provided by London overseers. It was made out of the old royal palace of Bridewell. "Houses of correction" were soon called Bridewells everywhere. The Poor Law was in use for more than 200 years.

A beggar – supposed to have refused work – is publicly whipped. He will then be sent home to his birthplace.

Catholics and Protestants

Edward VI was nine years old when he became king. As we have seen, a Protector, Edward's uncle, the Duke of Somerset, was appointed to rule the country with a council until Edward was old enough to rule on his own. For two years, Somerset struggled to deal with the country's many problems, until he was defeated by his rival the Duke of Northumberland, who took over from him.

Edward's father Henry VIII had always regarded himself as a loyal Catholic. He was proud of the pamphlet he had written in 1521 in defence of Roman Catholic beliefs and against the beliefs of the German Protestant, Martin Luther. The Pope had rewarded him by giving him the title *Fidei Defensor*, which is Latin for Defender of the Faith.

Although, as we saw, Henry then quarrelled with the Pope and set up a new Church of England, he had no intention of altering the Church's beliefs or customs. As he saw it, he was now head of the English Catholic Church. Henry instructed his clergymen to refer to the Pope as the Bishop of Rome, but otherwise to continue preaching and teaching as usual. In the majority of parishes the same priest held the same Latin services in the same church as before. The church was furnished as before, the priest was dressed as before, and the congregation attended as before. For Henry, like all Tudor monarchs, made attendance at church compulsory.

Even so, some changes were introduced during Henry's reign. A translation of the Bible in English was placed in each church. It had to be read in the church and it was chained to the reading desk so that no one could take it away. It was an offence to own an English Bible, or to have a copy in your home unless you were a priest or a nobleman. But men and women at least grew accustomed to hearing Jesus' teaching expressed in their own language instead of in Latin. Two years before Henry's death, the first English service was allowed to be used in the Church of England. It was written by the Archbishop of Canterbury, Thomas Cranmer, whose hand Henry was holding when he died. For years Cranmer had been trying quietly to make Henry more Protestant in his ideas.

Protector Somerset and the boy king Edward, who had strong Protestant beliefs, were determined to make the English Church properly Protestant. With their support, Cranmer put together in 1549 a new service book – the first *Book of Common Prayer* – which all clergymen

A chained English Bible in a church.

had to use. Much of it was translated word for word from the Roman Catholic Mass, but it was all in English.

The priests were now allowed to marry. Churches were told to remove or destroy holy images (pictures or statues) – of Jesus' mother Mary, for instance, or of the saints. This was because people were thought to treat such pictures as idols – as if they were holy in themselves rather than just illustrations of the Christian faith.

When the Duke of Northumberland became Protector, the English Church became completely Protestant. The second *Book of Common Prayer* had all traces of Roman Catholic belief, which was now called "Popery", removed from it. A special Act was passed to order the removal of all images from churches. This led to a spate of destruction which went even further than Northumberland and his friends wanted. Just as local landowners had made a fortune out of buying up the monks' farms cheaply, now they used the Act as an excuse for looting the churches of their works of art and gold and silver valuables. It was said that even the lead from the church roofs was being ripped off by "holy thieves". The frescoes and murals painted on many church walls, illustrating scenes

from the Bible or from the lives of the saints, were whitewashed over. Only in modern times have a number of these paintings been rediscovered under the whitewash, and some of their colour and beauty restored.

Somerset's reforms led to a rebellion in Cornwall. The people opposed the first *Book of Common Prayer* and demanded that the Roman Catholic Mass be continued. They marched to Blackheath in 1549 before they were defeated.

Other problems then crowded in. As we have seen, Robert Ket's rebellion against enclosures in Norfolk was suppressed, though only after fierce fighting.

The national finances were in chaos. Henry's French wars had bankrupted the country. Inflation was producing hardship and riots all over England.

In 1547 Somerset attacked the Scots. By so doing he made them ally once more with the French, with whom England was still at war. English troops burned Edinburgh and looted its houses. They made Scotsmen hate Englishmen even more. Henry VIII had hoped that Edward VI would one day marry the

The coronation procession of Edward VI in 1547 as it moves down Cheapside from the Tower of London. London has scarcely developed south of the Thames.

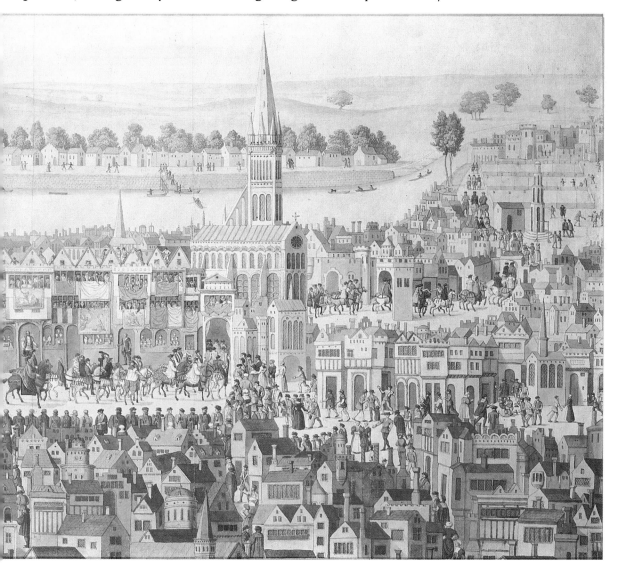

young Scottish queen, Mary Stuart, and unite England with Scotland. But instead 6000 French troops landed at Leith, near Edinburgh, and took Mary, who was then six years old, to France. Soon it was announced that she would marry the French heir to the throne.

Edward VI, who had never been very healthy, died in 1553 at the age of sixteen. The troubles during his reign made some people more convinced than ever that the country needed a strong ruler. The only person with a real claim to the throne was Mary Tudor, daughter of Henry VIII and Catherine of Aragon. But as well as being a woman, she was a Roman Catholic. Before he died, Edward VI and the Duke of Northumberland conspired to give the crown instead to Lady Jane Grey, aged sixteen, who was quickly married to Northumberland's eldest son.

Lady Jane Grey reigned for nine days. But the whole conspiracy seemed like a return to the Wars of the Roses. Court, Parliament and the people of London would have none of it. When Mary Tudor marched from Suffolk to London to claim her rights, support for Lady Jane Grey and Northumberland faded away. The gates of London were opened to her. Mary was crowned queen, and and Lady Jane Grey was executed.

Mary I, who reigned from 1553 to 1558, was a deeply convinced Roman Catholic. For many years, ever since Henry had left her mother Catherine, she had lived an unhappy life. She had felt friendless and, in the last year of Edward's life, had been afraid that she might be killed to prevent her becoming queen. She was determined to be loyal to her mother's memory and to the beliefs which had comforted and supported both of them.

The first step Mary took was to stop all clergymen using the English *Book of Common Prayer* for their services. Then she united England once more with the Roman Catholic Church, brought back Roman Catholic services, stopped the marriage of priests, and even tried to return all the monks' lands and property.

But Parliament refused to pass laws to give back the monks' lands. Almost all the Lords and Members of Parliament owned property themselves which had once belonged to the monks. Though they were prepared to see the return of the Roman Catholic faith, they were not prepared to give up their own wealth.

Parliament could do nothing to prevent Mary marrying the Spanish King Philip II, but it distrusted the marriage and insisted that Philip must have no power over English affairs. It passed a law that England must never go to war to support Spain without the English government's agreement. Sir Thomas Wyatt led a rising against Mary as a result of her Spanish marriage, but it was supported by only a few people in Kent, and was suppressed without great difficulty.

Though King Philip is always thought of as a loyal Roman Catholic, he advised Mary against trying to force Protestants to go back to the Roman Catholic Church by means of cruel persecutions. However, this is what Mary did, and it is for her policy of Protestant persecution that she is chiefly remembered. It earned her the title "Bloody Mary".

The title is rather unfair. Elizabeth I killed and tortured Roman Catholics, just as Mary persecuted Protestants. All over Europe, convinced Christians — both Protestants and Catholics — persecuted other Christians. Sometimes they burned them alive. They did so believing that it would be better for the victim to suffer a few minutes of agony on earth

than eternal agony in the world to come.

About 300 people were burned alive during Mary's reign, 60 of them women. They were mostly ordinary people (Protestant nobles and clergymen could afford to flee abroad). Many went to their terrible deaths singing their favourite psalms or hymns.

By the time of her death in 1558, at the age of forty-two, Mary had become a pathetic figure. Failures in the harvests and rising prices were looked on by her people as judgements of God upon her. She longed to have a child and heir, but she never succeeded. She adored her husband Philip, but he spent little time in England. When he knew she was dying, he did not come to her deathbed. She was jealous of her half-sister Elizabeth, Anne Boleyn's daughter. She feared a rebellion against her in support of Elizabeth. When, in the last year of her

This print shows the burning in Mary's reign of two leading Protestant Bishops, Latimer and Ridley. Archbishop Cranmer, who was himself burnt alive later, is shown praying that God will strengthen them. At the last moment Ridley said to Latimer: "We shall . . . light such a candle . . . as shall never be put out." Time was to prove him right.

reign, the French captured Calais from her army, which was fighting with Spain against France, Mary was deeply ashamed. Calais was the last piece of French soil which the English had held. Shortly afterwards she died.

Not everybody hated or despised Mary Tudor. After her death one of her admirers wrote:

Her perfect life in all extremes
Her patient heart did show
For in this world she never found
But doleful days and woe.

The Reign of Elizabeth I (1558–1603)

When Elizabeth became queen at the age of twenty-five, in 1558, there seemed no reason to expect that she would rule for long. Though Mary Tudor's persecutions had made her unpopular, a great many people, particularly those of an older generation, still supported the traditional Roman Catholic religion. As Anne Boleyn's daughter, Elizabeth I could never be recognized as the rightful monarch by any loyal Roman Catholic.

On the other hand, not all Protestants were satisfied with the Church of England. The Puritans, the most extreme English Protestants, wanted the Church to be "purified" of all its Catholic practices. They wanted the priest's clothing to be simple and all statues and images removed from churches. They wanted to end the appointment of bishops by the Queen and have all clergymen elected by their congregations.

Apart from these bitter disagreements over religion, Elizabeth had to deal with the troubles arising from prices, unemployment and the harsh Poor Laws. Then there were the threats from enemies abroad. The Scots and the French were now closer allies than ever after Queen Mary Stuart's marriage in 1558 to the heir to the French throne, Francis. They might unite to get rid of Elizabeth. An even more dangerous enemy was Spain, whose King Philip, a hater of Protestants, had just lost his power over England through his wife Mary Tudor's death.

But as most people wanted to live in peace, if Elizabeth worked to unite the country over religion, to remove Mary Stuart's challenge, and above all to avoid expensive or warlike policies, she might not only survive but be a successful ruler. Such an achievement would require intelligence, tact and cunning, as well as courage and determination. Elizabeth had all these qualities. She was highly educated, and able to carry on fluent conversation in French, Italian and Latin. The troubles in the reigns of Edward VI and Mary Tudor – when Elizabeth herself had been in danger of execution – had strengthened her determination to survive at almost any price.

First Elizabeth set out, with the help of Parliament, to settle the disagreements over religion. Nothing could change her loyalty to her mother's religion, or her determination to head a Church of England which would resemble her father's Church. But although she was a Protestant, she did not like the Puritans and would not let them have their way.

Westminster, with the first royal palace. The Abbey, and Westminster Hall where Parliament met, were nearby.

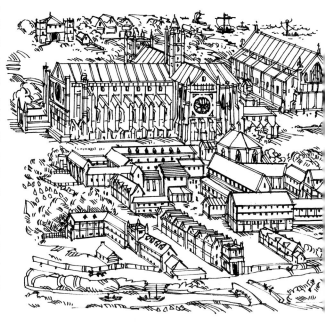

200

Her new Archbishop of Canterbury, Archbishop Parker, stopped any further looting and destruction of churches and cathedrals. Bishops were still appointed by Elizabeth, who relied on them to control the clergy in their area and see that they gave no trouble. Everyone had to attend the new Church of England, but the punishment for not doing so was only a fine of a shilling a month. A few brave Roman Catholics would have nothing to do with it. Everybody else accepted it, though many people probably went to church just to avoid trouble. If they did so and kept quiet, Elizabeth said that she had no wish "to open windows to look into men's souls" – in other words, they could believe what they liked.

The dangers from abroad soon grew less. For this, the Queen could thank both her good luck and the good management of her government – in particular, William Cecil, her Secretary of State, who served her quietly and skilfully throughout her long reign.

In 1559 King Henry II of France died. Francis II, aged fifteen and an invalid, became King. Mary Stuart was now Queen of France and Scotland. The worst had happened. But in 1560 Francis II died and Mary was forced to return to Scotland. There she found that there had been a Protestant revolution, led by the preacher John Knox and supported by many of the nobles. Roman Catholic churches in Scotland had been wrecked, Roman Catholic priests expelled, and, most important of all, French troops had been removed. William Cecil had shrewdly encouraged the Scottish Protestants and sent an English army into the Lowlands to support them. The French had been surrounded in their garrison at Leith, and blockaded at sea by the Engl-

The young Queen Elizabeth.

ish fleet. In the Treaty of Edinburgh, in 1560, it was agreed that all French troops would be removed from Scotland.

The fighting between England and France which was left over from Mary's reign was now ended by a peace treaty. Elizabeth made no attempt to get back Calais; she chose to secure peace abroad and end French influence in Scotland at little cost in money and lives.

During Elizabeth I's long and peaceful reign, many new private houses were built. Here the Countess of Shrewsbury, known as Bess of Hardwick, consults her architect, Robert Smythson (a local man) during the building of Hardwick Hall in Derbyshire. Her initials – ES (Elizabeth Shrewsbury) – already cap one tower. Most materials, like the stone blocks being wheeled on trolleys, came from the Hardwick estate. The marble, used in fireplaces and mantelpieces, was quarried in Derbyshire. The family and state apartments were on the first and second floors, as the height of the windows shows. The servants' quarters were, unusually, on the ground floor. Great Elizabethan houses like this were unfortified. The centuries of barons' wars were over at last.

From the moment she returned to Scotland, Mary Stuart was continually quarrelling with her Protestant government. There were rumours about her scandalous private life. Her second marriage, to the Earl of Darnley, was known to be unhappy. The couple made up their quarrel, and a baby son, James, was born. But then Darnley was murdered by a group of Protestant lords, led by the Earl of Bothwell. There were rumours that Mary had been involved in her husband's murder, though it was never proved. But when, shortly after the murder, Bothwell divorced his wife, and Mary married him, Mary's court and government could stand it no longer. She was imprisoned. In 1568 she escaped, fled across the border and threw herself on the mercy of her cousin, Elizabeth.

Mary Queen of Scots and one of her servants in captivity. After her escape from Scotland, Elizabeth kept her under house arrest.

For the next nineteen years Mary was Elizabeth's prisoner.

The year after Mary's flight into England, Elizabeth faced a dangerous rebellion – the Rising of the North. It was led by the northern Earls of Northumberland and Westmoreland, who wanted a Roman Catholic ruler. There were plans to release Mary Stuart from imprisonment and make her queen. She was to marry the leading English Roman Catholic, the Duke of Norfolk. The Spanish ambassador was involved in one of the plans – the Ridolfi Plot. The ambassador talked vaguely of landing Spanish troops in the north of England from his country's colonies in Belgium and Holland.

English spies heard of the plots, and the rising was prevented. The Duke of Norfolk was executed. But Elizabeth, against her ministers' advice, refused to put Mary Stuart on trial.

In 1570 Pope Pius V excommunicated Elizabeth from the Roman Catholic Church. After that it was the duty of every loyal English Roman Catholic to withdraw his support from Elizabeth. From that time onwards Pope Pius and Queen Elizabeth knew that there was no way in which they could agree. It was war between them.

English Roman Catholic missionaries began to work secretly to reconvert people in England and Wales to the Roman Catholic faith. They were hidden by other Roman Catholics who risked death to give them shelter. Some of these were Catholic nobles from families who remained faithful to their old religion. They would also hide priests, who held secret services in their houses, and hid in secret rooms ("priests' holes", as they came to be called).

The government hit back hard against the Catholics. Fines for refusing to attend Church of England services were raised to £20 a month. This was a huge sum which would bankrupt all but the richest families. The government did not stop there. Nearly 300 Roman Catholics were executed for their beliefs, most of them in 1588. This, as we shall see, was the year when the Spaniards set out on their campaign to invade Britain. The government looked on every Catholic as a friend of the Spaniards. This was certainly not the case (the commander of the English Navy which defeated the Armada was himself a Catholic), but it explains the persecution, which was seen as protecting the country.

The Catholic Spaniards now hated the Protestant English as enemies of God. The English thought the same, from the opposite point of view. Things were made worse when the English tried to "steal" trade which Spanish traders claimed as theirs in the Spanish empire in south and central America.

A Roman Catholic missionary hides in a "priests' hole" under a fireplace.

In 1568 Sir John Hawkins was trading slaves from west Africa to the Spanish colonies in the West Indies and Panama. The colonists wanted the slaves, but the Spanish government would not allow any foreign traders to enter their empire. Spanish sailors attacked Hawkins and his men while their ships were lying peacefully in a harbour in Mexico called San Juan d'Ulloa. Many were killed or captured and made slaves in the Spanish navy. Hawkins himself escaped with his young cousin, Francis Drake. From that time onwards they swore revenge on the Spaniards.

Though war had not been declared officially between England and Spain, English sea captains now did all they could to attack the Spanish empire and its bases in America and the West Indies. They wanted to seize as much wealth as they could lay their hands on.

The Spanish had found large quantities of gold in South America. Much of it was mined in Chile. From there it was taken a little way by sea, then strapped on the backs of mules and carried in convoy across the narrow Panama Isthmus. Here, in 1572, Drake lay in wait for the convoy. He captured gold valued at £200,000 in the money of that time and escaped with it.

Five years later Drake set off with five ships on a secret mission to sail round the world. He followed much the same course as Magellan along the east coast of South America. Only one of his ships, the *Golden Hind*, sailed through the Magellan Straits, south of South America, and entered the Pacific Ocean. Here by chance Drake found a Spanish galleon, the *Cacafuego*. He boarded it off San Francisco, and seized fabulous loot — 360,000 "pieces of eight" (Spanish gold coins), along with chests of gold and silver, diamonds and rubies.

From California, Drake and his men sailed across the Pacific and landed on the island of Ternate in Indonesia, where many of the world's cloves were grown. The ruler was in the middle of a dispute with the Portuguese. He agreed to let the English and not the Portuguese have the monopoly in his spices. In 1580, fifty-one out of the original 160 men who had set out with Drake returned – the first Englishmen to sail round the world.

Drake brought back £1,500,000 to share out among the people who had given money to pay for the expedition. Although the profit was kept secret, for every £1 invested in the voyage an investor probably received about £14. The Queen herself had secretly given money towards the expedition, and she did well out of it. It was reported that five pack-horses loaded with treasure from the *Golden Hind* secretly left Plymouth for the court. Elizabeth went down to Deptford, on the Thames, to knight Drake on board his ship. The Spaniards, not surprisingly, were furious.

In 1568 Spain's colonies, Holland and Belgium, revolted against Spanish rule. The Dutch were the most anti-Spanish and the most Protestant. They looked to the English queen for help. At first she only agreed to help them secretly, but when a Spanish ship, loaded with pay for the Spanish army in Belgium, stopped in Plymouth for repairs, she refused to let it go. Many Englishmen fought as volunteers with the Dutch armies. One of Elizabeth's favourite courtiers, Sir Philip Sidney, died fighting for the Dutch. Finally, in 1585, an English army under the Earl of Leicester went to help the Dutch. War between Spain and England had been declared.

All this time plots had been made to overthrow Elizabeth and put Mary Stuart in her place. In 1587 British spies reported that Mary had taken part in a plot to assassinate the Queen. Mary was found guilty and condemned to death. Reluctantly, Elizabeth signed her death warrant, and she was executed at Fotheringay Castle in Northamptonshire.

Mary's execution made King Philip II of Spain decide to go ahead with plans to invade and occupy England. (Philip saw himself as the champion of the Roman Catholic faith.) The Spanish fleet prepared for an expedition in 1587. But while many of its supply ships were anchored in Cadiz, Drake led his men in a surprise attack on the harbour. He

The fate of the Spanish Armada

SCOTLAND

North Sea

IRELAND

Howard pursues fleeing Armada 23 July 1588

ENGLAND

Armada attacked by fireships 22 July 1588

197 English ships mostly small & 16-17,000 men

Portland

Plymouth

Armada sighted 19 July 1588

Armada sighted 20 July 1588

Armada sighted 14 July 1588

Atlantic Ocean

The Spanish invasion plan was based on picking up troops in Belgium. These never materialized.

Armada scattered by squalls

4 June 1588

La Coruna

Santander

FRANCE

SPAIN

PORTUGAL

Madrid

Mediterranean Sea

Lisbon

14 May 1588 Armada leaves with 132 ships

destroyed thirty ships and burned warehouses full of supplies. The invasion was postponed.

The Spanish had decided not to invade England directly. Although their ships were carrying many troops there were not enough to ensure a successful landing. So the plan was for the troops to be escorted in convoy by Spanish galleons through the English Channel to Belgium. Here they would join forces with Spanish troops fighting the Dutch and Belgians. The combined force of 30,000 men would then sail to the mouth of the Thames, land near Margate and march on London.

The English had been expecting an invasion ever since the summer of 1587. But Elizabeth had always refused to spend much money on defence. The English toops in Holland were months behind with their pay. There was no proper army with which to defend the

The Armada. The crosses painted on the sails gave the expedition the look of a Christian crusade, as the Spaniards wanted.

south coast. However, Sir John Hawkins, who was treasurer of the Navy, had persuaded Elizabeth to strengthen her fleet. The English Navy, under the command of an English Catholic, Lord Howard of Effingham, had several advantages over the Spanish. The English ships were better suited to the rough seas of the English Channel and the Atlantic. The Spanish ships were top-heavy, for they stood higher in the water. They were too wide for bad weather and rolled in high seas. They were designed for sailing in the calmer waters of the Mediterranean. The English sea captains, such as Drake himself, Martin Frobisher and Walter Raleigh, were experts at handling their faster and slimmer craft. And they were fighting in their own waters.

Nevertheless, in July 1588, 132 ships left Spain in rough seas. An English warship sighted them off Plymouth on 14th July. The warning system of beacons sprang into use. From Cornwall to York beacons piled high on hilltops

warned that the invasion was finally coming.

The Armada, with the wind behind it, sailed up the Channel. In the middle the troop ships wallowed in the waves. At the rear and on each side sailed the big galleons, convoying the troop ships. Thousands of people lined the cliffs of the Isle of Wight to watch the Armada sail by. They cheered the English ships as they twisted in and out of range of the Spanish galleons, trying to isolate Spanish ships and destroy them.

On the night of 22nd July the Spaniards were anchored off Calais. The English sent in eight fireships. These were old merchant ships, crammed with bonfires and tar barrels. They had fully loaded guns aboard, which would fire when flames reached the gunpowder. Their crews had a dangerous job. As they sailed straight for the anchored Spanish ships, they set fire to the bonfires and took to their boats.

The arrival of the fireships caused panic in the Spanish navy whose ships were anchored close together in military formation. In the general confusion, it

Elizabeth I died on 24th March 1603. Her funeral procession, with its magnificent horses and its coffin draped in purple velvet must have been a splendid sight.

was each commander for himself. They cut their anchors and made for the open sea. One ship ran aground.

When day dawned, the English sailors moved in. Fighting began and continued all day. The wind was driving the Spanish ships onto the sandbanks off Gravelines and Dunkirk on the French coast. The English fired again and again from their cannons, sailing close to the Spanish ships. They sank one galleon. Two others ran aground on the sand.

Next morning the wind changed, and drove the Armada into the North Sea. The English ships followed as far as the Scottish coast, but gave up through lack of ammunition. The Spanish struggled home, sailing north of Scotland and west of the Irish coast. The storm continued, and many ships sank or ran aground.

Of the 132 Armada ships that set sail fifty-three never returned. The war continued, though by the time of Elizabeth's death, both sides were beginning to think of making peace. Elizabeth's government could not bring itself to enter into peace talks with Spain. It was left to the new government of James I to do so. As for the sailors whose skill and courage had destroyed the Armada, many of them were dismissed unpaid as soon as the fighting ended.

Plotters and Parliaments

Nothing unites a country as completely as fear of invasion. With the ending of the Spanish war by James I at the Peace of Westminster in 1604, the threat from outside was removed. James I of England, son of Mary Stuart and Darnley, was already James VI of Scotland when he succeeded Elizabeth. He was wise enough to see that the continuation of the war was futile, but there must have been times when he longed for the war to be brought back. For troubles which had been suppressed during Elizabeth's long reign now flared up again. National unity was broken.

The most important of these troubles was that Members of Parliament (MPs) were demanding more say in the government of England. They had been doing so since Mary Tudor's reign. All Tudor monarchs from Henry VII to Elizabeth I had the same attitude to Parliament. All were determined to rule in their own way and to call Parliament only when they wanted to raise money through taxes or when they wanted Parliament's support for their policies.

As we have seen, there were two Houses of Parliament – the House of Lords and the House of Commons. In spite of its name, the House of Commons did not represent the common people. Only one man in every thirty in England could vote. The other twenty-nine men and all women were unrepresented in Parliament. MPs were wealthy and powerful men, many of whom were representatives of the City of London and the other great merchant areas. They were involved in the cloth trade (like the Merchant Adventurers), or the trade with India, China and Indonesia (like the East India Company), or the slave trade.

Other MPs were great country land-owners. Their great houses ruled over the local districts in the same way as the castles had done before them. Like the medieval barons, they were often the uncrowned kings of their counties. They had no private armies, and their houses were not walled and moated, but they owned most of the farms round about them and employed the local labourers.

Henry VIII knew very well that Parliament only represented the rich. He knew that the landowners, in particular, had had their eyes on the monks' rich estates for a long time. So instead of passing a royal decree to close down the monasteries he let it be done by Parliament. The matter was debated (discussed) in both Houses and an Act of Parliament was passed. That way Parliament took some of the blame for closing down the monasteries. But Henry's example was to have an important effect in the future. If a change of such importance had been carried out through Parliament, MPs believed that in future Parliament itself could decide similar changes, whether monarchs approved of them or not.

We have already seen one of the first signs that Parliament could stop being just a royal servant and have opinions of its own. Mary Tudor was shocked when her Parliament refused to return the monks' lands to the monks. But there was nothing she could do about it.

However Elizabeth I would not even allow religious issues to be discussed in the House of Commons. Some MPs were imprisoned in the Tower, where they stayed for years, simply because of their Puritan opinions. At other times, Elizabeth stopped debates in Parliament on the spot and reprimanded the participants she disagreed with.

Elizabeth believed that anyone who criticized her was a traitor. MPs who claimed the right of "free speech" – the right to say what they believed to be true – were told that they could only express their opinions when the Queen asked for them. In her last ten years on the throne,

People laughed at James because of his strange manner, but he was shrewder than he seemed. One man called him "the wisest fool in Christendom".

Elizabeth was treated by her court more like an empress than a queen. People had great respect for her strength and courage. Any ruler who took over from Elizabeth was bound to face great difficulties. MPs and others, who had been prepared to wait till her death and the end of the war with Spain before making demands, would certainly not hold back afterwards. And James I, who became king at the age of thirty-seven in 1603,

made things more difficult than they would have been in any case.

James had been made king of Scotland at the age of two. In Scotland he always felt that he was a boy king, controlled by his council. Now that he had also become King of England, he was determined to rule as he liked.

James believed in a theory which became known as the "divine right of kings". This stated simply that as God was the ruler of the world, the king in any country ruled on God's behalf. He could not be disobeyed, just as God could not be. He could rule as he saw fit, and his people must not criticize him. James wrote:

"As it is atheism and blasphemy to dispute what God can do, so it is presumption and high contempt in a subject to dispute what a king can do."

Or, as he put it in his stuttering speech, "I would be the great s-s-s-schoolmaster of the whole land". (Elizabeth I, like Henry VIII, privately believed very much the same. But she had the sense not to say so publicly.)

As well as objecting to this attitude, the English disliked James I merely because he was a Scotsman. One advantage of having the same king for both countries was that at least the two were not at war. But the prejudice in England and at the English court against the Scots was strong. (Some Londoners even pretended to believe that Scotsmen had tails curled up beneath their kilts.) James did not make it any better by bringing with him a crowd of Scottish courtiers, greedy for positions at court and English lands.

As a person, James was not likely to convince people that he was specially chosen by God to rule. He had a bad stammer. His tongue was said to be too big for his mouth, so he slobbered when he spoke. He loved sweet food and was a messy eater, dribbling his food down his doublet jacket. He had thin, bandy legs. They could not always support his rather fat body, so at one point during his coronation service, he fell down.

Assassinations were common at the Scottish court. (James' own father had been blown up.) So it was not surprising that James I went in daily terror of losing his life. He had his doublets specially padded to protect him from assassins' daggers and slept surrounded by thick mattresses for the same reason. He was terrified, too, of witches.

James was to prove himself as wily a politician as Elizabeth, but he never commanded the respect which she had. This was unfair, for he was often wise and far-seeing. It was James who risked great unpopularity by ending the war with Spain at the beginning of his reign. It was James who hoped to make Scotland and England properly united instead of just having the same king. But though he managed to prevent civil war breaking out during his reign, there was no doubt that the disagreements between different groups in England grew deeper.

James' first concern was with religion. He arranged the best known of all English translations of the Bible – the Authorised Version or King James' Bible. Sunday after Sunday its magnificent prose was read in every church in the land for centuries. Until modern times it was often the only book to be found in many English homes.

In 1605 a group of Roman Catholic conspirators planned to blow up James and his ministers when they were all assembled together at the opening of Parliament on 5th November. A Roman Catholic soldier called Guy Fawkes had been stacking gunpowder and firewood in the cellar under the Houses of Parliament for months. He was acting under orders from Robert Catesby and other Catholic noblemen.

News of Fawkes' plot leaked out, and the conspirators were rounded up. They were terribly tortured, and executed as traitors. Ever since then, great bonfires have been built, and stuffed "guys" or effigies of the Pope burned on them. Even today an effigy of the Pope is burned on top of a great bonfire on the South Downs above Lewes, in Sussex, on Guy Fawkes' night. Crowds come from miles around to watch the stuffed Pope blaze. By such means hatred of Roman Catholics was kept alive for centuries.

Guy Fawkes and his fellow conspirators. Fawkes stacked firewood and gunpowder under the Houses of Parliament. He planned to set fire to them when James I came to open Parliament.

The troubles with Parliament started with James I's first Parliament in 1604 and continued until the king's death. Behind them lay the government's financial troubles. Elizabeth I had had difficulties over money and her government, desperate for cash, had sold monopolies to favoured businessmen. This meant that they were the only people allowed to sell a particular article, such as coal or soap or candles. They could therefore charge what price they liked for them. Since candles were the main means of lighting, people were bound to be indignant if their price, for instance, was unnecessarily high. Some MPs protested about this, but Elizabeth ignored them.

James was more fortunate than most English rulers. Elizabeth did not leave him a great heap of debts. She left him £200 – and 3000 dresses! But the king soon got into debt. The cost of governing was rising steadily, but much of the government's income remained the same. Rents from royal lands, for instance, could only be raised when a tenant's lease ran out. Many leases were for periods as long as ninety-nine years. Other regular sources of income were the customs' taxes. But these could only be raised if Parliament agreed.

This was how Parliament, particularly the House of Commons, began to exploit its power. If the king wanted more money from Parliament, they told him, he would have to put their grievances right – especially over religion – and give them more say in government. The conflicts which were to lead to the outbreak of civil war in 1642 were beginning.

James I's financial difficulties grew steadily worse. Unlike Elizabeth, he did not have to pay for the war with Spain, but he himself did not help matters by the extravagance of his court. Elizabeth had used the traditional money-saving

A crowded market square in a 17th century English town. The gabled roofs, red tiles and leaded windows of the houses are typical of a time when merchants and craftsmen were growing richer.

trick of English monarchs of spending months away from London in the summer travelling round her noblemen's houses "on progress". The arrival of the Queen and 500 courtiers to stay with a nobleman for a fortnight might have bankrupted the lord but it saved the taxpayer money. James, too, loved to go "on progress", but his courtiers were more unruly than Elizabeth's. The nobles he visited began to complain, and Parliament took up their complaints.

In Scotland James had been closely supervised by his Scottish ministers and forced to live simply. When he moved to Whitehall Palace as King of England, he reacted by spending money. So did his wife Anne, a Danish princess, who did not help matters by becoming a Roman Catholic. During the first three years of his reign, James spent £92,000 on jewels. Anne ran up debts of £40,000 with just one of her jewellers in ten years.

Plays had become very popular during Elizabeth's reign, both at court and among the people. Men, women and children (boys played the female parts in plays at this time) flocked over the Thames to visit the Globe Theatre in Southwark in south London. Here a young actor, William Shakespeare, was one of a number of popular playwrights whose plays were performed. The audience sat on the stage itself, and liked to show their feelings about the plays or the actors by cheering, booing and throwing refuse.

Shakespeare's greatest plays — such as *Macbeth*, whose Scottish story was well suited to James I's taste, and *Othello* — were performed at James' court. Though they were well received, the King and Queen's favourite entertainment were lavish masques.

These were half plays, half ballets. The clothes of the actors and dancers were magnificent, and so was the scenery. One of Shakespeare's fellow playwrights, Ben Jonson, wrote masques for the court. The great architect Inigo Jones, who designed the banqueting chamber of Whitehall Palace — the only part of the palace still standing today — and the Queen's House at Greenwich for James, made the scenery for one of Jonson's masques. The performance must have provided a breathtaking spectacle; but it cost £3000.

Most unpopular of all, James spent thousands of pounds of taxpayers' money on his favourites, most of whom were Scottish. By 1610 he had given them £220,000 in cash — roughly a quarter of his total debt.

When the Duke of Buckingham took over as leading minister, the position grew worse. It is true that Buckingham was a capable minister. But other ministers had never lived with such open extravagance at the taxpayers' expense. It was not surprising that Parliament began to dig in its heels and refuse to grant the taxes James demanded.

James replied with defiance. If Parliament would not give him the money he needed to govern the country, he would look round for other ways of raising money. He and his ministers won an important victory in Bate's Case (1606) when the judges ruled that the king could increase customs duties without Parliament's approval. James' ministers used every legal trick they could to find more money for their ruler. Landowners were made to become knights, whether they liked it or not, and to pay the king for the privilege. Fines were increased. If you lived on land which had once been forest land, though it had long been cleared, you were forced to pay forest taxes.

Soon James I gave up calling Parliament altogether. Between 1611 and 1621, he called only one Parliament. The Parliament of 1614 lasted three weeks before James closed it.

Although the Spanish were hated in England, James had a secret plan to marry Prince Charles, heir to the throne, to a Spanish princess. Buckingham and Charles were sent to Madrid to arrange the marriage. When the arrangements failed, and the couple returned, offended with the Spanish, James I and his Parliament at last reached agreement. An English expedition would be sent to Holland to fight the Spanish.

In return James agreed not to oppose the impeachment of Lionel Cranfield, the king's Treasurer, who had nearly achieved the impossible and got rid of the government's debts. He also agreed that all monopolies were illegal. James' reign ended with an unusual feeling of agreement between King and Parliament, when he died suddenly in 1625.

The Parting of the Ways (1625–1642)

Charles I, who reigned from 1625 to 1649 was not brought up to expect to be king. The crown should have passed to his elder brother Henry, but Henry died in 1612. Charles accepted being king as a duty; but he did not enjoy it. In his boyhood there had been talk of him going into the Church. Certainly, when he became king, he was already a deeply religious man.

Like his father, James I, Charles I believed in the "divine right of kings". Courtiers noticed that Charles altered the coronation oath. He swore to main-

A fashionable lady and gentleman outside Whitehall Palace in the time of Charles I.

tain the liberties and laws of England only in so far as they did not clash with his royal prerogative (rights).

Charles' disagreements with his Parliaments started as soon as he was crowned. The expedition to fight the Spanish in Holland was a disaster. The English soldiers scarcely fired a shot; 9000 out of 12,000 of them died of diseases. Parliament blamed the government. Charles said that Parliament had only granted him about an eighth of the money the expedition required. Parliament replied by criticizing the unpopular Duke of Buckingham, on whom Charles was very dependent. Charles dismissed it. If a Parliament gave Charles trouble, he dismissed it. "Parliaments", he said, "are like cats. They ever grow cursed with age."

Before his next Parliament was called, in 1626, Charles I had married a French princess, Henrietta Maria. She was a Roman Catholic, and the English court became a centre for Roman Catholics, many of them French. She and Charles were devoted to each other. Their life-long love is moving to recall. But Henrietta's religious and political influence on her husband was disastrous. She encouraged him to defy Parliament and to rule like a royal dictator.

After the failure of the expedition to Holland, Buckingham planned a raid on the Spanish port of Cadiz. The sailors who landed there looted the wine shops and got drunk. The raid was a complete failure. The year after, Buckingham organized another raid in Brittany to give support to French Protestants in their civil war with the Catholics. It proved the third failure in three years.

Such failures cost money. Parliament refused to increase taxes, so the government ordered "forced loans". Taxpayers had to "lend" the government the same amounts as they would have paid if Parliament had passed the taxes Charles demanded. Many influential men refused to pay. Some were imprisoned. When Charles called Parliament in 1628, both Houses presented him with a simple petition to sign. It became known as the Petition of Right. Like the Magna Carta it has been regarded ever since as one of the foundations of Britain's liberties. Its first two clauses were the vital ones:

1. No man should be forced to pay a tax which has not been passed by Act of Parliament.

2. No man can be imprisoned without a reason which has been clearly shown.

The King accepted the Petition of Right, but his acceptance made little difference to his behaviour. When Buckingham was severely criticized by the House of Commons, Charles dismissed the MPs again.

Buckingham was in Portsmouth, planning a second expedition to Brittany, when he was stabbed to death by a naval officer who had a personal grievance against him. His corpse was taken from Portsmouth to London and all the way to Whitehall Palace the crowds turned out to cheer and jeer. When Charles heard the noise, he retired to his room and wept. A writer at the time wrote that Charles never forgave the people for

Charles I painted from three different angles by the Dutch portrait painter, van Dyck.

their reaction to Buckingham's death. After more disputes with Parliament during 1629, Charles dismissed both Houses. From 1629 to 1640 he ruled without once calling Parliament.

During those eleven years Charles I governed by himself with a small group of ministers, which included three outstanding men. One was his Treasurer, Sir Richard Weston. He was so successful at finding methods of taxation which did not involve Parliament that by 1635 Charles was no longer short of money.

Another was Charles' Archbishop of Canterbury, William Laud. He opposed the influence of Puritans in the Church of England. He and Charles believed that the Church should use every means to teach the people about the Christian faith, just as the medieval Church had done. Stained glass, images, statues and musical compositions were encouraged and not frowned upon. During the first half of the 17th century some of the finest poets in the country – George Herbert, Henry Vaughan and the Dean of St Paul's, John Donne – were clergymen in the Church of England.

Archbishop Laud was determined to drive the Puritans out of England. In 1620 a few brave Puritans had sailed in the *Mayflower* to North America. They wanted to start a new life abroad, worshipping God in the simple way they believed was right. The area where they settled became known as New England. As a result of Laud's persecution of the Puritans, thousands of others left Eng-

In 1620 a number of English Puritans, persecuted for their strong Protestant faith, set sail in the "Mayflower" in search of a new life. Months later, they landed in Cape Cod in Massachusetts. Thousands soon followed them and settled in the area they called New England. Their hard work, disciplined lives and modest ways deeply influenced American life.

land to join them. But those who remained in England became more and more certain that at some point they would have to stand up to Charles and fight for their beliefs.

The most powerful of Charles' three ministers was a wealthy Yorkshire landowner, Thomas Wentworth, who later became Earl of Strafford. He was never forgiven by Charles' opponents in the House of Commons for going over to the king's side. He had started his political life as one of their leaders. In 1627, he had been imprisoned for six months for refusing to pay Charles' forced loans. But after Buckingham's murder, he accepted Charles' offer to make him president of the Council of the North. Five years later, in 1633, he was appointed Lord Deputy of Ireland.

Throughout Tudor times, English governments had used Ireland as a source of land with which to reward courtiers or others who were in favour. In this way thousands of hectares had been given to English landlords, many of whom lived in London and never visited their estates. By 1633 English government in Ireland had become thoroughly corrupt. It did not even provide Charles with much money. English landlords, civil servants and politicians all took as much money as they could from the Irish and lined their own pockets.

Strafford was determined to "clean up" the English government in Ireland and make the colony profitable. He greatly increased taxes, and ensured that the rich paid more tax. He reorganized the army and strengthened the navy. He improved roads and bridges, helped the Irish industries producing woollen and linen cloth, and encouraged the breeding of horses by the Irish, for which they became famous.

Strafford also began a "plantation" scheme, which the governments of Oliver Cromwell and William of Orange were later to follow. In the north-west – Sligo, Mayo and Galway – he expelled Roman Catholic landlords and "planted" Protestant English in their place, who would be more loyal to him. Although these strict policies made Ireland less corrupt, they made Strafford hated by the people there. He was also feared by MPs in England – with a man like Strafford to help him, Charles might be able to go on ruling without Parliament until his death.

Charles I's personal government was at last brought to an end by the Scottish war. Like his father, Charles was King of Scotland as well as England. He was determined to make the Scottish Church use the English prayer book. But the ruling group in Scotland were Protestants who belonged to the Presbyterian Church and believed in a simple Puritan faith. Many of their services were written by the most respected of their early leaders, John Knox. When Charles ordered that clergymen in Scottish churches should use the English prayer book, national feeling was violently aroused. There was a riot in St Giles' Cathedral in Edinburgh. (One of the congregation, Jenny Geddes, was reported to have hurled a stool at the minister's head.) Within a few months a defiant Scottish army was raised. They were known as the Covenanters, as they covenanted (promised) to end Charles I's religious changes.

Charles, who could not afford to fight a war, marched north to face the Scottish forces who had crossed the border. He had no alternative but to enter into peace talks with his Scottish subjects, while calling on his English subjects to elect a new Parliament, which would pass taxes to pay for a war.

There is no reason to think that during the eleven years from 1629 to 1640 the English people were longing for the recall of Parliament. The country had been at peace, since Charles had soon ended the wars with France and Spain. Taxes were low, and the people generally prosperous. Unlike James I's unruly court, Charles' court was dignified and restrained. Charles was keen on music and loved to listen to his private orchestra. For the only time in British history the court was renowned for its love of art. Charles owned paintings by Titian, Tintoretto, Raphael and Rembrandt. He commissioned work from the great painter Rubens, and was himself painted many times by Van Dyck. After Charles' execution, Oliver Cromwell's government sold his art collection. What, one Puritan revealingly asked, did the taxpayer want with "old rotten pictures and broken nosed marbles?"

Yet English landowners had been alarmed by the "ship money" case in 1637. One of Parliament's future leaders, John Hampden, had refused to pay ship money – a tax which paid for the Navy. This tax had always been provided by people living in coastal areas. Charles extended payment to all taxpayers because, he argued – quite reasonably – the whole country was defended by the Navy, and not just the coast. Hampden refused to pay on the ground that the extension to inland areas had not been agreed by Parliament. The King was clearly breaking the Petition of Right. But by a majority of seven votes to five the judges sided with him. The case convinced many people that without the recall of Parliament the King would soon be able to do exactly as he liked.

When Parliament met in the spring of 1640, it lasted only a few weeks before Charles dismissed it again. That summer the Scots occupied Newcastle. It was obvious that the King had no army capable of defeating them. He entered into peace talks, in which the Scottish leaders demanded the removal of Strafford and Laud from Charles' council. From now on the Scots and MPs who opposed the King worked closely together. Charles was forced to call another Parliament at Westminster in the autumn of 1640. It was to meet on and off for the next twenty years and to earn

The peaceful, prosperous England of 1629–1640.

the title the Long Parliament.

As soon as the Long Parliament met, John Pym announced that it was going to try Strafford for treason. However, there was, of course, no evidence to prove that Strafford was a traitor to the King, since he was the King's devoted minister. So a bill was introduced in Parliament which required no evidence, but merely said that Strafford was guilty of treason. It was rushed though the Commons and presented to the House of Lords in 1641.

When the time came for the Lords to vote, huge crowds surrounded Parliament. The names of the fifty-nine MPs who had voted against Strafford's death were posted up all over London. Their houses were besieged. Some MPs had transported their servants and labourers to London so that they could crowd round the House of Lords shouting "Justice!", jeering at the coaches of the bishops, or crying out "There goes a Straffordian!". The air was full of rumours that Queen Henrietta Maria and the leaders of the Army were about to take over the country by force. Charles feared for the Queen's life. His French mother-in-law, who was staying at the palace, refused to go to bed she was so frightened.

Only forty-five Lords turned up for the vote. The Act ordering Strafford's death was passed by twenty-six votes to nineteen. Charles, urged by his council, the bishops, and even by Strafford himself to do so, signed his minister's death warrant. He was to blame himself for the rest of his life.

One hundred thousand people crowded Tower Hill to see the execution of "Black Tom the Tyrant". When the executioner held up Strafford's head to the crowds, they chanted: "His head is off! His head is off!" That night bonfires were lit all over London.

Throughout the summer of 1641 Pym and his supporters made the most of their advantage. Acts were passed which ordered that Parliament must meet at least once every three years and could not be dismissed without its own agreement. Ship money could not be levied on inland areas without its consent, and Parliament was to have control of customs duties. The King signed them all in a daze. Archbishop Laud was imprisoned, and later executed.

But not all MPs supported Pym. Many disagreed when he proposed, in the autumn, to abolish bishops. Then Parliament demanded the right to control the army which was being raised to suppress a rising in Ireland. Soon it went further and claimed the right to appoint the King's own council of ministers. About half of Parliament thought that Pym was going too far. It was one thing to prevent a royal dictatorship. It was quite another to establish a parliamentary government and to do away with the need for a king.

Charles, by now, had regained his nerve. He decided he would give up no more of his power. He announced that he would never surrender "his Church, his Army or his friends". Then in one ill-planned move, he threw away all the support he had won.

On 3rd January 1642 the King's Attorney rose to his feet in Parliament and accused Lord Kimbolton and five MPs — Pym, Hampden, Holles, Haslerigg and Strode — of high treason. Next day Charles I, urged on by the Queen, marched down to Parliament, surrounded by four hundred guards. He broke the custom of centuries by marching straight into the House of Commons and demanding that the five members be handed over. No previous king had ever entered the House of Commons. But news of his plans had been "leaked" and the men concerned had left the House by river for the City of London. The frustrated King returned empty-handed to Whitehall Palace.

The next day Charles drove to the Guildhall where he told the Council of the City that he hoped they were not hiding the MPs. All the way along his route crowds swarmed round his carriage shouting, "Privilege of Parliament! Privilege of Parliament!" On 10th January, Charles left Whitehall and took up residence at Hampton Court. He was never to return to London until his trial

In the 17th century, many important scientific discoveries were made, including Newton's theory of gravity, Boyle's chemical theories and Harvey's discovery of the circulation of the blood (below is an illustration from his book).

and execution, seven years later. On 11th January, the five MPs were carried back in triumph to the House of Commons, escorted by City soldiers and armed ships on the Thames.

The failure of Charles I's attempt to seize the five MPs made civil war inevitable for the first time. The Queen fled abroad with her children. Both King and Parliament gave public statements of their position, while beginning to organize their armies. In June 1642 Parliament repeated its demands. All bishops must be removed. The Army and Navy must be controlled by Parliament. The king's ministers must be appointed by Parliament. Parliament must control even the education of royal children. On 22nd August 1642, Charles I raised the royal standard at Nottingham. He called on all his loyal subjects to take up arms in his defence.

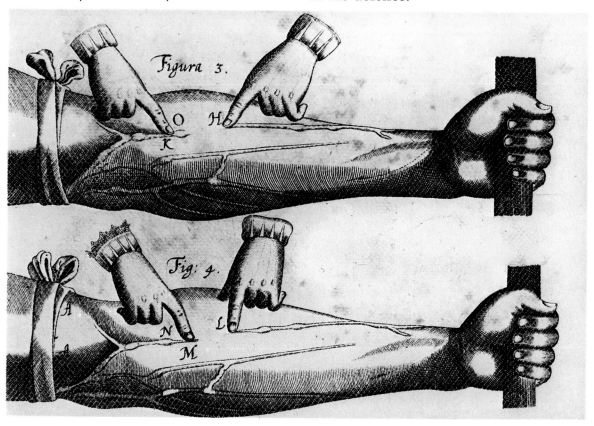

Civil War

The Civil Wars of 1642–1645 and 1648 involved a tiny proportion of the British population. Most of those who felt passionately about the matters in dispute were wealthy. A great many of them lived in the south-east or east of England. The armies who fought would seem small today. Yet the leaders on both sides knew very well the seriousness of the war. Behind the fighting lay one great question: "Who is to rule the country – King or Parliament?"

Both sides had solid support. The King could rely on most of the great landowners, though this was not always the case. The Earl of Bedford, for instance, supported Parliament, and the comman-

der of Parliament's armies when war broke out was the Earl of Essex. The University of Oxford and the leaders of the Church strongly supported Charles I. Parliament had most followers in London (among them were many leading merchants), as well as the Puritans. As for the Scots, both sides knew that if the Scottish armies could be persuaded to fight for them they would be bound to win.

The two groups were known as Royalists and Parliamentarians, or Roundheads and Cavaliers. This was because many of Parliament's supporters wore their hair cut short, while Charles' men had long hair and were thought of as courtly gentlemen, like knights of old (chevaliers).

Parliament had control of London. It was therefore up to the Royalists to advance on the capital quickly and recapture it before it was too late. But first Charles had to recruit more troops. From Nottingham, his armies moved west to Shrewsbury to recruit infantrymen from the Welsh borders. After he had strengthened his army, Charles marched south to London and the two armies met at Edgehill near Warwick on 23rd October 1642.

Each of the armies at the battle of Edgehill contained about 14,000 men. The pattern of the fighting was to be repeated in later battles. The Royalist cavalry, under the command of the

Puritans believed that services should be simple and held in undecorated churches, as the illustration shows. The most important parts of their services were the sermon and the Bible-reading.

King's nephew, Prince Rupert, swept aside all the troops on the left wing of Parliament's forces. Riding with the speed and dash which was to make them famous, they chased their opponents for 15 kilometres across country, looting as much booty from them as they could. But in their absence, the Earl of Essex's cavalry, on the right of his army and in its centre, attacked the King's forces and broke through. The King was very nearly captured and sixty of his bodyguards were killed. At the end of the day neither side could claim victory.

Charles went on to London, and entered Brentford, to the west, on 12th November. Essex marched the London Trained Bands to meet him. These were part-time soldiers, many of whom were teenage apprentices. They had been encouraged to join up by Parliament's decree that any time spent with the Bands counted towards their apprenticeship. It was said that as they marched out of the city, drums beating and colours flying, all the girls from Cheapside to Hammersmith ran out with baskets of baked meats for them.

The Trained Bands outnumbered Charles' forces by two to one. The King retreated, and spent the winter in Oxford. His army was never again to come so close to London.

One of the Parliamentarians at Edgehill was the MP for Cambridge, Oliver Cromwell. He took no part in the battle, but watched the fighting closely. He decided that the Parliamentarians would never win unless they had better troops, so after the battle he went home to East Anglia to see if he could build up a better army. Within a year, his new Eastern Association had 15,000 well-disciplined men, commanded by Sir Thomas Fairfax, the Earl of Manchester, and Cromwell himself.

During the next year, 1643, Charles I tried once more to capture London. He planned to advance on the capital from three directions. The Duke of Newcastle would march south from Yorkshire, while Royalist forces in Cornwall would march up from the south-west. But both were prevented from advancing by soldiers stationed in towns such as Hull, in the north, and Plymouth and Southampton, in the west, who supported Parliament. The garrisons in these towns were brought supplies by the Navy, which had gone over to Parliament at the beginning of the Civil War. The third Royalist army was led by Charles from Oxford. It captured Bristol – the Royalists' greatest triumph of the war – but when Charles tried to march on London, the Earl of Essex's forces stopped him at Newbury.

During the winter John Pym completed an agreement with the Scots, known as the Solemn League and Covenant of 1643. The Scots agreed to enter the Civil War on Parliament's side so long as the English Churches were reformed after the war along the lines of their own Presbyterian Church.

In the summer of 1644 Scottish armies crossed the border and marched on York. Charles sent Prince Rupert to help the Duke of Newcastle's garrison there. Rupert's army met the Parliamentarians at Marston Moor, 15 kilometres to the west of York, on 2nd July 1644. The result was a complete victory for the combined Scottish and Parliamentary armies, who outnumbered the Royalists. Rupert and most of his cavalry escaped, but many infantrymen were killed.

Oliver Cromwell's horsemen from the Eastern Association had been largely responsible for Parliament's victory. That winter he and Sir Thomas Fairfax pushed aside the Earls of Manchester and Essex, who favoured peace talks with the King. Cromwell and Fairfax organized a new army, called the New Model Army, which could be described as the first genuinely British army. Before, armies had been organized by local landlords using whatever men were available in their area. The New Model Army was national, professional and well-disciplined.

When choosing recruits for the Eastern Association, Cromwell had insisted that the officers should be "God-fearing men", which meant Puritans. If possible they should be gentlemen. The horsemen must charge hard, and be trained to realign themselves the moment they broke through the enemy's ranks. (Cromwell had seen what had happened

to Rupert's forces at Edgehill when they failed to do this.) All the soldiers must be well-behaved and sober. There were fines for swearing and drunkenness.

These principles were transferred to the New Model Army. More than half of its 21,000 men were volunteers. They were paid regularly and well equipped with good artillery. They wore uniforms. The infantry wore scarlet tunics, the cavalry brown leather coats. The men sang psalms before battle.

On the 14th June 1645, the King's forces met Parliament's at Naseby, near Market Harborough, in Leicestershire. The Royalists were outnumbered and ill-equipped. Soon,

"there was not a horse or man of the King's army to be seen except the prisoners."

A Parliamentary landowner and his wife pore over battle plans during the Civil War.

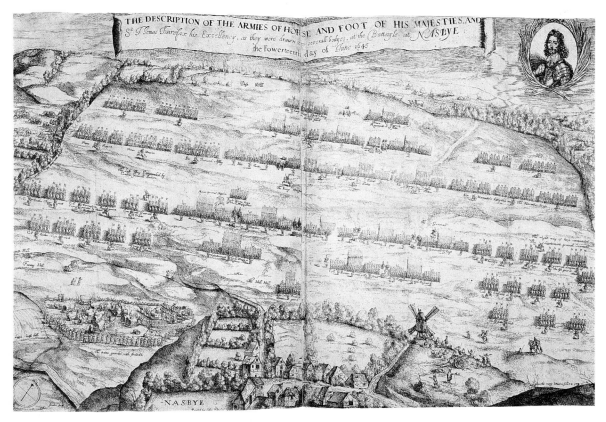

THE DESCRIPTION OF THE ARMIES OF HORSE AND FOOT OF HIS MAJESTIES, AND
S.r Thomas Fairefax his Excellency, as they were drawn in severall bodyes, at the Battayle at NASBYE
the Fowerteenth day of June 1645

NASBYE

Though fighting continued until March 1646, the Civil War was really over after the battle of Naseby. Peace talks began between the King and the Parliamentarians. But the great political and religious issues were still no nearer solution, for the King would not surrender any of his power. He wrote to one of his ministers at the peace talks:

"If you would put my enemies in mind that they are errant knaves and blaspheming dogs it might do some good."

There was disagreement among the Parliamentarians about what to do next. Ever since Charles had left London after his failure to arrest the five MPs in May 1642, Parliament had been practically ruling the country. Its officials had been particularly efficient at raising taxes. They even taxed beer and salt. People

The Parliamentarians confront the Royalists at the Battle of Naseby in 1645, after which peace talks began.

were now paying more taxes than they had ever paid under Charles I and this was unpopular. Most of the money was being spent on the New Model Army, though its soldiers were not up to date with their pay by the end of the war.

Many MPs wanted to disband the Army now that most of the fighting was over. But there were two problems with this. Firstly, an army had to be sent to Ireland to suppress the rising which had started when Strafford left in 1640. Secondly, the New Model Army simply refused to disband until it received its back pay, and until it was convinced that Parliament would not reach an agreement with Charles which would amount to a sell-out of the Parliamentary cause.

The majority of MPs wanted to reach

224

an agreement with Charles to bring back the King but make him more dependent on Parliament for his power. They also wanted to set up a new Church of England, without bishops, whose services would be similar to those used by the Presbyterian Church of Scotland. All people would have to attend this Church.

The Army, whose members were now deeply interested in politics, would have nothing to do with Parliament's plans. They had not fought the Civil War in order to be ruled by a King they did not trust. Nor would they agree to a national compulsory Presbyterian Church. They wanted people to worship God as they liked, so long as their worship was neither Roman nor Church of England.

But except on these two points there was little agreement among the soldiers. One group under Colonel Lilburne, called the Levellers, wanted a democratic system of elections – one man one vote. Others, called the Diggers, wanted all common lands to be returned to the people. They wanted the big estates split up, and only small farmers allowed to farm. There was talk of a free education system for everybody, and even a free health service. The large landowners such as Oliver Cromwell thought that groups like the Levellers and Diggers were wild revolutionaries. But they bided their time, waiting for the right moment to suppress them.

In 1648 Charles I escaped from Hampton Court to Carisbrooke Castle on the Isle of Wight. Here he held secret talks with the Scots, and reached agreement with them. When the New Model Army heard this, Cromwell marched them north to Lancashire. They defeated the Scots at Preston. Royalist risings in Kent and Essex were easily suppressed.

This second Civil War only lasted the summer of 1648.

In August 1648 the Army held a great prayer meeting at Reading. Here it was decided to put "Charles Stuart, that man of blood" on trial for his actions. But in September Parliament reached agreement with Charles. The King was to be restored to the throne with limited power. The agreement horrified Cromwell, who, like most of his officers and men, had become convinced that it was impossible to trust Charles.

On 1st December the Army took over London. A group of soldiers under Colonel Pride marched into the House of Commons and expelled all but a few MPs. (What was left of Parliament, its "rump", became known as the Rump Parliament.) On 23rd December Charles was taken to Windsor Castle. He was to be tried for treason "in the name of the Commons and Parliament assembled, and all the good people". The court was supposed to consist of 135 judges or commissioners, though in fact only fifty-two appeared on the opening day.

When the trial began, in Westminster Hall, the King refused to answer questions put to him by the commissioners and their president, John Bradshaw. He said they had no right to try him.

The commissioners were reluctant to find Charles guilty. But Cromwell reminded them that it had been thought necessary to execute Mary Queen of Scots and get rid of Edward II and Richard II because of the harm they had done the country. Charles, he said, was the "hardest-hearted man on earth". With grim humour, Cromwell went round flicking ink in the commissioners' faces, as he urged them to sign the death warrant. Those who did so became known as the "Regicides" or "King-killers".

Charles I's execution was set for 30th January 1649. A special scaffold draped in black was built outside the banqueting hall of Whitehall Palace so that the King could step straight on to the platform from the hall. It was bitterly cold. The ground was frozen hard. Charles dressed at six o'clock in the morning. He wore two shirts so that he would not shiver and appear frightened when he laid his head on the executioner's block. After he had dressed, he took Holy Communion.

At two o'clock in the afternoon a party of soldiers came for the King. He walked through the banqueting hall between two lines of soldiers, standing shoulder to shoulder. He walked straight on to the scaffold from an open window. Here stood a party of soldiers, three shorthand writers, and the executioner with his assistant. The last two were masked, and disguised with wigs and false beards. Bishop Juxon, who had given Holy Communion to Charles, stayed with him.

The crowds in the packed street were held back from the scaffold by mounted troops. Charles made no attempt to speak to them. He took from his pocket a small piece of paper and spoke to the party on the scaffold.

He said that though the sentence which the commissioners gave him was unjust, he now saw it as God's judgement on him. Remembering how he had signed Strafford's death warrant, he continued: "An unjust sentence that I suffered to take effect is punished now by an unjust sentence on me". Charles then forgave those who had brought him to the scaffold, and turned to the reasons which had brought him there:

"As for the people, truly I desire their liberty and freedom as much as anybody whomsoever; but I must tell you their liberty and freedom consists in having from government those laws by which their life and their goods may be most their own. It is not for having a share in government ... A subject and a sovereign are clear different things ..."[13]

Finally he spoke about his religion:

"I die a Christian according to the profession of the Church of England, as I found it left me by my father ... I have a good Cause and a gracious God; I will say no more."[13]

He laid his head on the executioner's block. The crowd and the troops fell silent. The King made a sign to the executioner, who at one blow severed his head from his body. A man who saw the axe fall wrote that he would remember the sound that broke from the crowd for as long as he lived:

"Such a groan as I never heard before, and desire I may never hear again."[13]

It is easier to say what was wrong with Charles' trial than it is to see what else the Army leaders and Rump Parliament could have done. Charles had very fixed opinions. If he gave away some of his power when he was in trouble, he would only scheme to recover it when his affairs improved. A permanent agreement between King and Parliament would have been impossible.

John Cook, the chief Parliamentary prosecutor at Charles' trial, wrote, shortly before his own execution:

"We are not traitors, nor murderers, nor fanatics but true Christians and good Commonwealth men ... We sought the public good."

Cromwell's Protectorate (1653–1658)

After Charles I's death, Britain became a republic, a country without a king. The Rump Parliament – those MPs who survived Pride's purge – declared that Britain was now a "commonwealth". It was to be ruled by one House of Parliament only. The House of Lords was abolished. The MPs sat all the year round, Christmas Day included – for the Puritans regarded Christmas as a Catholic festival, which they did not recognize. No attempt was made to hold new elections.

The new Commonwealth had many enemies. European governments had been shocked by Charles' execution. All over the Continent, kings were regarded as representatives of God Himself. Ex-ecution of a king was blasphemy. Holland – whose King William II had married Charles I's daughter Mary – as well as France and Spain, declared war on Britain. Prince Rupert had taken to the seas. His warships sailed the Mediterranean and the Atlantic, hunting Commonwealth ships. The Scots were at war with the Commonwealth government; the Irish were rebelling.

At home, the Royalists were not the Commonwealth's only enemy: those MPs who had been purged by Pride awaited the right time for revenge, while the Levellers and Diggers declared that the Army chiefs had betrayed the soldiers' cause. One of the Levellers' leaders, Lieutenant-colonel Sexby, hated Oliver Cromwell so much that he later called on Englishmen to assassinate him in a pamphlet called *Killing is No Murder*.

On its side, the Rump Parliament had a good professional navy under Admiral Blake, which soon cleared the seas of its enemies, and an army now double the size it had been when it had first been raised. It also had a strong leader in Oliver Cromwell.

After the trial of Charles I, Cromwell was accepted as the new ruler of Britain. This moody, dominating landowner had no rival in either Parliament or the Army. The other main Parliamentary leader, Sir Thomas Fairfax, disapproved of Charles' execution and left Parliament. For the next nine years Cromwell found himself surrounded by continual troubles, as he struggled to make the country united and peaceful again after the Civil War.

Cromwell moved first to suppress a rising of the Levellers in the New Model

The executioner's assistant holds up Charles I's head to the crowd. The soldiers control the crowds who packed Whitehall to see the King's execution.

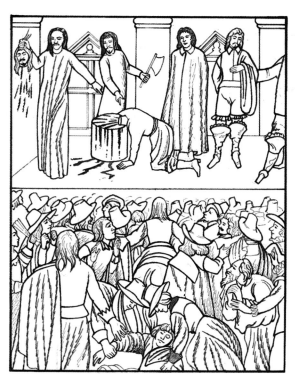

Army. At Burford in Oxfordshire he rounded up the rebels and shot four of their ringleaders. They spent the night before their execution locked up in Burford Church. Their names can still be seen where they scratched them on the church walls. With the suppression of the Levellers, democratic ideas were scarcely to be heard again in Britain for 200 years, until the Chartists in the 19th century again campaigned for one man one vote.

In the summer of 1649 Cromwell took personal charge of the New Model Army's expedition to Ireland. In a swift and ruthless campaign, he completely suppressed the rebellion there. The methods he used were to make his name still hated in Ireland today. As a result of them one third of the Irish population died. From that time onwards the Irish never stopped hating English occupation of their country and looking for ways to become independent.

Two atrocities in particular stayed in Irish memory – those at Drogheda and Wexford. In both cases, Cromwell called on the towns to surrender. They refused. When the Army had captured the towns, they cold-bloodedly killed large numbers of civilians – particularly Roman Catholic priests – as well as soldiers. Cromwell offered no apologies for what his men had done. He believed he had followed the customs of war accepted throughout Europe. Both towns had been given every chance to surrender before the attack. They had refused and must take the consequences of defeat. Cromwell wrote to Parliament a short time after the murders at Drogheda:

"I am persuaded that this is a righteous judgement of God upon those barbarous wretches who have imbrued [stained] their hands in so much innocent blood, and that it will prevent the effusion of blood for the future."

When Cromwell defeated the Scots, he never treated them in such a cruel way. But then the Scots were fellow Protestants, while the "barbarous wretches", the Irish, were Roman Catholics, to whom Cromwell and his fellow Puritans would show no pity.

As we saw in Chapter 30, Strafford's policy of "plantation" had tried to replace Roman Catholic landowners in Ireland with English Protestants. Cromwell's government in Ireland continued this policy. Two thirds of Irish lands were confiscated and given to English landowners and farmers. Just as Elizabeth I had found that giving Irish lands to her courtiers was a cheap way of

Cromwell's troops outside Edinburgh in 1649. The New Model Army was England's first professional army – uniformed (with leather coats and scarlet tunics), disciplined and well paid.

rewarding them, so Cromwell thought an Irish farm was a good way of rewarding his Puritan soldiers. Cromwell's chaplain, Hugh Peter, wrote of Wexford:

"It is a fine spot for some godly [Puritan] congregation where houses and land wait for inhabitants and occupiers."

Roman Catholic worship was now forbidden in Ireland. Priests were to be transported to colonies overseas. Instead they went into hiding.

Next year Cromwell fought in Scotland with the New Model Army. Charles I's twenty-year-old son, Prince Charles, had been declared King of Great Britain in Edinburgh. He hoped to win back the English throne with the help of Scottish troops. But in September 1650 Cromwell won one of his most amazing victories. Although they were outnumbered by two to one, his Army defeated the Scots at Dunbar.

Prince Charles, however, escaped, and in 1651 he invaded England, advancing from Carlisle as far south as Worcester. Here Cromwell won a total victory, capturing half the nobility of Scotland. Charles went on the run until, finally, he reached Brighton and found a boatman to sail him across to France, where he stayed in exile. He never forgot that many of those who risked their lives hiding him during these dark days were Roman Catholics, particularly priests.

After the battle of Worcester, Cromwell made peace with the Scots and had no further trouble from them. He returned to London in triumph. A grateful Parliament gave him Hampton Court to live in. As an MP, Cromwell still regularly attended debates in the House of Commons. But he was growing dissatisfied with the Rump Parliament.

By the end of 1652 the Commonwealth could claim a remarkable set of victories. The Irish rebellion had been suppressed. Scotland had been defeated. France and Spain had sought peace. The Levellers' days were over. The Royalists had to content themselves with secret toasts to the young king "over the water". But many Puritans and soldiers now wanted Cromwell to take action against the Rump.

Parliament had said that it would reform the Church and the law, but nothing had been done. Peace had been made with England's Roman Catholic enemies, France and Spain, but war was still dragging on with the Dutch, who were fellow Protestants. As a result of the war, taxes remained high. Above all, MPs seemed curiously reluctant to call a general election to choose a new Parliament. When at last they did produce their plans, they seemed – to put it mildly – strange. All existing MPs would automatically keep their own seats without any election. In the remaining constituencies, Parliament would judge whether or not a voter's opinions made him suitable to vote. It would also decide whether or not those elected were suitable to sit in Parliament.

These proposals decided Cromwell. Like Charles I and Colonel Pride before him, he brought soldiers into the House of Commons. "Call them in, call them in!" he shouted to one of his generals during a debate in April 1653. The general went out and returned with a group of musketeers. They turned out the Speaker from his chair and ejected the MPs. Cromwell pointed to the mace, the Speaker's symbol of office. "What shall we do with this bauble [toy]?" he asked. "Here, take it away."

So ended the rule of Parliament, in

whose name the King's forces had been defeated and the King himself beheaded.

Yet someone had to govern, and Cromwell was reluctant to become a dictator, relying on the Army to keep him in power. For a few months, Britain was ruled by a new Parliament, elected

serving for a year without pay. Such extremism not only horrified the Army leaders, it also caused fierce disagreements among the MPs themselves. They became deeply divided, and in December 1653 abdicated (gave up) their power.

Cromwell now believed that he had no

not by ordinary voters but by members of the Puritan churches. A hundred and forty men, chosen by their Puritan congregations and agreed by the Army council, assembled in Westminster in the summer of 1653.

Nobody could accuse these men of lacking enthusiasm for reform. Within a few hectic months, they planned to change the Church and the legal system completely. They made it possible for marriages to be held in registry offices. And they proposed that the Army leaders should set an example to the country by

A contemporary engraving of Cromwell expelling the Rump Parliament. The Speaker is surrounded by soldiers. Written on the wall is "This house is to let".

alternative but to become ruler of Britain. He was supported by many of the English people, and by the all-powerful Army (now 70,000 strong). He was declared Lord Protector, and held the position until his death five years later. His rule was known as the Protectorate.

Cromwell genuinely tried to treat his enemies in England fairly. In 1655, when there was a Royalist plot to overthrow him, known as Penruddock's Rising, he treated his Royalist opponents generously. He allowed local church congregations to elect their own clergymen and leaders. Roman Catholics were quietly tolerated in England. So were supporters of the Church of England so long as they did not use the *Book of Common Prayer* for their services. Cromwell also allowed the Jews back into Britain. For more than 350 years, no Jew had been allowed into the country.

When a group of Christians called the Society of Friends (also known as the Quakers) were being persecuted, their leader George Fox asked to see the Lord Protector. Fox was taken from prison to Whitehall, where for an hour the two men discussed different interpretations of Christianity. When the interview ended, Cromwell shook Fox's hand and released him from prison. He said to Fox as they parted: "I beseech you to consider that you might be wrong."

Parliaments were called during the Protectorate, though Cromwell dismissed them in much the same way as Charles I had done. At one point Parliament even urged him to become king himself – its views had altered strangely since Charles' time. But Cromwell would have none of it.

The most unpopular thing about Cromwell's Protectorate was that he tried to make people obey "godly" – in other words, Puritan – laws. He never tried to ban public amusements, but his officials kept a close eye on race meetings, largely because they were known to be places where Royalists met together. As in the New Model Army, swearing, drunkenness and cockfighting could be punished by death, though in fact no one was ever convicted. Sunday was strictly observed. No shops or public houses could open, and no work could be done. Even "vain walking" was not allowed.

However, many justices of the peace disagreed with these laws and did not enforce them. In desperation Cromwell decided, for a few months, to divide the country up into districts. Each was to be supervised by a major-general, who would strictly enforce the "godly" laws. He soon abandoned this – the only example in British history of the country being directly ruled by the Army – but it did not stop his enemies talking as if Cromwell's rule was always military.

Although the Army was gradually reduced in size, taxes remained high, chiefly to pay for the country's defences. Whereas Charles I's government was spending £600,000 a year in the mid-1630s, the Protector's was spending £2,000,000.

Britain's military power under Cromwell came to be feared in Europe. After his death, Englishmen, whatever their political or religious opinions, came to look back on Cromwell's foreign policy with admiration. Peace was made with Holland on good terms. Jamaica became a British colony. In 1658 – 100 years after Mary Tudor's loss of Calais – the Army won Dunkirk from Spain. To many people this success seemed a symbol of the power of a Protestant leader compared with the weakness of a Catholic. One took Britain out of Europe, the other led it back in.

On 3rd September 1658 Cromwell died. (The day was the one he thought of as his "lucky day", for on it he had defeated the Scots at Dunbar, and Prince Charles at Worcester.) At the time of his death his power as Lord Protector was unchallenged. The Royalists had given up hope of overthrowing his government. Prince Charles was wandering from one European country to another, permanently bankrupt.

Yet within eighteen months, the Protectorate system fell apart. Oliver Cromwell had been a successful ruler not only because of his forceful character, but because he was accepted by various important groups in England. To Parliament he was a fellow MP and landowner. To the country squires – the local rulers of England – he was a fellow squire. To the Puritans he was a devout man. To the soldiers, he was not only their unbeaten general but their champion. So long as he was Protector they would remain members of a highly respected and well-paid profession.

But Oliver's son, Richard Cromwell, held no such position. He was neither well respected by the Army nor well liked by Parliament. Above all he appeared to have no wish to govern. He became Protector, but by the spring of 1659 he had abdicated.

After that there were further rapid changes of government. The Rump – nineteen years after it had first been elected – was restored (or, at least, those of the MPs who were still alive). Then the Army disbanded it again. The Army itself split up into sections led by Generals Lambert, Fleetwood and Monk. Finally General Monk, who was in charge of the forces occupying Scotland, marched his soldiers down to London, which he took over in early 1660.

Monk knew that, for the moment, the Army and only the Army could keep law and order in the country. But he was a professional soldier and, unlike earlier leaders of the New Model Army, he did not want the Army to be permanently involved in governing the country. He organized new parliamentary elections.

The new Parliament issued an invitation to Prince Charles, who was in Holland, to return to his kingdom. This might not have happened if Charles had shown signs of behaving like his father. But he promised to be tolerant in religion and to share political power with Parliament. On May 1660 he landed at Dover, knelt down and kissed the stony beach. Looking around him at the cheering crowds, Charles was heard to wonder why, if he was so popular, he need ever have gone on his travels in the first place.

Oliver Cromwell's death mask. By the time he died Cromwell was virtually King. He was the only man whom soldiers, Puritans and Parliamentarians supported. His son Richard succeeded him, but Britain soon became a monarchy again.

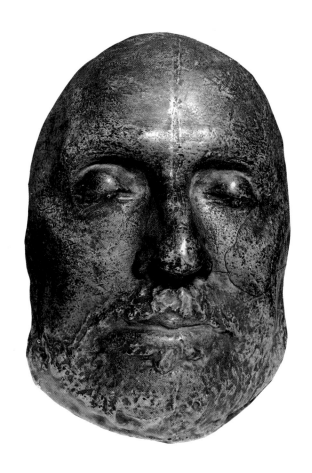

Plague and Fire

The London which Charles II entered, dawdling deliberately on his way from Dover so that he could ride into his capital on his thirtieth birthday in May 1660, was one of the wonders of the northern world. Generation after generation, it had grown in size. By 1660 the population was well over half a million. (Paris had 350,000 citizens.) The populations of York, Bristol and Norwich – rivals for second place – were about 25,000. London had more citizens than the next biggest fifty towns in England combined.

London was still dominated by the Thames, as it had been ever since Roman times. The great houses of the nobility, like Whitehall Palace itself, were built with gardens running down to the river. They had their own private quays. The boatmen, like their boats, proudly displayed their masters' colours as they rowed to and fro. Two such houses were Savoy House, looted by the peasants in their revolt of 1381, when John of Gaunt lived there, and Somerset House, built at the time of the destruction of the monasteries by Protector Somerset from the wealth of Westminster Abbey.

The roads were still as narrow, overhung and filthy as they had been in medieval times. Progress along them, through a tangle of coaches, carriages, carts and sedan chairs (a closed box carried on poles by two servants, one in front and one behind) was slow. So, if you lived anywhere near the river and were in a hurry, you walked down one of the many narrow streets that ran down to the Thames, and hired one of the boatmen. They tied their boats to the

Many Londoners preferred to travel by boat rather than along the crowded streets. Great houses had their own riverside quays, while boatmen offered a taxi service.

quayside and seem to have been available at any time of the day or night.

But for all its great size London was still a town in one piece. Hyde Park, where the New Model Army camped before its occupation of London, was well outside the city's earthwork defences during the Civil Wars. So were Paddington, Tottenham, Islington and Bethnal Green. The road between Kensington and London was so bad that when a coach overturned one winter in one of its deep ruts, a passenger was drowned. When a private messenger service carrying letters across the capital was widened to include Chelsea in the west and Hampstead and Highgate in the north, it was thought remarkable that such outlying villages could be included in a London service.

Charles II's London, like that of Edward III, had two great daily enemies – plague and fire. Plagues, otherwise known as "the sweating sickness", had been common during James I's reign.

233

The poet John Donne, who was Dean of St Paul's Cathedral, wrote of the funeral bell tolling ceaselessly for victims of the plague. No important circumstances had changed since the Black Death in the 14th century. The streets were just as dirty and the water supply as scarce. The fleas which spread the plague were now more plentiful, for the black rats who carried them came in the holds of ships trading from Europe, and London had become the largest trading port in northern Europe. But one thing distinguishes the Great Plague of 1665 from the Black Death of 1349 – the diary of the civil servant, courtier, man-about-London and gossip, Samuel Pepys.

Pepys kept a diary which describes his daily life during the 1660s in great detail. The first entry in his diary which mentions the plague is for 7th June 1665:

"The hottest day that ever I felt in my life. This day, much against my will, I did in Drury Lane see two or three houses marked with a red cross upon the doors, and 'Lord, have mercy upon us!' writ there."[14]

No method of curing the plague was known. The parish authorities could therefore only rely on isolating the plague victims. If a death had occurred in a house two "searchers of the dead", generally old women, would be sent to it. They would decide the cause of death. If the corpse had died of the plague, it was carried at night in a cart to a special plague pit in a nearby field. Here all the bodies were thrown together and covered with lime. The drivers of the carts performed a dangerous service and were well paid. As they toured the streets they rang a handbell and cried, "Bring out your dead!"

If someone in a house was certified as sick of the plague, he or she was taken to the parish pest house. This was a small hospital of sorts, often merely a shed, with some beds in it. There would be a doctor and some nurses. Here the patient lay until he or she recovered or died.

An infected person's house was shut up for forty days; the occupants were forced to stay there, and no one was allowed in. Food and water were left on the doorstep. Sometimes fires were lit in the streets to purify the air. Because they were supposed to be carriers all dogs in the area were killed. If you fell ill, the odds against recovery seem to have been about three to one. On 11th June Pepys noted:

A Dutch trading ship docks in London.

"I walked out of doors a little to show … my new suit. I saw poor Dr Burnett's door shut; he hath, I hear, gained great good will among his neighbours; for he discovered it himself first and caused himself to be shut up of his own accord: which was very handsome."[14]

Dr Burnett was Pepys' doctor. He died of the plague.

On 21st June Pepys noted that many people were leaving London. On 22nd June he sent his mother to the country. On 29th June he noted that the King and court were packing up. On 5th July he despatched Mrs Pepys with two maids down river to Woolwich. On 19th July he recorded that at Westminster the dead were being buried in the open fields. The plague pits were full. A week later the plague was in his own parish.

Although most of his friends left London, Pepys stayed on. The streets were empty. Pepys' curiosity was so great that he even walked to Moorfields to see if he could see a corpse being carried to the plague pit, but he had no such luck. The official death toll for the week before 31st August was 6000, Pepys wrote. Soon it was to reach 7000 – one thousand a day – and then slowly decline. November frosts cut the weekly death toll to 600. On 31st December Pepys noted that "the plague is abated [died down] almost to nothing".

The total death toll is believed to have been about 70,000, though nobody can be certain. Many other parts of England were stricken, but London's suffering was the worst. Such plagues, known as bubonic plagues from the "buboes" (boils) which appeared on the bodies of the victims, never returned to England. London was largely rebuilt after next year's Great Fire. Streets became wider,

A red cross, sign of the Plague.

lighter and cleaner. The water supply was improved. Most important of all, brown rats migrated into Britain and drove out the black rats who spread the plague.

Fires were part of town life. One of the main duties of the nightwatchmen who toured the streets of each town parish was to report a fire. The only hope of putting out a fire in crowded streets of wooden houses, many of which were still thatched, was to detect it early. Fire-fighting equipment consisted of pumps, tanks and buckets. If you lived close to the river, neighbours would form a human chain and pass full buckets from the river to the scene of the fire. The first firemen were London watermen, appointed in 1658 by one of the first insurance firms. Once fire caught hold of a house, the only way to prevent it spreading was by blowing up all the houses round about with gunpowder.

Pepys was again in London during the first week of September next year, 1666. He was wakened at three in the morning on 2nd September by one of his maids:

"Jane called us up about three in the morning, to tell us of a great fire she saw in the City. So I rose, and slipped on my night-gown and went to her window ... I thought it far enough off; and so went to bed again, and to sleep."[14]

The fire began in a baker's shop in Pudding Lane to the east of London Bridge and spread with appalling speed. It had been a hot summer and the flames were spread by a high wind. When, later the same morning, Pepys walked to the Tower and climbed up on its walls to see what was going on, he noticed that houses on both ends of London Bridge were on fire. (The bridge had houses all the way across it on both sides, like a London street.) Pepys walked through the city to Whitehall Palace. The King told him to take a message to the Lord Mayor of London. He was to pull down all the houses surrounding the area of the fire. Pepys found the Mayor and delivered the order. In the evening he took a boat again on the Thames:

"All over the Thames, with one's face in the wind, you were almost burned with a shower of fire-drops ... When we could endure no more upon the water, we to a little alehouse on the Bankside ... it being darkish, we saw the fire as only one entire arch of fire from this to the other side of the bridge, and in a bow up the hill for an arch of above a mile long: it made me weep to see it. The churches and houses on fire and flaming; and a horrid noise the flames made, and the cracking of houses of their ruin."[14]

On 4th September St Paul's Cathedral on Ludgate Hill, which had towered over the capital for centuries, caught fire. The lead from the roof streamed down dangerously and the building was completely destroyed. Pepys lost hope. He dug a pit in his garden and in it stored his papers and valuables – especially his beloved Parmesan cheese and wine. Next morning he took a boat down river to Woolwich with his wife, who had charge of his gold (valued at £2,350 in money of that time). There he settled her in a friend's house, telling her never to leave the room where the gold was stored. Then he returned home.

There he found, to his delight, that all the houses between the fire at its easternmost point and his street had been destroyed. The men had been under particular orders to clear that area because it was near the Tower, where quantities of gunpowder were stored. It was probably fear of the great explosions which would follow the burning of the Tower that saved Pepys' house.

About five-sixths of the old city had been destroyed in the Great Fire: 13,000 houses were burned and 100,000 people made homeless. The capital was quickly rebuilt, though now in brick and stone. There were more tiles on the roofs, and wider streets. The new city had drains in it and a system of refuse collection. Water was now piped from the Thames to the streets through wooden pipes. Fire plugs set into the pipes could be opened with a key which the parish officer kept, and water would then – it was hoped – gush out. A waterworks was built in Chelsea to serve west London.

Sir Christopher Wren was given the job of rebuilding St Paul's Cathedral. His domed cathedral, modelled on St Peter's in Rome, took forty years to build. It managed to survive the next great fire of London, in 1941, when German bombers set fire to most of the City round it.

The rebuilding of London was done

quickly – too quickly. Many of the plans to improve the crowded town were forgotten in the rush. In particular Wren's plan for allowing a large open space around St Paul's, stretching down to the river, was forgotten. The cathedral was partly hidden by the houses, shops and offices which crowded round about it, up to its very steps. After the Second World War, when once again the City was rebuilt after destruction by fire, no attempt was made to revive Wren's plan for an open space. Such a space would have made it possible for observers to stand back and admire his masterpiece. Daniel Defoe, in his *Tour of England and Wales*, written fifty years after the Great Fire, commented:

"Private property on this occasion, as it does on most others, got the better of . . . Public Spirit."

Part of Hollar's engraving of The Great Fire of London, seen from Southwark, south of the river. St Paul's Cathedral was destroyed, but the Tower of London, near Samuel Pepys' house, was spared.

Charles II and the Popish Plot

Shortly before he returned to England to become Charles II, Prince Charles had issued a simple statement of his policies. In it he made clear that he did not plan a return to the 1630s, when Charles I had ruled without Parliament.

The laws of 1641 which Charles I had signed were not overturned by his son. Taxes had to be raised through Parliament. Parliament could not be dismissed except with its own consent. Charles II, like his father, insisted on controlling the Army and appointing ministers himself. He was also determined that the Church of England should continue in its traditional form, governed by bishops. But for the rest, he was happy to work with Parliament. The elections of 1660 had produced a large majority of Royalist MPs. The House of Lords was restored, along with the Church. Charles II, who was an optimist by nature, had good reason to foresee a long period of political calm. After his dreary years of exile, he thought he could settle down to enjoy himself. His hopes were not fulfilled.

At first things went smoothly. Charles, who did not bear grudges against his opponents, announced that he would offer them a general pardon. Parliament was not so generous. It proposed the execution of all those who had signed Charles I's death warrant (the Regicides). Twenty-eight of them were to meet a traitor's death by hanging, drawing and quartering. Ten did so. Charles reprieved the remainder and returned them to prison. Cromwell's remains were taken from their tomb in Westminster Abbey, hanged for a day on the traitors' gallows at Tyburn and buried in an unmarked pit. The New Model Army

was paid off and disbanded.

The religious differences of the past remained. Roman Catholics were persecuted, though Charles tried to help them. (His mother Henrietta Maria, now back in England, was a devout Roman Catholic. And Charles never forgot how Catholics had saved his life after the battle of Worcester and smuggled him out of the country).

In 1661 Parliament passed the Corporation Act, which said that all members of town councils had to take Holy Communion in the Church of England. This meant that all Puritan councillors – such as those who had run London during the Civil Wars – had to resign.

Puritan clergymen had gained the respect of Londoners. Many of them stayed in London during the Plague to care for their congregations, while many Church of England clergymen fled the city. Puritan churches became much better attended. Parliament passed the Five Mile Act in 1665 to try to make the life of a Puritan minister as difficult as possible. No Puritan minister was supposed to live – or visit – within 5 miles (or 8 kilometres) of a town.

The Society of Friends – the Quakers – were singled out for especially cruel treatment. The Quakers were disliked because they refused to take part in war – they were the first pacifists. Thirteen hundred of them were imprisoned following a special Act of 1662.

Once again there were arguments between King and Parliament over taxes. The King had hoped for an income of about £1,200,000 a year from Parliament. He and his advisers regarded this as the bare minimum needed to govern the state in peace time. Parliament refused to let Charles have more than about £800,000 a year.

Then, in 1664, the country drifted into another war with the Dutch. They were rivals over the slave trade from west Africa, and over colonies in North America. The two sides were equally matched at first, but the English fleet grew steadily weaker. Plague and the Fire of London weakened English resistance, while Parliament's grants of money were so small that ships were laid up through lack of funds and crews unpaid.

One of the most humiliating events in English history occurred in 1667. The

way – the Dutch were generous. The English were given the lands at the mouth of the Hudson River in North America which were previously Dutch. New Amsterdam became New York, named after Charles II's brother, James, the Duke of York.

After the disgrace of the *Royal Charles*, the King decided that things could not continue like this. He cruelly dismissed his chief adviser, the Earl of Clarendon, who had brought about his return to the throne and served him in day-to-day affairs of government as loyally as William Cecil had served Elizabeth. Using his sister Henrietta

Dutch sailed up the Thames estuary, and turned south into the River Medway. They brushed aside what defences there were, broke the chain across the entrance to Chatham harbour and sailed in. After putting ashore a few raiding parties, who caused some damage, they attached their tow lines to the deck of the royal flagship *Royal Charles*. They then set sail for Holland, where they moored the *Royal Charles* off Amsterdam and invited the Dutch public, on payment of a small fee, to come on board and inspect the enemy's most famous man-of-war.

Soon afterwards a peace treaty, known as the Treaty of Breda, was signed between England and Holland. Surprisingly – after the way English weakness had been shown in the Med-

Dutch ships sailing up the Medway.

who lived at the French court as a go-between, he arranged a secret treaty with King Louis XIV. The French agreed to give Charles money, and even, if necessary, some French troops with which to suppress any trouble in Britain. In return Charles would announce that the laws against Roman Catholics were repealed, and help France in a planned invasion of Holland.

When news of the secret terms leaked out, there was as much uproar in London as there had been at the time of Strafford's execution. English fears of Roman Catholics and the French blazed up again. Had not Guy Fawkes and his cronies tried to blow up Parliament?

Had not French spies started the Plague by poison and tried to burn down London a few years ago?

In 1672 Charles dismissed Parliament and announced his Declaration of Indulgence, which abolished the laws against Roman Catholics. Many people were convinced that the King was about to become a Roman Catholic dictator, like Louis XIV who was ruling France at this time without a Parliament and did almost what he liked. But Charles II was not Charles I. Faced with such determined opposition he withdrew the Declaration and recalled Parliament. He even signed the Test Act in 1673. By this Act, no man could hold any position in the government of the country – or even go to university – unless he took "the Test". To take the test, you had to take the bread and wine of Holy Communion regularly in the Church of England and produce a signed certificate to show you had done so. No Roman Catholic could possibly do this. James, Duke of York, who was a devout Roman Catholic, gave up his position as head of the Navy. Clifford, Charles' chief minister, committed suicide.

From 1673 to 1678 Charles II cooperated with Parliament. The King and his Portuguese wife, Catherine of Braganza, had no children, so the Duke of York was heir to the throne. Charles agreed to the marriage of the Duke of York's daughter Mary to William of Orange, the Dutch king, who was now regarded as the "Protestant champion" of Europe. Then suddenly both King and Parliament were caught up in the explosion of the "Popish Plot".

For several years two men, Titus Oates and Israel Tonge, had been trying to convince anyone who would listen to them that a Roman Catholic group at court was plotting with the French to overthrow the King and Parliament and put James, Duke of York, on the throne. James would then rule like Charles I, without Parliament, and force everybody to become Roman Catholics. So far no one had taken the idea seriously because of the untrustworthy character of Titus Oates himself.

Oates was a man on the make. He had been a clergyman in the Church of England, and had pretended to be a Doctor of Divinity which he was not. He had been convicted of perjury (lying when on oath) in 1675. And he had spent some time – nobody knew how much – at a college for Roman Catholic priests in Europe. There, he said, he had heard all about the plot.

In autumn 1678 Oates and Tonge were called in front of the Privy Council and cross-examined. Charles himself questioned Oates and caught him out in some lies. This convinced him that nothing Oates said could be believed. But the council was not so sure.

Then one of London's best-known magistrates, Sir Edmund Berry Godfrey, who had been hearing Oates' accusations, was murdered. His body was found in a ditch by the Hampstead road and there was candle wax on his clothes – a sure sign, it was said, that Catholics were responsible. (It was generally believed that Catholics were always burning candles to honour their saints.)

Lord Chief Justice Scroggs, urged on by the House of Commons, sentenced twenty-one Catholics to death. Parliament gave Oates the title "Saviour of the Nation" along with apartments in Whitehall, a salary of £1200 a year and an armed bodyguard. The capital buzzed with reports of French spies, and of French troops secretly landing in the

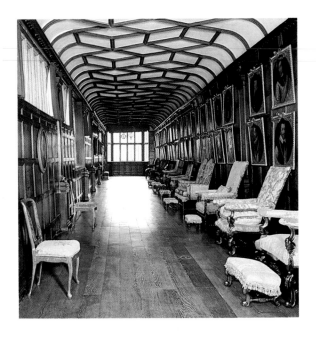

The long portrait gallery at Knole, Sevenoaks, Kent. This 15th-century house with its great deer park was greatly improved and extended in the 17th century.

Thames estuary to advance on London.

The government was now dominated by the Earl of Shaftesbury. He had been Chancellor of the Exchequer and Lord Chancellor, but Charles had dismissed him early in the 1670s. Shaftesbury believed passionately in a strong Parliament. In the autumn of 1678 Charles' chief minister, Danby, was sent to the Tower. Shaftesbury demanded that the Duke of York be removed altogether from Charles' government, and excluded from ever becoming king.

At this point, Charles II took his stand. He would not see Danby go to the executioner's block, as Charles I had been forced to see Strafford executed. And although he did not believe his brother James would be a good king — he felt he had no political commonsense — he saw him as his only rightful heir. He dismissed Parliament and called for new elections.

Right through 1680, London raged. Many innocent men, chiefly Catholics, were executed for treason. Crowds marched through the London streets, carrying images of the Pope. Shaftesbury put pressure on the small minority of wealthy men who had the vote to support him in the elections. Charles bided his time, and waited for Shaftesbury to go too far. This he did when he named the Duke of Monmouth as the next King of England.

The Duke of Monmouth, aged thirty, was Charles' handsome and popular illegitimate son by an Englishwoman, Lucy Walters, who had been at Charles' court in Holland when he was in exile. Charles himself was very fond of him but sent him at once into exile when Shaftesbury tried to make him his heir.

Parliament then proposed a bill to exclude his brother James from the royal succession, and Charles returned to the ways of his grandfather and father. He dismissed Parliament and decided to rule without it for a while. The dismissal was shrewdly timed. The day afterwards, the first instalment of the money promised by Louis XIV arrived. Overseas trade was prospering and customs duties provided sufficient taxes for Charles to rule England, with secret French money, for the next few years. Shaftesbury and Monmouth, who had defiantly returned from exile, fled abroad. Danby was released. It was left to James, when he became king, to take revenge on Titus Oates. He was twice whipped through the streets of London, "roaring", it was said, "like a bull" and imprisoned.

In 1685 Charles II died. He had outwitted his enemies and died peacefully (a last-minute convert to the Roman Catholic faith) in his bed.

The End of the Dictator-Kings

James II became king at a time when royal power was stronger than in any period since Elizabeth's reign. Within three years he had been forced to flee to France, where he later died.

James' reign opened with a meeting of Parliament in 1685. Although he was known to be a devout Roman Catholic, James promised to maintain the Church of England in its present state, and this satisfied both Houses of Parliament. The MPs showed their confidence in the new king by letting him have all the money from customs to spend as he wished for the rest of his life. Customs duties formed a large proportion of the taxes needed to govern the country. No Stuart king had ever been in so strong a position.

A few months later, the Duke of Monmouth landed in Dorset to lead a rebellion against James. Monmouth believed that people would want to get rid of a Roman Catholic king, but his past popularity had made him overconfident. People did not flock to his banner of rebellion as he hoped and James' army had little difficulty in defeating his troops – many of whom were armed only with scythes and pikes – at the battle of Sedgemoor.

Monmouth broke down and knelt at his uncle's feet, begging him to spare his life. James kicked him away contemptuously. Monmouth was beheaded and his supporters rounded up. A hundred and fifty men were hanged and eight hundred more were transported as slaves to work on the plantations in the West Indies.

James' easy victory made him too sure of himself. He immediately asked Parliament to give him special sums of money to pay for his victorious army of 20,000 men, who were now camped on Hounslow Heath outside London. He had to keep them there, he said, in case other rebels followed Monmouth. He also proposed the immediate repeal of the Test Act. Parliament had seemed likely to give James little trouble, but it turned down both his suggestions. He dismissed it. Parliament was never to meet again during his reign.

James then set out on the familiar Stuart road of government by king alone. By appointing a well-known Roman Catholic, Sir Edward Hales, as Governor of Dover Castle, he simply ignored the Test Act. He then began steadily to increase the number of Catholics in important positions both in government and in the Army.

James knew that Puritans had been as unfairly treated by the governments of Charles I and Charles II as Roman Catholics. Although he himself had persecuted them when he was governing Scotland during Charles' reign, he was prepared to help them now. In return, he hoped to count on their support if it was needed. In 1687 he announced, in the Declaration of Indulgence, that all Acts which in any way harmed either English Roman Catholics or Puritans were cancelled. By 1688 three-quarters of the local justices of the peace – the magistrates who did so much of the government in each town and village – had been dismissed. In their place Catholic and Puritan justices were appointed.

These actions horrified the local squires and merchants who were the day-to-day rulers of the country. Not only was there still strong prejudice against Catholics, but James was altering the whole nature of the country's religion and government without consulting Parliament. Once again people feared that the King was going to become a dictator.

A group of seven bishops in the Church of England announced their opposition to James' policies and advised their clergy not to read the Declaration of Indulgence to their congregations, although they were required by law to do so. The bishops were put on trial; they attacked the King for ignoring the Test Act and other Acts and so claiming to be above the law of the land. They also promised to use their influence to bring about toleration of Puritans in the future, once Parliament was recalled. The judges declared them not guilty. The cheers of the London crowds – even, it was reported, of the soldiers on Hounslow Heath – should have alerted James to the dangers ahead for him.

Shortly before the verdict in the bishops' trial was announced, James' second wife, Mary of Modena, gave birth to a baby boy. She and James had been married fifteen years without children, and it had been assumed that they would never have any. For that reason, many of the influential men who feared James' policies had been quietly waiting for his death, when his daughter by his first marriage, Mary, with her "Protestant champion" husband William, would take over.

But now all that was changed. With the birth of a Catholic male heir, England might be ruled by Roman Catholic dictator-kings for ever. A small group of leading Englishmen wrote to William of Orange in Holland and asked him to invade Britain.

On 5th November 1688, William landed at Torbay in south Devon with an army of 24,000 men. The day – that of the Gunpowder Plot – was carefully chosen. It reminded English people of what they had to fear from Roman Catholics. William said only that he had been asked to supervise free elections for a free Parliament. He said nothing about the overthrow of James, who was still the rightful king.

Fortunately, there was no need for fighting. As William marched slowly towards London, James marched his army to Salisbury Plain to meet him. There he learned that the Commander of the army, John Churchill (later Duke of Marlborough), had deserted to join William. So had James' second daughter by his first marriage, Anne. James returned to London and secretly boarded a boat for France. He was stopped in the Thames estuary by Kentish fishermen, and returned in shame to London. Here William was already in occupation, preventing riots and maintaining order. He provided James with a group of Dutch guards who escorted him to France. James II was never seen in England again.

After James' flight, William and Mary were declared joint rulers. During their reign (William III was king from 1689 to 1701, but Mary II died in 1694) a series of Acts were passed, known as the Revolution Settlement. Between them they established by law a number of rights on which the people of Britain have come to rely ever since.

One of these, the Habeas Corpus Act, had first been passed in Charles II's time in 1679. Kings and queens had for centuries imprisoned their enemies without trial if they did not have enough evidence against them to charge them with any crime. They often left them in prison for years. Under the Act – *habeas corpus* means "you must have the body" – people had to be arrested by a warrant giving reasons for their arrest. They must then quickly be brought to trial.

The Bill of Rights (1689) laid down that no Roman Catholic could become King or Queen of Britain. Nor could a British king or queen marry a Catholic. (This remains the law today.) The Bill also said that future monarchs must no longer simply ignore the law and claim to be above it, as James II had done. Kings and queens must obey the law, like everyone else. Nor were they to raise taxes without Parliament's consent. Under the Mutiny Act (1689), Parliament had to decide every year whether to go on keeping an army in peace time.

Under the Toleration Act (1689), Puritans were free to worship as they chose, though they could not be appointed to responsible positions in government or attend universities. Roman Catholics were still not allowed to worship freely, though in practice the authorities increasingly left them alone.

By the Act of Settlement (1701), judges could not be dismissed because the government disapproved of their verdicts. In 1695 the royal power of censorship of the press was quietly dropped and has never returned.

Everyone who hoped to be noticed at court or in high society in the 17th century had to be sure to dress in the latest fashion.

These Acts ended a long battle for power which had stretched back to Tudor times. Kings could no longer rule as they liked; they could now only govern if Parliament agreed with their policies.

In 1689 James II landed in Ireland with a French army, calling on the Catholic Irish to rebel in support of him. Not surprisingly, many of them did so. James' army of Frenchmen and Irishmen then besieged the Protestant garrison at Londonderry. During the 105 days of the siege, 15,000 men, women and children starved to death before the English fleet came to their rescue. But the next year, William himself landed in Ireland. At the battle of the Boyne, James' forces were utterly defeated. James fled back to France where, in 1701, he died.

The treatment of the Irish by their English conquerors now grew even worse. Half a million hectares of land belonging to Catholics – particularly in Ulster in the north – were confiscated and given to Protestant English or Scots as a reward for their services to William of Orange. Ever since, the descendants of these "planters" have been known as Orangemen. Roman Catholic priests were forbidden to hold services or go about their duties and no Catholic could carry arms or teach in an Irish school.

William III's life work was to defend his native Holland against Louis XIV's France. Over and over again, the French, who had the greatest army in Europe, threatened to overrun Holland. But they never managed to do so, any more than the Spanish before them. In taking over the British crown, William had gained the support of the British Army and Navy in his battle against France. From 1689 to 1697 British troops fought alongside the Dutch, while British and French ships clashed in the Channel.

After William's death in 1701, James II's younger daughter, Anne, carried on the wars against France. Under her great general, the Duke of Marlborough, British armies in Europe won a number of victories against France, of which the battle of Blenheim, in 1704, was the most remarkable. It seemed as if the days of Agincourt had returned.

As we have seen, English governments were always afraid that the Scots would take advantage of an English war with France to invade England. Now it was decided to remove this problem, by uniting England and Scotland. Such a union had been dreamed about by far-sighted individuals for centuries, but the hostility of ordinary people on both sides had prevented it. Even when the Act of Union was signed in 1707, many doubted if it would last.

Under the Act, all customs barriers between the two countries were removed and there was to be a common currency. The Scottish parliament at Edinburgh was closed down and Scottish MPs sat in the House of Commons at Westminster. But the Presbyterian Church of Scotland continued as the national Church, with Queen Anne at its head, and Scottish law continued to apply in Scotland, as it still does today.

In the 18th century, the Scots rebelled in support of James II's son, James Edward, and later, his grandson Charles (Bonnie Prince Charlie), in an attempt to win back Scotland and England for the Stuarts. Their so-called Jacobite risings – in 1715 and 1745 – failed. The battle of Culloden ended the 1745 rebellion once and for all. The brutal English occupation of the Highlands under the Duke of Cumberland afterwards was long and bitterly remembered by the Scots.

England in the 18th Century

The final success of Parliament in its long battle with the King led, in the 18th century, to a time when Britain was governed by its country gentlemen and rich merchants. Although the King retained important political powers – such as the right to appoint members of the government and to control Parliamentary elections – there was no possibility of a return to the dictator-kings. Moreover, the new line of kings, the Hanoverians, started by George I, had no wish to challenge the power of Parliament as the Stuarts had done.

Queen Anne had died childless in 1714, and George – who was Elector (king) of a German state, Hanover – was the next in line. He was James I's great-grandson and a Protestant. He was fifty-four and could not speak English when he took the throne. Neither he nor the later Hanoverian kings – George II (1727–1760), George III (1760–1820) and George IV (1820–1830) – were popular.

Just as the sign or symbol of the feudal system was the castle, the typical image of 18th-century Britain was the great house. Great country houses like the Duke of Marlborough's Blenheim Palace at Woodstock, near Oxford, or Houghton Hall in Norfolk, where Sir Robert Walpole, Britain's Prime Minister in the 1720s and 1730s, lived, were worlds of their own. Local farmers paid their rents to such noblemen or their bailiffs. On the noble's own farms – the home farms, as they were called – the latest agricultural methods were tried out.

In the medieval three-field system, as we have seen, one field was always left fallow (unfarmed) every three years. Thus the goodness was restored to the field. For a long time, however, people had been trying to think of ways which avoided such a waste of productive land.

Heaveningham Hall in Suffolk is a typical 18th-century great house, with its lake and huge grounds.

This contemporary painting by Thomas Weaver portrays local farmers inspecting Robert Bakewell's famous rams.

Jethro Tull wrote a book called *The New Horse-Hoeing Husbandry*, in which he described methods he had seen at work in French vineyards which made a fallow period unnecessary. He invented a horse-drawn hoe which penetrated deeply into the ground while crops were growing, so that the roots were kept moist and the weeds destroyed. He also invented the horse-drawn seed-drill. Now the old wasteful method of broadcast sowing was ended. Seeds were sown in straight lines so that hoeing could take place in between, and covered up so the birds did not eat them. The gain in production was staggering.

The Dutch had started to use root-crops, such as swedes and turnips. These could be grown on land instead of leaving it fallow, because they restored fertility to the soil. Even more important, they could be stored during the winter and fed to the animals. Now, at last, it was no longer necessary to slaughter the animals at Christmas time. An 18th-century Foreign Secretary, Lord Townshend, who became known as "Turnip Townshend", particularly encouraged farmers to use root-crops.

The supply of sufficient winter food made the careful breeding of animals possible. Robert Bakewell was one of the first to breed much better sheep and cattle, on his Leicestershire farm. Soon farmers were producing much heavier animals, and sheep with much thicker fleeces. This table of average weights of animals sold at Smithfield Market in

London at the beginning and end of the 18th century tells its own story:

	1710	1795
Oxen (bullocks)	370lb	800lb
Calves	50lb	150lb
Sheep	38lb	80lb

George III earned his nickname of "Farmer George" by his enthusiasm for the new methods. He made part of Windsor Park into a "model" farm, which was visited by thousands. Thomas Coke, a great landowner at Holkham in Norfolk, made his tenant farmers use the new crop rotations – planting root-crops and corn alternately. His sheep-shearing fairs were attended by farmers and land-lords from all over Europe.

New methods meant new farms. From 1793 to 1815 Britain was at war with France, and there was a need for even higher food production. During this time in particular, many small farmers sold out to the richer, more productive far-mers. Special Acts of Parliament were passed so that the big farmers could take over the village commons. The enclosure of farmland was complete. As always, the poor were the losers.

The estate of the great house was self-sufficient. Not only did the owner's workers produce all the crops needed, they brewed all the beer. The laundry-

By about 1800 fields had been enclosed all over Britain. The landscape resembled a patchwork quilt. At Stanbury in West Yorkshire (shown below), as in most parts of northern Britain, the fields were enclosed by drystone walls.

maids washed and ironed all the clothes. The dairymaids churned butter from the home farm's prize herd of cows. The estate even levelled out its own football and cricket pitches, for its own home-produced teams.

The nobles competed with each other as to who had the finest houses and estates. They loved to landscape their grounds. The landscape artist "Capability" Brown was in great demand. He designed not only formal gardens, but striking vistas (views). It was not enough to have a fine house; it must be properly shown off. Carriages must drive up to its front terrace down a long avenue of trees. Wherever possible a lake should be visible from the main sitting-rooms, with a ruined castle behind it. If there was no natural lake, one must be constructed. If no castle ruins stood within view, they must be specially built. If — as at Mereworth Castle in Kent — a village spoilt the view, it must be destroyed and its people moved out of sight.

The lesser landowners — the squires — modelled their ways of life, their houses and their estates on those of the nobility. But they mixed more easily with those beneath them on the social ladder, the local merchants, the yeomen (small farmers), and the lawyers from the local town. They were glad to see their sons or daughters marrying into such families. They needed their money, apart from other considerations.

The style of life enjoyed by the great English merchants was the envy of their fellows all over Europe. As we shall see, English trading companies were, by this time, roaming the world. During the reign of William III, the Bank of England had been set up, based on the national bank in Holland. The directors of the bank and the heads of the great trading companies lived like kings. Indeed one Frenchman wrote in 1727:

"Some English merchants are certainly far wealthier than many sovereign princes of Germany and Italy."

Not only did these men live lavishly and buy large estates which they left to their sons. They were proud of their gifts to schools, hospitals and the poor. The Bristol slave trader Edward Colston helped the poor of thirty different parishes with his bequests (gifts) and set up nineteen charity schools.

The English nobles were also deeply involved in trade. They invested money in trading companies such as the East India Company or the Royal African Company, which organized the slave trade, in return for huge profits.

Frequently, however, the nobles might lose all they invested. The Duke of Chandos lost the enormous sum of £700,000 (in money of that time) in the South Seas Company. Along with others, he believed its claims that it would take over all the trade of the Pacific Ocean. When the claims were found to be lies, this "South Sea Bubble" — as the financial crash was called — burst. Thousands lost their savings.

Though the population of the towns was growing fast, most people still lived in the country. Farmworkers worked on the estates of the great house, or for the local squire. Their cottages, often no more than two rooms, were provided by their employer. If they lost their job, they lost their house. Their wages were barely enough to keep them and their families alive. They were skilled poachers of game from the squires' estates. Many had a smallholding and combined work for a farmer with work on their own land, or with fishing if they lived by the sea.

At all levels of society, the life of a married woman was determined by her husband's work. The nobleman's wife entertained guests alongside her husband. The squire's wife supervised the work of her cooks, maids and other house servants. (In a great house that job was done by a housekeeper.) The labourer's wife not only had to cook for her family; she also worked in the fields, particularly at harvest time, and in her garden. Or, with her children, she made money spinning and weaving wool at home. An unmarried woman would often spin or weave as a full-time job, as the word "spinster" still shows.

But it was easier than in the past for country people to change their lives. Some boys ran away to sea, and more and more married couples left England behind them to start a new life as a labouring couple on a lord's estate in North America. (They would be transported across the Atlantic free, in return for signing an "indenture", or contract, promising to work for an employer for a period of five years or more.) But most of

For hundreds of years the wool industry – one of Britain's main export trades – was organized in people's homes. Here the farm labourer's wife is spinning the wool while her daughter winds it off the spindle into a ball. The balls were then taken to weavers' cottages to be woven into cloth.

all, country people left home to find work in the towns.

In London, such people often added to the thousands of unemployed men and women who lived in great poverty and easily turned to crime. There was no police force, though there were men called the "Bow Street runners" who tried to maintain some sort of law and order in the capital under the control of the Bow Street magistrates. Public houses were open all through the day and night. Drunks were seen everywhere, among them children. Publicans advertised the popular spirit, gin, with the slogan:

"Drunk for a penny,
Dead drunk for twopence."

There was no street lighting. Servants escorted their masters, carrying strong cudgels to protect them. A boy would accompany them, holding a "link" (flare) to light their way. Street gangs carried out muggings without much difficulty. All men who possessed any wealth carried a sword in London.

The crowd of unemployed men and women could always be organized into an angry "mob" by unscrupulous men who wanted to use them for their own purposes. A mere rumour or cry – about Catholic shopkeepers, for instance – would start a stampede by thousands of chanting, angry people, smashing shop windows and burning property.

The most terrifying example of the London mob on the rampage occurred in 1780. Two years earlier a law had been passed by Parliament which allowed Catholics to own land and permitted Catholic priests to enter Britain. A group of Protestants petitioned Parliament to repeal the Act. For a week, a huge mob, led by Lord George Gordon, ran wild through London, shouting anti-Catholic slogans, burning, smashing and looting. When the crowd destroyed a gin distillery, men and women rushed into the burning building. An eye-witness described how:

"They rushed down the stone steps into the cellar and came up choking with blackened faces and bloodshot eyes, carrying untapped [unopened] casks of gin, or pails and jugs, bowls and even pig troughs overflowing ... Soon the gin came gushing up into the streets and ran in warm streams in the gutter ... The people knelt down and dipped their faces in the river of fiery spirits and gulped as much of it down as they could before it

Hogarth's engraving "Gin Lane" (1751) warns of the terrible dangers of gin. The baby falls from its drunken mother's breast, and a man and a dog gnaw on the same bone next to her. The skeletal-looking man at the bottom of the picture and the man who has hung himself in the background show that, where poverty is, death is never far behind.

A concert at fashionable Bath. The singer tries but fails to attract the audience's attention. Is the woman in the front planning to strike the singer with her fan in disgust?

made them choke ... Men and women lay down prostrate in the streets, incapably drunk; some of the women had babies in their arms."[15]

More than 800 people were killed during the week of the Gordon riots.

Fashionable men and women liked to spend the summer "taking the waters" in a spa. Here those who had eaten and drunk too much during the year could drink the waters from the springs at places like Tunbridge Well, Leamington Spa, Cheltenham or Bath. The waters were believed to be medicinal.

During the day these well-to-do men and women would parade their new clothes, gamble, or take tea or coffee in the tea and coffee houses which had now become fashionable. In the evenings they would dance in the Assembly Rooms under the direction of a Master of Ceremonies, who would supervise the orches-tra's choice of music, and decide what clothes were in fashion and what behaviour could be classed as bad manners. The most famous Master of Ceremonies was Richard Nash, who became known as "Beau [Handsome] Nash".

Squares and crescents, such as Lansdowne Crescent in Bath, were built in the most formal and elegant of styles to suit the formal and elegant men and women who came to live in the spa towns for the summer. The furniture which was built for them by great craftsmen such as Chippendale and Sheraton, and the clocks which stood on the fireplaces designed for them by men like Robert Adam, fetch huge prices today.

Although the majority of English people belonged to the Church of England and went to church, many people had become half-hearted about Christianity. After the persecutions and wars of religion in previous centuries, they mistrusted anything that might be thought of as extremism, or "enthusiasm" as it later came to be called. The clergy of the Church of England were now appointed by local landowners. Many village parsons did just as good and important work as ever. They spent their lives visiting the sick of the parish, helping the poor, and educating the cleverest of the local children. But often they were afraid to criticize the squire – if he was unjust in dealing with his workers, or ignorant and domineering over matters of religion, for example – in case they were dismissed.

The greatest criticism that can be made of the 18th-century Church was that it had little contact with the poorest people in the towns. Industry was growing, along with the towns, and new churches were not built in the new areas of work and living. It was in these areas – coal-mining areas such as Kingswood, outside Bristol, or tin-mining districts such as those in Cornwall – that the great 18th-century preacher John Wesley gained some of his strongest support.

John Wesley was a clergyman of the Church of England and never wanted to leave it. But he and his brother Charles, together with a small group of supporters, became convinced that the Church needed to be brought to life. It had lost touch with many people, was too easy-going and did not teach the beliefs of Jesus with sufficient fire.

John Wesley set out to travel the country preaching wherever he went, in the manner of Christ and his disciples.

Many of the local clergy distrusted him and would not allow him to preach from their pulpits. So he preached in the open air, on the village commons or in the open spaces of the towns. He began to draw great crowds.

For over fifty years John Wesley rode up and down Britain on his horse. He covered 400,000 kilometres and preached 40,000 sermons. He and his preachers were howled down, jeered at, stoned and thrown into ponds. Their meetings were highly emotional. Men and women who heard the words and teachings of Jesus for the first time would often shout out, and weep and groan. They loved to sing the hymns which John's brother Charles Wesley produced in great numbers.

In the end, John Wesley, against his will, set up his own Church, which became known as the Methodist Church. He knew that a large, enthusiastic meeting in the open air had little real effect in making true Christians. Men and women soon forgot what they had felt in the heat of the moment. So whenever he left an area, Wesley always tried to leave behind him a little group of keen Christians. He would keep in touch with them by letter, and organize them "methodically" into groups by areas. They would "methodically" study the Bible together, pray, and try to bring the Christianity of the local church to life.

Finally, when the Church would not appoint some of Wesley's followers as missionaries to work abroad, he appointed them himself. After Wesley's death in 1791, Methodist churches were to spread all over Britain. They were to reach thousands of working people who were unaffected by the Church of England, and to be one of the main Christian influences in Victorian England.

The American War of Independenc

The first British colonies were founded in America in Elizabethan times. Traders and explorers, such as Sir Walter Raleigh, led the way and were followed by ordinary men and women wanting to start new lives in a different country.

As we saw in Chapter 26, one of the first British settlements was in Newfoundland, where Bristol fishermen began profitable deep-sea fishing for cod. Sir Humphrey Gilbert claimed official possession of Newfoundland in the name of Queen Elizabeth in 1583.

The prospect of finding gold has dazzled the imaginations of explorers and settlers for many centuries. The success of the Spanish in finding and working the gold and silver mines of Chile and Peru in South America encouraged thousands of British adventurers. The most famous was Sir Walter Raleigh. He was convinced – along with many others, including the Spanish – that a kingdom of Gold, "El Dorado", was to be found in the Guiana highlands in South America. But an expedition led by Raleigh up the Orinoco river failed to find the fabulous land. And when he returned to Britain, Raleigh was executed for disobeying James I's orders not to fight the Spanish.

The lure of wealth remained as strong as ever. Gold was supposed to be everywhere in North America. Rubies and diamonds were said to lie like pebbles on the beach. Admittedly you ran the risk of being killed by men with heads below their shoulders, dog's teeth and eyes in their chests. But to many the risk was worth running.

In 1607 three ships sailed into Chesapeake Bay in modern Maryland. They saw "fair meadows and goodly tall trees, with fresh waters". The party was landed and a fort was built at Jamestown. The settlers overcame malaria, typhoid and shortage of food. Half of the original 104 colonists died in the summer of 1607. Eventually the colony prospered, chiefly because of their plantations of tobacco, a crop which they had learned how to cultivate from the local Indians. Later the colonists began to import black slaves from west Africa to work in the tobacco fields.

A few years later, a very different colony was formed further north on the North American coast by English Puritans fleeing from persecution. These colonists became known as the "Pilgrim Fathers". On 15th December 1620, their ship, the *Mayflower*, dropped anchor off Cape Cod with 100 colonists. The ship was 30 metres long and 6 metres wide. The height of the space below deck was about a metre and there were no portholes. Here the passengers had rolled about and vomited their way across the Atlantic for 100 days. The only water available for washing was sea water.

The first winter brought worse suffering. Half the colonists died of disease and cold. But somehow or other, helped again by local Indians, they planted and harvested 8 hectares of maize. In the autumn of 1621 they held their first harvest supper. They killed geese and turkeys and invited the Indians to the first "Thanksgiving Day". That day – towards the end of November – is still a national holiday in the United States.

Families and neighbours meet together in the evening for the traditional Thanksgiving meal – turkey, cranberry sauce, pumpkin pie and sweet potatoes.

During the 17th century, thirteen separate British colonies grew up along the North American coast. By the end of the century a million colonists, mainly British, had started new lives there.

The colonies were of two very different types. Those in the north – known as New England – were dominated by their Puritan leaders. Like the Pilgrim Fathers, many of them had left England because James I and Charles I had persecuted them for their Puritan beliefs. They were religious, independent and extremely hardworking. They lived very strict private lives. None of them was aristocratic, and they did not believe in having different social classes as in Britain. Not surprisingly, they supported Parliament during the Civil Wars.

The southern colonies were mainly founded by large British landowners. They were granted huge areas of land by the British king and they farmed these at first, as we saw in Chapter 36, with "indentured" workers from Britain. When the landlords or their tenant farmers found they could not attract sufficient labourers, they turned to importing slaves who would do the heavy work on their tobacco or cotton plantations.

The transportation of slaves from west Africa to the West Indies had been started by Portuguese and Spanish traders in the 16th century. Spanish farmers in the West Indies and South America almost exterminated the original inhabitants by overworking them on their plan-

An early settlement in the woods of New England. The houses are built from nearby trees though the chimneys are made of stone. Curious Indians have crept up to the clearing to see their new neighbours.

tations. (The Caribs, in the area of the Caribbean Sea, were wiped out, for instance.) They then found they were short of labourers and turned to slave traders to supply them with slaves from the other side of the Atlantic.

Sir John Hawkins and his father were the first Englishmen to break the monopoly of Spanish and Portuguese slave traders. By the middle of the 18th century more than 100,000 slaves a year were being transported to North America or the West Indies, half of them in British ships. The main British port trading slaves at the beginning of the 18th century was Bristol. By the end of the century Liverpool had taken its place.

The slave traders' agents built forts along the coasts of modern Gambia and Ghana in west Africa. Local chiefs were paid with guns, beads of glinting glass and rings, alcohol and tobacco, to bring the slaves to the forts. The slaves were often criminals, or prisoners of war. One of the worst aspects of the trade was the way it encouraged the chiefs of the tribes who lived along the African coast to raid the inland tribes and carry off their strongest young men.

The slaves were chained together and taken to slave ships which were waiting for them off the coast. Here they would be packed, still chained, below decks, lying shoulder to shoulder. Such conditions encouraged the spread of epidemics. Often a quarter of the cargo of "black gold" – as the slaves were called – were dead when they reached the slave markets of the West Indies or the southern colonies in North America.

The traders returned from America not only with money, but with the holds of their ships packed with sacks of sugar, or bales of cotton and tobacco. It was one of the richest trades known to men. Modern West Indians and black citizens of the United States are descended from the slaves who were sold.

The British were not the only settlers in North America. French explorers had founded the first Canadian colonies along the St Lawrence River at Quebec and Montreal. In the reign of Charles II, British fur traders around Hudson Bay in Canada developed a profitable trade and took over a large area of land. This led to competition between the two countries. There was also rivalry between British

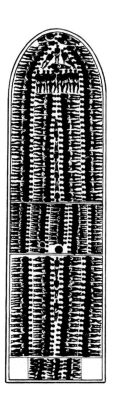

The interior of a slave ship. The slaves lay shoulder to shoulder, chained to each other below decks, during the long passage across the Atlantic. This horrific drawing was part of William Wilberforce's evidence which he presented to Parliament during his campaign to end the slave trade.

and French traders in India, where they had two rival East India companies.

The 18th-century wars between Britain and France in Europe led to fighting between the two countries in Canada and India. The British were victorious. Canada became a British colony but with a large minority of its people speaking French. In India, the British East India Company became the dominant trading company. The English now made huge fortunes in India from tea or diamonds, jute or cotton, and returned home to spend their last days in places like Cheltenham or Hampstead, which became known as "nabob land". (Nabob was a wealthy Indian prince.)

The removal of the French from Canada by the Treaty of Paris in 1763 had an important effect on the thirteen British colonies in North America. They had long been dissatisfied with the British government's treatment of them. But they relied on the British Army to protect them from the French, who had ideas of building a New France which would stretch from their colonies around the banks of the St Lawrence to their colony of Louisiana at the mouth of the Mississippi. Now that the French had no power to fulfil their dream, British Americans wanted to stand on their own feet.

The Americans particularly disliked the way British governments interfered in their trade and made them pay taxes they considered unreasonable. The British expected their colonies to send their valuable raw materials — such as tea, cotton and tobacco — to Britain, where they were turned into finished products in British factories. Then the products were exported back to the colonies.

The British disliked the colonists trying to develop their own industries.

They forbade them to use non-British ships for their trade, even if these provided a better and cheaper service, as the Dutch did, for example. If the Americans imported goods from Europe, they had to pay British taxes on them.

The British government also tried to prevent American colonists travelling west to open up their great country. (Up to now they had lived only along the eastern seaboard of the modern United States.) If they did so, the British argued,

A Canadian fur trapper.

an army would be needed to defend them from attacks by Frenchmen, Spaniards or Indians. And who would pay for that?

The wars with France had left the British with a national debt of £140 million. They were determined that the colonists should pay at least some of the cost of the wars. After all, the British said, it was the Americans who had gained from the removal of the French from Canada. The Americans replied with the strongest of their arguments in the dispute. If they were to be taxed, they should be consulted. Taxes were passed by British Parliaments, in which the Americans had no representatives. There should be, in the words of their slogan, "No taxation without representation".

The troubles started when the British Parliament passed a Stamp Act, which said that all legal documents in the colonies had to carry a stamp. This was really a form of tax — the money for the stamp was to go to the British government. When the Americans protested, Parliament withdrew the Act, but instead imposed small taxes on American imports of tea, paper, glass and other articles. The colonists replied by boycotting (not buying) those goods. Again the British withdrew the taxes — on all imports except tea. In December 1773, a cargo of specially cheap Indian tea, to be taxed at threepence a pound, entered Boston harbour in Massachusetts. A group of young Americans, with blackened faces and dressed as American Indians, threw the 342 chests of tea into Boston harbour. This event was known as the "Boston Tea Party".

Boston had been the centre of trouble for several years. In 1770 an incident occurred which became magnified until it was known as the "Boston Massacre".

A group of young Americans had been taunting and snowballing British soldiers. In the end the soldiers could stand it no longer. They fired, without orders, into the crowd, and killed five civilians.

After the Boston Tea Party, the British closed the port of Boston. They then declared that the whole colony of Massachusetts was in revolt. Fighting broke out and the thirteen colonies issued their famous Declaration of Independence in 1776. They declared themselves to be the thirteen United States of America. Their justification to the world of their break with Britain has been taught to American schoolchildren ever since. It starts:

"When, in the course of human events, it becomes necessary for one people to dissolve the political bands which have connected them with another...a decent respect to the opinion of mankind requires that they should declare the causes which impel them to the separation ... Governments are instituted [set up] among men, deriving their just powers from the consent of the governed...Whenever any form of government becomes destructive of these ends it is the right of the people to alter or to abolish it, and to institute new government laying its foundation on such principles...as to them shall seem most likely to effect their safety and happiness."

The Declaration sums up the principle of democracy — that countries should be governed according to the wishes of their people. After seven years of fighting, the war ended with the battle of Yorktown in 1781. With the surrender of the British army, the first British empire ended, and independence was declared in 1783.

The first British empire was not built by British governments, though sometimes colonies were encouraged by governments. It was built by trading companies, landowners or persecuted individuals and groups. Individuals were led to settle overseas – Puritans because of religious persecution, the unemployed because they sought work, farm labourers because they hoped for better pay, all sorts of people because they believed that the colonies offered them chances of new and better lives. Governments followed the companies and individuals, and protected them, grudgingly, with a few ships and soldiers.

The loss of the American colonies made many English leaders doubt the value of acquiring an empire. What was the point of setting up colonies if they then broke away and became independent? Nevertheless, during the 19th century, more and more ordinary English men and women – desperate with poverty, frustrated by snobbery, or penalized for their political beliefs – sold all that they had and sailed abroad to start a new life. We shall see where they settled, now that the United States was independent, in Chapter 40.

American troops surrounding the British base on the Yorktown peninsula, Maryland, at the end of the American War of Independence. They were helped by French soldiers and sailors. The British surrender led to the creation of the new United States.

Roads, Railways and Factories

The changes that occurred in Britain between the end of the 18th and the middle of the 19th century altered the whole nature of British life. No such great changes had occurred since the Roman occupation. Instead of a country largely empty of people, Britain became overcrowded. For the first time more people began to live in the towns than in the country. There they earned their living mainly by working in factories rather than by farming. These changes are known as the Industrial Revolution.

Between 1780 and 1851, the population of Britain grew from thirteen million to about twenty-seven million. One of the reasons for this great rise seems to have been that safer methods were now used by the midwives who delivered the country's babies. Far fewer children died at birth or in the first year of their life. Moreover, people were beginning to understand the importance of cleanliness, and to wear more washable cotton clothes. Cleanliness meant better health. People began to live longer.

A number of circumstances combined to cause Britain's industrial revolution. Long before it became a great manufacturing nation Britain had become a country which traded all over the world. It is ideally placed as a centre of world trade. To the south, Europe is only 30 kilometres across the Channel; to the west there is no land between Glasgow, Liverpool and Bristol and the ports of North America. Ships can sail deep into the country up rivers like the Thames, the Humber, the Clyde, the Mersey and the Severn. Nowhere in Britain is more than 90 kilometres from the sea.

In France, local taxes discouraged businessmen from transporting goods and raw materials from one part of the country to another. But this did not happen in Britain. The building of canals and railways and the improvement of roads in the 18th and 19th centuries made transport much easier than it had been. (It had taken a year to move the wood for the ships of Cromwell's navy 50 kilometres from the Weald of Kent to the building yards at Chatham.) Profits made from trade gave nobles and businessmen plenty of money to spend on improvements and inventions.

The pioneer of canal-building was the Duke of Bridgewater who had large supplies of coal on his estate at Worsley, 10 kilometres from Manchester. He was looking for a better way of moving coal than strapping it on the back of packhorses, the method of the day.

The Duke employed James Brindley, an engineer of genius who never learned to read and write properly, to build a canal from Worsley to Manchester. It took Brindley five years, from 1759 to 1764, to build the Bridgewater Canal, which, with its 10-metre-high aqueduct over the River Irwell at Barton, was one of the wonders of the age. Experts came from all over Europe to admire it and to learn from it. Later Brindley extended the canal for 60 kilometres to the Mersey, so that Manchester was linked with Liverpool. Now ships could sail up the Mersey estuary and then sail on to tie up alongside quays in the heart of Manchester. One horse pulling a barge along a canal could transport more coal than sixty packhorses. The cost of carrying cotton from Liverpool to Manchester was cut by eighty-three per cent.

The Bridgewater Canal proved an example which local groups of landlords, farmers, manufacturers and bankers were quick to follow. By the 1770s all Britain's main rivers were linked up with each other by canal.

Brindley's most ambitious scheme was the Grand Trunk Canal. This started at the Bridgewater Canal and ran south-east to Stoke-on-Trent. From there it continued till it joined the River Trent. Then ships could sail north-east straight to the Humber and Hull. Josiah Wedgwood invested a lot of money in the scheme, and was well rewarded for his foresight. He built a pottery works on the banks of Brindley's canal at Stoke. Here his factory could receive china clay dug in Cornwall and brought by sea to Liverpool and by canal to Stoke. From here his delicate pottery could travel by

The Bridgewater Canal aqueduct (above), built by James Brindley, ran from his master's, the Duke of Bridgewater's, coalmines at Worsley, to Manchester. Early canals were used chiefly for carrying coal, and boats were pulled by horses.
Thomas Telford's iron bridge (below), the first one of its kind, was built over the river Severn in Shropshire.

canal barge to Liverpool or Hull instead of risking breakages on the backs of packhorses. His china was exported all over the world.

Canals enjoyed seventy years of prosperity. Then, in the 19th century, railways beat them for speed and price, and they lost popularity with factory owners. Today they are busy not with business traffic but with pleasure craft.

In 1745 it took nearly a fortnight to travel by stage coach from London to Edinburgh. In 1796 it took two and a half days. During those fifty years the road system of England was revolutionized.

The deep ruts and bumpy surfaces of roads in the early 18th century made journeys by coach unpopular. They were long and uncomfortable. The coaches had no springs. They were expensive. They were dangerous, for coaches were easy targets for highwaymen. Here is how Charles Dickens describes a coach carrying letters from London to Dover:

"The Dover mail...lumbered up Shooter's Hill. The first of the persons with whom my story has business walked uphill in the mire by the side of the mail, as the rest of the passengers did; not because they had the least relish for walking exercise...but because the hill, and the harness, and the mud and the mail were all so heavy, that the horses had three times already come to a stop ...With drooping heads and tremulous tails, they mashed their way through the thick mud, floundering and stumbling between whiles as if they were falling to pieces at the larger joints...

In those days anybody on the road might be a robber, or in league with robbers...So the guard of the Dover mail thought to himself, that Friday night in November...as he stood...keeping an eye and a hand on the arm-chest before him, where a loaded blunderbuss lay at the top of six or eight loaded horse-pistols, deposited on a substratum of cutlass."[16]

As for trade, fleets of packhorses with baskets of coal or bales of wool or cotton strapped on their backs were the usual method of moving goods by road. Cattle and sheep were driven by drovers along the roads, all the way from the farms – in Wales, for instance – to Smithfield market in London. The drovers would leave the Welsh farms in the spring and return in the autumn.

With the roads, as with the canals, improvement came through enterprising groups of squires, bankers and businessmen. They banded together to form groups called turnpike trusts, which were given the right to improve stretches of road by Acts of Parliament. The trust provided the money and hired the engineers to survey and build the road. Then they charged people a regular toll (tax) for using the road. On stretches of main road in Britain today you can still see the toll-house by the side of the road, where the gate was closed until the horseman, coach driver, or waggoner had paid his toll.

One of the most remarkable road builders was John Metcalfe. He was blind, and used to feel the lie of the land over which his turnpike roads would pass in Lancashire and Yorkshire with his stick. Metcalfe used jagged, broken stones for his surfaces and not round pebbles, for they crushed better. If he found a round stone on one of his roads with his stick there was trouble.

The road-builder John Macadam, a Scotsman, also laid great emphasis on

the surfaces of his roads. They were made up of thousands of small chipped stones of standard shapes and sizes which packed tightly together when they were rolled. Prisoners or people from the workhouses broke the stones into the required shapes with a hammer. We still use his methods. Later the "Macadamized" surfaces were sprayed with tar to make "Tarmac" roads.

But the most famous of all road engineers – who also designed canals, docks, lighthouses and bridges – was Thomas Telford, another Scot. Like the Romans, he believed that a well-built road must be well drained and built on a solid foundation of stone blocks laid by hand. He built more than a thousand kilometres of roads. His Caledonian Canal linked northern Scotland from coast to coast. His suspension bridge over the Menai Straits, linking Anglesey to the mainland of north Wales, is still used today.

The first large factories ran on water

A toll-gate keeper comes to open the gate to a post-chaise on a toll road through the woods. The state of British roads was revolutionized during the 18th century by private companies. They paid for the improvements by charging tolls.

power and were to be found in the cotton industry. The import of slaves to the southern United States greatly increased the amount of cotton produced on the plantations. So did a machine for cleaning cotton invented by Elias Whitney. One of his machines (called "gins" or "engines") cleaned as much cotton as fifty slaves working by hand.

John Kay's flying shuttle loom and James Hargreaves' "spinning jenny", invented in 1766, had doubled the output of weavers and spinners in Britain. But they were both used by men and women working at home. Now great factories were built in the country valleys of Derbyshire, south Lancashire, and Clydeside, using new machines run by water power.

The first cotton-spinning factory was built by Richard Arkwright in 1771, at Cromford near Derby. He built it over the River Derwent so that the waters of the river moved wheels which provided the power for his machinery. As the factories resembled the old mill-houses which ground flour by water power, they were called mills. Later Edmund Cartwright developed looms which could be used in factories and driven by Watt's steam engines.

Steam power had been known for many years. Steam pumps were used in coal and tin mines to prevent flooding, which was a matter of life and death. In designing his steam engine in the 1760s James Watt developed the ideas of a previous inventor, Thomas Newcomen. With money from a Birmingham businessman, Matthew Boulton, he built engines which could drive machinery with steam produced from boilers heated by coal. By 1800 Boulton and Watt's machines were being used by any factory owner who could buy coal cheaply. From now on industry moved to be near the coalfields, and no longer relied on fast-running streams and rivers.

In 1793 Britain and France again went to war. The French wanted to control Belgium and dominate Europe. The wars, which lasted till 1815, were the first wars in the history of Britain which really affected the lives of the British people. Before the armies had been small and casualties were low. When the news reached Britain in 1709 that 600 British soldiers had been killed in the battle of Malplaquet against the French there was a public outcry. But between 1793 and 1815 one-sixth of the adult male population of Britain was in the armed forces and 210,000 fighting men died.

The soldiers and sailors who fought so

Children at work in a Manchester cotton mill. The hours were so long and their work so physically exhausting that children often fell asleep while working and suffered serious injuries from the moving machinery.

An early railway locomotive carrying coal. The first trains were used only for this purpose. When they began to carry people too, they spread all over Britain.

During these latest wars with France, the British once again faced invasion. In 1798 the French tried to invade England through Ireland. They landed in County Mayo and fought for two weeks before they were defeated. In 1805 everybody believed that the French would invade along the south coast. A military canal was dug along the edge of Romney Marsh. Special towers called Martello towers were built along the coast. Mothers terrified their children by telling them that "Boney"(the English nickname for the French emperor Napoleon Bonaparte) would deal with them unless they behaved themselves.

After Admiral Nelson had won the most famous naval victory in British history at the battle of Trafalgar, in 1805, the fear of invasion faded away. The British Navy controlled the Channel and blockaded the French coast. As a result Britain captured much trade which had previously been carried by French ships. By 1815 half the world's trade in manufactured goods was transported by British ships.

After 1805 British armies fought a long campaign in Spain. They drove the French out of the Spanish peninsula from 1808 to 1812. Finally their troops, under the command of the Duke of Wellington, formed a large part of the army which defeated Napoleon once and for all at the battle of Waterloo in 1815.

The wars with France involved the British people in other ways. Foreign food was not imported so British farmers could charge high prices. There was plenty of work for the men who made

bravely and made Britain one of the world's leading nations were often recruited from the poorest classes or were former criminals. Army recruiting sergeants used to tour the gaols offering service with the army as an alternative to years in prison; they also recruited the unemployed and young farm boys eager to leave home. The Navy's sailors were kidnapped by the "press gangs" – naval recruiting parties. The sailors were generally fishermen or others with experience of the sea who were seized when they walked along the streets of their home town or reeled out of a pub at closing time. The press gang would rush them straight to the quayside and they would be rowed to ships which were on the point of sailing. They would not see their homes again for three years or more. Both the Army and the Navy maintained discipline by continual flogging. Some of these punishments were so severe that men died of them.

guns and boots. (French generals continued to buy British boots for their soldiers throughout the war.) The women and children who made the British uniforms worked hours of overtime.

Another industry which gained from the French wars was the railway industry. The cavalry needed all the fodder it could get for its horses, so feed was in short supply at home. As a result, the mine owners were forced to look for alternatives to packhorses for moving

Locomotion. He was made a public engineer, with orders to join the coal mines of south Durham with the river port at Stockton. The *Locomotion* pulled twelve wagons loaded with coal and twenty-one open passenger cars along 40 kilometres of track in front of cheering crowds. The "railway age" had begun.

So far the railways had been developed mainly to carry coal. Now a group of Lancashire businessmen formed a com-

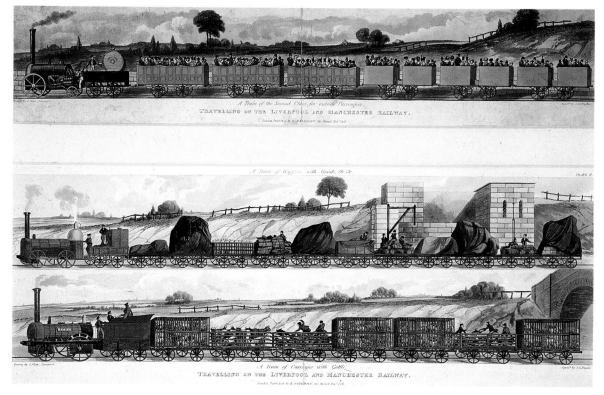

coal from their pits. A Cornishman, Richard Trevithick, invented a high-pressure steam engine in 1802. In 1804 his locomotive drew five wagons of coal, a coach, and seventy passengers along 15 kilometres of track in south Wales.

Others worked on his ideas. In 1812 a regular steam railway was dragging coal trucks outside Leeds. In 1825 George Stephenson designed a locomotive called

An early print of the Manchester–Liverpool railway. The trains carried sheep, cattle, goods and passengers. Notice how even the passengers' carriages were open to all weathers.

pany to carry both goods and people to and from Manchester and Liverpool. George Stephenson and his son Robert designed a "locomotive steam engine", the *Rocket*, which reached a speed of

266

nearly 50 kilometres per hour in 1830.

Over the next twenty years railways spread all over Britain. By 1850 almost all the main modern railway lines had been laid, and a fast service provided. Because the fares were too expensive for ordinary people, Parliament laid down that every railway company had to provide at least one train a day in each direction which stopped at all stations. Passengers must be given a covered seat – at first they sat in the open – and charged not more than a penny a mile.

Isambard Kingdom Brunel, chief engineer of the Great Western Railway, was the greatest engineer of his day. His iron ship, the *Great Eastern*, weighed 18,000 tonnes – an unheard-of weight in those days. His bridge across the river Tamar, which divides Devon from Cornwall, was as famous as Telford's bridge across the Menai Straits. His tunnel on the London–Bristol line at Box Hill was three kilometres long. He designed it on such an incline that the rising sun shone through it from end to end on his birthday (9th April).

The roads, canals, and railway lines were not built by engineers and surveyors alone. There were about 250,000 workmen – many of them Irish – building railways in 1850. They were known as "navigators" – navvies. They lived in their own shanty towns, which they built along the line of the track as they went. They liked to wear sealskin caps, or white felt hats whose brims they would turn up. They wore rainbow waistcoats and moleskin trousers. They waved brightly coloured handkerchiefs.

The navvies were well paid, by the standards of those days. They spent much of their cash on food and drink. Indeed it was said that the railways were built at the cost of £1000 a mile on drink. Their casualties were very high. A hundred and thirty-one seriously injured men were taken to Bath Hospital during twenty-one months' work on the Great Western Railway.

One of the greatest gains brought by the railways was the introduction of the penny post in 1840. Before that year it was the receiver of a letter, not its sender, who had to pay for it. Charges were based on weight and distance, and they were high. Rowland Hill had the simple and revolutionary idea of charging the sender a penny a letter to anywhere not just in Britain but in the British Empire. As he forecast, the amount of postage rose so greatly that the Post Office – a government-run service – soon showed a profit.

Navvies walking along a new railway. If companies planned routes close to great country houses, the owners tried desperately to move them.

Social Reform and Change

The mass movement of British men and women into towns to work in factories made Britain for a time the wealthiest nation on earth. It also made many people deeply unhappy.

Men, women and children crowded into the new mining villages, mill towns and industrial cities in a manner which had never been known before. The new workers lived as close to the factories as they could. Builders never kept up with the demand for small houses, built back to back, with outside earth toilets and one street pump to serve the row. So families crowded into old buildings, which were now let to them by floors or even single rooms. The only place where children could play was in the street, which was made of crushed earth and ash. A man, wife and three or four children crowded into one room, and slept together in one bed. By day, the air was thick with the smoke belching out of the factory chimneys. By night the only light came from the fires of the factories or iron works.

There was nothing new about children working. In the past, boys had worked alongside their fathers on the land and girls helped their mothers. Most children had never gone to school, so they started work soon after they could walk. But now boys and girls, aged six upwards, worked — and lived — in factories.

Cotton-factory owners liked to use children in their works. They had nimble fingers. They did exactly what they were told to do, or if they did not, they could easily be bullied. They did not argue or answer back. Under the Poor Law, if a boy or girl had neither mother nor father

A child staring out over a filthy town. Factories often developed in old established towns which they polluted with their smoking chimneys. Workers were forced to live nearby.

and no other relatives, he or she had to be brought up in the local poor house. Employers obtained many of their child workers by paying a fee to the overseers of the poor house. The children would then be sent to Lancashire or Derbyshire to the cotton factory. After that, the overseers were no longer responsible for them, and the local ratepayers did not have to support them.

As a result, nobody took much notice of how the children were treated in the factories, until Parliament carried out an inquiry in 1816. Here are extracts from the evidence of Mr John Moss, master of the apprentices at Backbarrow Mill in Lancashire, where 150 children and young people, aged seven to twenty-one, were employed.

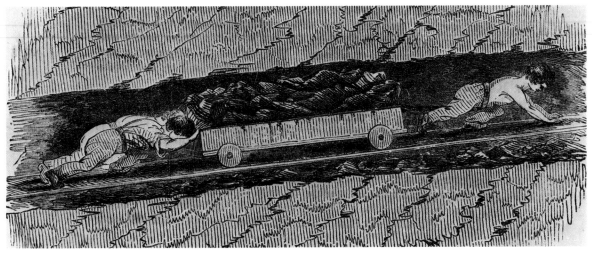

Question: What were the hours of work?

Answer: From 5 o'clock in the morning till 8 at night all the year through.

Question: What time was allowed for meals?

Answer: Half an hour for breakfast and half an hour for dinner.

Question: Would the children sit or stand to work?

Answer: Stand.

Question: Were there any seats in the mill?

Answer: None.

Question: Where did they sleep?

Answer: In the apprentice-house.

Question: Did you inspect their beds?

Answer: Yes, every night.

Question: For what purpose?

Answer: Because there were always some of them missing, some sometimes might be run away, others sometimes I have found have been asleep in the mill, upon the mill floor.

Question: Were any children injured by the machinery?

Answer: Very frequently. Very often their fingers were crushed, and one had his arm broken.[17]

In the coal mines, boys and girls as young as four years old were made to work for an average of twelve hours a day.

In 1815 the same sort of people governed Britain as had done in the 18th century. Members of Parliament still only represented about one man in thirty. The constituencies they represented – the counties and the old medieval towns – were unchanged. Not only did no farm or factory worker have the vote; hardly any of the owners of the new factories and mines had the vote either. New industrial towns like Leeds or Birmingham or Manchester had no MP to represent them. Old towns which now had tiny populations, like Old Sarum in Wiltshire or Winchelsea in Sussex, had two MPs each. Many people felt that no improvements would be made in living and working conditions, until Parliament was reformed so that it represented more people.

The Levellers, as we have seen, had been asking that each man be allowed to vote at the time of the Civil Wars. John Wilkes, who became an MP in 1768, campaigned to make the House of Commons more representative of the people. Wilkes became Lord Mayor of London,

269

and at one time was the hero of the city. But the wealthy classes were afraid of reformers, or Radicals as they were called. They feared that their campaigns might lead to a bloody revolution, as had happened in France after 1789.

At the end of the war, in 1815, half a million men were demobilized all at once from the Army. Many of them could not find work. Thousands of desperate men and women faced starvation. Bad harvests made matters worse. There were marches of unemployed men and women, and a riot in London when looters broke into a gun shop and the Lord Mayor's life was threatened. In what later became known as the Cato Street Conspiracy, Arthur Thistlewood hatched a wild scheme to assassinate all the leading members of the government

and run down the Strand in London with their heads displayed on silver platters. Magistrates, fearing that their towns might be overrun by wild mobs and the new mills in the north be set on fire, turned to the local troops to provide security. An army of 12,000 soldiers was on standby in the north of England in case of trouble.

Gangs of workers went round smashing stocking factories in Nottingham, where new machines threatened their jobs. They said they were commanded by a secret general named Ned Ludd. They

Hogarth's painting "Polling At The Elections" (1754). Election days, until long after the first Reform Bill, were days of drunkenness and rioting. The few men who had the vote voted publicly on a platform. Voting did not become secret until 1872.

became known as "Luddites".

On 16th August 1819, a large Radical meeting was held outside Manchester on some open fields called St Peter's Fields. Unlike the Luddite rioters, the crowd of about 70,000 men and women were well-disciplined and peaceful. They had come to hear William Hunt, a well-known Radical speaker, demand a reform of Parliament.

Hunt had hardly started speaking when the local magistrates ordered soldiers, some of whom were mounted on horses, to disperse the people. They rode into the crowd with drawn swords. Terrible casualties occurred, most of them from suffocation, as men and women fell on top of each other, rushing to avoid the soldiers and their horses. Within a quarter of an hour the Fields were empty of crowds, but eleven men had been killed, and 500–600 people seriously injured. The event was called the "Peterloo" Massacre by the government's enemies in sarcastic memory of the battle of Waterloo. The name stuck.

"Peterloo" changed the government's policy. Before 1819 the Conservative leaders seemed to believe that sheer brute force would prevent a revolution. After "Peterloo" they moved very slowly towards the reform of the conditions which were causing such demonstrations.

One of the new group of Conservative reformers was the Home Secretary, Sir Robert Peel. He carried out several important reforms in the 1820s. At this time you could be hanged for 200 different offences. You could be hanged, for instance, for shoplifting or sheep-stealing. So rather than sending shoplifters or sheep-stealers to their deaths, juries were just letting them off altogether. Peel reduced the number of capital (hanging) offences by half. Public hanging continued for the other hundred offences and thousands of jeering, drunken crowds came to see the sight.

The state of British prisons was a scandal at this time. If you had money, or could persuade your friends and relatives to help you, you could live fairly comfortably in prison. But if you could not afford to pay for decent conditions, you were locked in a dark and filthy room, given foul water to drink, and half starved on bread and potatoes. Peel was impressed by the reports of Christian men and women, such as Elizabeth Fry, a Quaker, who visited prisons regularly for thirty years, and reported what she saw. He started a slow improvement in the conditions of prison life.

As with his reform of capital punishments, Peel faced bitter opposition when he proposed to set up a British police force. Perhaps it was feared that such a force would be like Cromwell's army, dominating the lives of the people. But Parliament realized that "Peterloo" had shown what happens when soldiers are asked to control great crowds. They are not trained for such work, and cannot fairly be blamed if they lose their heads and open fire on the crowd or draw their swords. In 1829 Parliament agreed to set up a police force in London only – the Metropolitan Police Force – so long as it was unarmed. Within thirty years similar police forces had spread to every part of Britain. (For many years policemen were called "bobbies" after Robert Peel.)

Other reforms were also passed in the 1820s. For the first time trade unions were allowed. Their power was at first very limited. A group of local farmers and landowners managed to find a loophole in the law and used it to prosecute six farm labourers at Tolpuddle in Dorset merely for organizing a trade union. These men, who were transported to Australia, became known as the "Tolpuddle martyrs".

Other reforms, such as the repeal of the Test Act, made it possible for all Britons, whatever their religious beliefs, to take part in governing the country (so long as they had enough money). Catholics and nonconformists had been able to vote for many years.

But the most important reform – the reform of Parliament – was not even considered by the Conservatives who dominated Parliament for fifteen years from 1815. In 1830 the opposition party, who were called the Whigs, formed a government under Lord Grey. In the same year wealthy landowners were frightened by the outbreak of a second French Revolution and news of disturbances in the English countryside. In Kent, for example, new threshing machines which put men out of work were systematically smashed. Farm labourers set fire to barns all over southern England. Nine men were hanged, and 457 transported to Australia for these and many other similar acts of vandalism. Something had to be done to prevent a British revolution.

The new government decided to make the constituencies more up to date. They also decided, at last, to give more men the vote. Their reform proposals were passed in the House of Commons by 345 votes to 246, but they were rejected by the House of Lords.

A hundred and fifty thousand people attended a meeting in Birmingham to show their support for the Reform Bill. The windows of the Duke of Wellington's house in Piccadilly were smashed. Bristol's city centre was vandalized. The House of Lords was advised to pass the Bill. If it refused, the King, acting on the advice of the government, promised to create enough new peers who were supporters of the Bill to make its passing certain. In the end, the Lords agreed and the Bill became law.

There was nothing extraordinary about the 1832 Reform Act. The new industrial towns were now properly represented, but constituencies were still unfair and only one man in twenty had the vote. Voting was still in the open, so everybody knew how you voted. But the 1832 Act led to further changes. In 1867 most working-class men in the towns could vote. In 1884 the vote was extended to farm labourers. In 1918 all men over twenty-one could vote.

All this, however, was in the future. In 1838 the campaign to make Parliament properly representative of the people began again. The aims of a group of campaigners called the Chartists were expressed simply in the six points of their charter. They wanted all men to have the vote. They wanted voting to be secret. They wanted all constituencies to be of roughly the same size, and general elections to be held each year. They said that any man should be able to become an MP – whether or not he owned property – and that MPs should be paid.

Although the Chartists had many supporters, they were scorned as wild and dangerous men by those who had wealth and power. In 1848 a huge meeting was called to present a petition for the reform of Parliament, which had been signed, the Chartist leaders said, by six million people. Half a million men and women were expected to meet on Kennington Common in south London. The government took no chances and raised 170,000 special constables to keep law and order. They need not have bothered. Only 20,000 people turned up. Only two million signatures were found on the petition, and many of them were forged. The Chartists were made to look ridiculous, and never regained wide support.

Nevertheless, we can see now that the Chartists were among the founders of our democratic system. In time their points were accepted, and all their demands, apart from annual general elections, are now British law.

The Reform Act was followed by other reforms. In 1833 the first of the Factory Acts was passed, preventing the employment of young children in cotton factories. Two men of deep Christian beliefs – the Earl of Shaftesbury and Richard Oastler – were particularly responsible. It was bitterly opposed by businessmen, who said that the changes were examples of government interference in matters of business. Later Factory Acts stopped child labour altogether in all factories. The Mines Act of 1842 stopped the employment of women and children in coal mines. Here women, in particular, had often been employed dragging trucks along railway lines for twelve hours a day in the dark.

If the British have a shameful record of profiting from the slave trade behind them, they can also claim to have led the campaign to end it. In 1807 Parliament banned all trading in slaves. After the peace with France in 1815 the British Navy patrolled the Atlantic to prevent slave traders of all nationalities reaching their markets in the West Indies or the southern United States. In 1833 slavery was ended by law in all parts of the British Empire. William Wilberforce, the Christian who had given a large part of his life to bringing about the abolition, died shortly before the Act abolishing slavery was passed.

Not all reforms improved people's

A Victorian street scene.

lives. The reform of the old Elizabethan Poor Law system by the Poor Law Act of 1834 led to the building of the grim Victorian workhouses which can still be seen in all British cities. So determined was Parliament to make all men and women stand on their own feet that in future anyone who wanted help from public funds had to enter a workhouse to receive it. Here husbands and wives were separated. The food was scarce and of the poorest quality. The inmates slept on hard beds in great dormitories, and were set to work long hours on monotonous work like breaking stones for the new "Macadamized" roads.

The workhouses were so feared and hated that many people preferred to starve to death or to turn to crime, rather than ask for help from public money. If you had a job, you worked to keep it at all costs. If you were unemployed, you went anywhere, however low the wages, to find work. Or perhaps you emigrated.

As we have seen, far fewer children died in the 19th century, partly because there was greater knowledge of the importance of cleanliness. Many more lives were saved by Edward Jenner's discovery of vaccination.

Jenner was a country doctor in Gloucestershire. Many of his patients held the old country belief that if you caught cowpox – a mild disease common among milkmaids – you would not catch smallpox. (One in ten people died of smallpox at this time, most in childhood.) After careful experiments, Jenner became convinced of the truth of the belief. He began injecting his patients with the virus of cowpox to prevent them catching smallpox. This is called vaccination, from the Latin *vacca* (a cow). His methods soon caught on. In 1840 free vaccination was made available to everyone in Britain. Forty years later smallpox was more or less unknown.

Towns had always been centres of disease. In 1851 the national census showed that if you lived in Manchester or Liverpool you were lucky if you lived past twenty-five. If you lived in the country, you could hope to live twice as long. The terrible epidemics in the towns hit poor and rich alike. But such diseases as typhus, typhoid fever and cholera always started in the areas where overcrowding and ventilation were worst, where there were no proper drains and no running water – that is, in the poorest areas. In such areas the sewage from the outside earth toilets was dumped in the streets or thrown in the nearest river or pond. The only water pump was 50 metres away and would often have run dry by the time you reached it with your bucket.

A great cholera epidemic in 1831 so alarmed Parliament that an inquiry into the causes of epidemics began. Edwin Chadwick took the lead in this. He pointed out that far more British people died from filth each year than from wars.

Chadwick's Public Health Act of 1848 set up a Board of Health in London with power to set up local boards where death rates were exceptionally high. They organized street cleaning, the building of pavements, and, above all, proper sewers. Many of their tasks were later taken over by local Medical Officers of Health. One such officer for London was John Simon. He insisted on inspecting the poorest houses to discover whether they were fit to live in. Landlords opposed him. They said they could not afford the changes he tried to make them introduce or the rates which paid for new streets and street lighting. But slowly, decent sanitation, public water supplies and street lighting were to be found even in the poorest areas of Victorian cities.

The great improvements in the nursing profession at this time are always associated with Florence Nightingale. Before her, nurses were regarded with contempt. They were thought of as dirty, lazy and often drunken. Florence Nightingale saw what happened to wounded soldiers in hospitals during the Crimean War of 1854–1856. The wards, corridors, kitchens and laundries were filthy. Soldiers lay on blood-stained beds which were never washed. Their excrement – and most had diarrhoea – lay stinking in unemptied buckets on the wards. Their bandages were never changed.

Florence Nightingale was determined to clean things up when she was sent to improve the soldiers' hospitals in the Crimea. She came from a wealthy family and was used to getting her way. After six months, instead of 420 patients dying out of every 1000 soldiers admitted to hospital, only twenty two died.

After the war was over, Florence Nightingale founded the first training school for nurses at St Thomas' Hospital in London. She supervised a strict method of training nurses which lasted from two to four years and ended with a final examination. Her methods were adopted by every hospital in the land.

From the earliest times the usual anaesthetics, or painkillers, available to doctors were alcohol and opium. Sometimes men – particularly soldiers – were just knocked hard on the head and made unconscious before an operation.

It was James Simpson who pioneered the use of chloroform as an anaesthetic. Now surgeons could operate without their patients writhing in agony. Meanwhile Joseph Lister worked to overcome the danger of wound infections. Because of the filthy conditions of wards and operating tables, a surgeon could never carry out an operation without the cuts he made getting infected and turning septic. Lister realized through reading the work of Louis Pasteur, the great French scientist, that infections came from germs. If you killed the germs, you killed the infection. He insisted that the surgeon's hands, clothes and instruments should be disinfected before use. Carbolic acid was used to disinfect the wound as well as anything which might come into contact with it. Deaths from infected wounds now virtually ended

Much of what is called "history" is the record of people's cruelty and aggression against other people. It is good to record the work of men like William Wilberforce and Joseph Lister and of women like Elizabeth Fry and Florence Nightingale. Thanks to them and many other reformers, politicians, civil servants and medical pioneers, our lives have been transformed during the last 200 years. They too have made "history".

Joseph Lister in the operating theatre. The patient is anaesthetized with a cloth soaked in chloroform. The surgeon's instruments stand in carbolic acid to disinfect them. Notice that the surgeons are in suits and wear no gloves or masks.

The British Empire

During the years 1815–1914 Britain became a great power in the world. This power had nothing to do the the Army; it grew out of world-wide trade, the Navy and the Empire.

British money was invested in companies which did business all over the world. British ships carried a high proportion of the world's trade. British railway engineers designed many of the railways in South America and Asia. British road builders and bridge builders were at work all over Africa.

The British Navy was to be found at anchor in harbours all over the world. Wherever there was trouble, and British interests were threatened, Royal Navy gunboats and frigates would be seen patrolling the coasts, their polished guns

Sydney, Australia, in the early 19th century. This Empire town, originally a convict settlement, had been established for thirty years. The great days of the country's wool trade were about to begin.

glinting in the sun, the Royal Navy flag – the White Ensign – flying in the offshore breezes.

In 1815 ministers from the countries who had joined together to defeat Napoleon's France – Britain, Austria, Russia and Prussia (Germany) – met at the Congress of Vienna. They divided between them lands they had gained from France. The British were no longer interested in gaining an empire in Europe. They wanted lands which would provide valuable raw materials, or which could be used as bases by the Royal Navy or by

British trading ships.

At the entry to the Mediterranean the British already possessed Gibraltar. Now the Congress gave them Malta. At the southernmost tip of Africa they took over the settlement of the Cape of Good Hope from the Dutch. They were given Ceylon (Sri Lanka) off India, and Mauritius in the Indian Ocean. They took over some more islands, rich in sugar and tobacco, in the West Indies. Britain's gains at the peace treaty soon led to others. By 1850 the British Empire extended all over the world.

If a party of Britons decided to take a cruise round the world when the British Empire was at its height at the end of the 19th century, they would find themselves on British soil or in lands under British control wherever they landed.

After Gibraltar and Malta in the Mediterranean, they would come to Egypt, which Britain controlled at the end of the 19th century. In 1870, a French firm finished building the Suez Canal and after that all British ships bound for India sailed down the canal from the Mediterranean to the Red Sea and into the Indian Ocean. The canal was owned by several companies, but from 1875 onwards the British government owned the largest share. At the southernmost point of the Red Sea was Aden, a British colony.

Across the Indian Ocean were more British colonies – India and Sri Lanka – and at the southernmost tip of Malaysia, Singapore, which became British in 1819. If their ship turned north to China, it would come to Hong Kong, a colony which the British had seized by force from China in 1842, or Shanghai which British merchants controlled, protected by British ships.

By sailing south, the ship would eventually reach Australia. The British had originally used Australia as a settlement for convicts. The beginnings of sheep-farming in New South Wales and the discovery of gold in Victoria and Western Australia had turned it into a prosperous country. Although it still belonged to Britain, Australia was more and more in charge of its own affairs. Millions of men and women, the majority of them British, had boarded the packed emigrant ships which regularly sailed from Britain to Australia to start a new life.

From Sydney or Melbourne the British captain would sail south-east to New Zealand. It had been taken over by Britain in 1840, when France was supposed to be interested in colonizing the islands. Here, too, men and women had come from Britain to start a new life. Here, too, sheep-farming made the country prosperous, while the export of butter back to Britain became a thriving trade.

On the other side of the Pacific, there was Vancouver on the west coast of Canada, which Britain had gained from France in the 18th century. The ship might then sail south and its passengers might cross the narrow Isthmus of Panama by horse or mule under British guard to pick up a British ship on the Atlantic coast. If the ship sailed the rough seas south of South America it would be protected by ships of the South Atlantic Fleet based on the Falkland Islands. On her way home she would be sure to stop off at a British West Indian island, Jamaica, say, or Trinidad, before returning to London.

When the travellers docked they could tell their friends that at no point in their voyage round the world had it been necessary to speak a word of any language other than English. They would have seen for themselves that the lands of the British Empire, painted red on all the maps and globes they used, covered one quarter of the world.

Some writers who have studied the lives of working people in 19th-century England have said that only emigration prevented a British revolution to match the revolutions in France in 1789 and

There were two main reasons for this harsh treatment. After the defeat of Bonnie Prince Charlie's rebellion at the battle of Culloden in 1745, the British government was determined to teach the Highlanders a lesson. Troops occupied the area, and their commanders were encouraged to expel any family they thought might take up arms against the British again. But another, more impor-

"The Last Evening" by J.J. Tissot (1873). This painting celebrates the days of the "grand tour" or world cruise which the rich were able to enjoy.

1830, in Germany in 1848 and, later, in Russia in 1917. Certainly, emigration to Canada, Australia, New Zealand and South Africa gave new life and hope to millions of desperate people.

Among those who went to Canada and Newfoundland were Scottish families from the Highlands. They left home because of the Highland "clearances" in the 18th century, when thousands of Scottish farmers were driven off their lands.

tant reason was that the rich Scottish landlords, or "lairds", wanted the land for sheep-farming. They knew that they could get much richer from sheep-farming than from the tiny rents paid by the small farmers. So they evicted them.

The troubles of the desperate men and women who left Scotland to start a new

278

life overseas – and left much of the Scottish Highlands the empty land it is today – were not ended when they boarded the emigrant ships. Many must have believed the promises which they read in advertisements like this one:

"NOTICE TO PASSENGERS
for
NOVA SCOTIA AND CANADA

All those who wish to emigrate to these parts in summer will find this an excellent opportunity, as every attention will be paid to the comfort of passengers."

The fare across was seven guineas for an adult and three guineas for a child aged two to seven.

But some of the emigrant ships were more overcrowded than slave ships. Men, women and children were crammed between decks in filthy, dark, un-ventilated conditions. The food was poor and scarce. The water was stale. The wood was rotten. The journey often took twice the time promised – two months instead of one. Many died of disease on the way. When, finally, the survivors landed in the "New World", as America was known, they found that there was no job or farm awaiting them, as had been promised.

One Governor of Canada wrote of these emigrant ships:

"I really do believe that there are not

During the 19th century English landlords evicted thousands of Irish farmers and destroyed their cottages. Here, the battering ram has already started work. Rather than face such experiences, many Irish emigrated like the Scottish Highlanders during the "clearances".

many instances of slave-traders from Africa to America exhibiting so disgusting a picture."

Like the empire in Elizabethan times, the new British Empire was not planned – at least, not at first. Bases were given in peace treaties, or seized by force because they were useful to traders or needed by the Navy in its task of patrolling the world's waters. British men and women went to settle in new continents because they were restless, or ambitious, or desperate at home. However, after the Indian Mutiny in 1857, Conservative governments in Britain did carry out a policy of empire-building (although the Liberals, who were now the main opposition party, were against the idea).

After the French had been defeated, India was still controlled by the British East India Company rather than the British government. But in 1857 a serious mutiny of Indian troops against their British masters occurred. After it was suppressed, the British government had to decide what future policy to adopt. Were they merely to protect British traders as they carried on their profitable trade in jute, tea and cotton? Or were they to take over India as a colony?

The British chose to colonize India, and their power was firmly established with astonishing speed. Burma and Malaya were soon thoroughly colonized also, along Indian lines.

Great areas of India, Burma and Malaya were now ruled over by British district officers. Often young Englishmen in their early twenties, these men were in sole charge of the lives of thousands of people in their districts. They could never have been so successful if their rule had not been quietly accepted by the people they governed. In this way the British Empire resembled the Roman Empire. No wonder the schools which educated the young British district officers made their pupils spend so many hours studying Latin!

After 1870 more and more colonies were established by Britain. British governments were particularly concerned to take over large parts of Africa before the French, Belgians and Germans got there first. This competition between the European countries was known as the "scramble for Africa". The British gained colonies on the coasts of both west and east Africa. On the west coast, they colonized Gambia, Sierra Leone, the Gold Coast and – the richest prize of all – Nigeria. On the east coast, they colonized Uganda and Kenya. After the First World War they were given the old German colony of Tanganyika.

British governments always remembered the revolt of the North American colonies. So when in the 19th and early 20th centuries Australia, New Zealand and Canada wanted to govern themselves the British did not oppose them. They became dominions – countries which governed themselves but which were closely linked with Britain through trade and fellow-feeling. (As we shall see they fought side by side with Britain in both the First and the Second World Wars.) Just as the colonies became dominions, so the idea of an empire, in which Britain ruled the colonies, gave way to a commonwealth in which Britain and its dominions were partners pledged to help each other. Later in the 20th century, when other British colonies wanted to govern themselves, the idea of dominions and a commonwealth was extended to include them too.

In South Africa the position was more complicated. When the British had bought the colony from the Dutch for £6 million in 1815, they took over a settlement of Dutch people whose forefathers had first landed at the Cape of Good Hope more than 150 years before. The British and the Dutch settlers – Afrikaners, as they called themselves – never got on together. Matters got worse when the British government tried to make English, instead of the Afrikaners' language, Afrikaans, the official language in South Africa. The British also ordered the Afrikaners to free their slaves, following the abolition of slavery in all British lands in 1833.

The Afrikaners now travelled – or "trekked" – north, in the Great Trek of 1835. They set up their own states of Transvaal and the Orange Free State. Here they lived their own lives, and the British left them alone.

But trouble arose again when fabulously rich gold mines were discovered near Johannesburg, the capital of the Transvaal. The two groups of white colonists – ignored by most of the black population – finally went to war.

The South African War (1899–1902) which the British insultingly called the Boer War – from the Afrikaans word "boer" meaning peasant – was a bitter war. The British were shocked when, to begin with, the Afrikaners won some important victories. How could the soldiers of the great British Empire suffer such defeats at the hands of a tiny group of settlers? Eventually the British won and at the end of the war the South African colonies became part of the British Empire. But in 1909 the South Africa Act was passed, making South Africa a dominion with equal rights for British and Afrikaners. The two white communities, however, continued to distrust each other. Finally in 1960 South Africa, under its Afrikaner leaders, left the British Commonwealth altogether.

Throughout the 19th century, British governments avoided making alliances with other powerful European countries. They did not want to have to fight in a major European war again, but they were determined to protect British trading interests in the East, using the power of the Navy.

The Turks controlled a large empire at the eastern end of the Mediterranean, which the Russians were trying to take over. The British feared that if either of these countries became too powerful, they might stop British traders from passing through the area on their way to India and China. In 1827 the British Navy fought to help the Greeks gain independence from their Turkish rulers. At the battle of Navarino Bay the British fleet sank many Turkish ships. From 1854 to 1856 Britain and France fought against Russia in the Crimean War. In 1878 Britain took over the island of Cyprus as a base for her ships in the eastern Mediterranean.

Britain was always keen to support rebels who were fighting for their nation's freedom. In the 1820s, when Canning was Foreign Minister, the British Navy was used to support South American republics in their fight to become independent of Spain, their colonial ruler. Later, Palmerston, the best-known and most feared of all British Foreign Ministers, supported those Italians, such as Mazzini, Cavour and Garibaldi, who were fighting to create a united Italy. Britain was always prepared to welcome refugees who were expelled from their own countries because of their political beliefs or their part in revolutions against dictators. For many people in Europe, Britain was the home of freedom.

The end of the 19th Century

For most of the 19th century, Britain's governments believed in free trade. They believed that countries should not tax foreign goods to prevent them competing with their own. But it took many years of argument and political campaigns before policies of free trade were adopted.

Until the 1832 Reform Act, Britain was still governed mainly by landowners. They wanted to encourage farming at all costs, because their own wealth came from the rents which their tenant farmers paid them.

The years of war with France were prosperous years for British farmers and landlords. Foreign corn did not enter the country, so the price of British corn was high. After the war was over, Parliament feared that millions of sacks of foreign corn – particularly wheat – would be imported into Britain. Their importation would lower the price of British corn, and the days of prosperous farming would be over. The Corn Law, passed in 1815, said that foreign corn could not be imported unless the price of British corn stood at £4 a quarter – a high price. This law was followed by other similar ones.

British farmers and landlords may have liked the Corn Laws but British businessmen hated them. Their businesses depended on exporting their goods (cotton, for instance, or wool) abroad. When the British government protected its own farmers, foreign governments replied by banning or limiting the entry of British manufactured products into their countries.

After 1832, businessmen at last had the vote. Some became MPs themselves. Others urged their local MPs to repeal the Corn Laws. All over Britain, anti-Corn Law meetings were held; anti-Corn Law advertisements were placed in newspapers; and even anti-Corn Law tea-sets were sold. In 1846 the businessmen converted the Conservative Prime Minister himself, Robert Peel.

The Conservatives had always been the landlords' party. Peel was the Conservative leader. But he was also the son of a successful Lancashire cotton manufacturer and reformer. Now he faced an agony of conscience. Should he follow the principles of free trade, which he now believed in, or continue to support the Corn Laws, which his party believed in? In 1846 Peel announced his conversion to the cause of the Anti-Corn Law League. The Corn Laws were repealed: the protection of British farmers was ended.

To repeal the Corn Laws, Peel had had to rely on the votes of the Whigs (the main opposition party of the time) and MPs of no party, as well as the group of Conservatives who supported him. Now they came together to form the Liberal Party, which in time took the place of the Whigs. But Peel's career was over. The Conservatives would no longer have him as their leader.

One of the younger MPs who most admired Peel was William Gladstone. He became the leader of the Liberal Party and, in 1868, Prime Minister. His first government (1868–1874) set out to free Englishmen from unfair restrictions and to give them more opportunities.

It seemed unfair to the Liberals that voting for Parliamentary elections still took place openly in market squares or

A school in the 19th century. Children of all ages are assembled in one room. Notice the the children in the front doing exercises.

The most important of all the reforms passed by Gladstone's first government was the Education Act of 1870. The majority of British children still did not go to school, though in most districts there were schools, run by the local churches. Gladstone's government set up elected authorities, School Boards, in each area. The authorities had to build schools for children up to the age of thirteen in any district which did not already have a church school. Where a church school existed, the government subsidized (paid money towards) it. The boards got money from local taxpayers to build schools and pay the teachers. Schools were not yet free and children did not have to go to them. However, twenty years later, it was made compulsory for children to attend school up to the age of thirteen, and it became free.

Gladstone and the Liberal Party did not have such a good record over the improvement of people's working and living conditions. Just as they believed in free trade, they believed governments should not interfere with the running of employers' businesses. They were not supporters of trade unions. However, Gladstone did pass a Trade Union Act which guaranteed trade unions the right to exist and go about their business. But it did not allow picketing.

When an employer and his workers completely disagree — over wages, for instance — the only power the workers have which can balance the employer's power to sack them is to go on strike. A strike can only work if all the workers are united and remain on strike together. If some return to work — or if new workers are taken on — the strike is bound to fail. The best way of maintaining unity among the strikers is by picketing. Pickets are workers — generally

similar public places. Voters raised their hands for the candidates of their choice, and could be victimized by their employers if they were seen to be voting for candidates the employers disliked. The Liberals passed the Ballot Act of 1872, which made all voting for Parliamentary elections secret.

It seemed unfair and inefficient to Gladstone and his Cabinet (his leading ministers) that men often became civil servants not because they seemed likely to do their jobs well but because their families were influential. So it was decreed that you had to pass an examination to become a civil servant. Another Act was passed which said that men could no longer become officers in the Army simply by paying for their positions. Instead they had to show that they would be good at the job. At the same time flogging in the Army was abolished.

strong union men or women – who stand at the entrance to the factory or mine and try to persuade their fellow workers not to work until the strike is over.

In 1874 Gladstone's government was defeated at the general election. A new Conservative government, with Benjamin Disraeli as its Prime Minister, took office. Disraeli was more sympathetic to the trade unions. He allowed picketing, so long as it was peaceful. Peaceful picketing has been legal ever since.

Disraeli believed that over matters of public health it was a government's duty to interfere. By his Public Health Act of 1875, all houses had to be supplied with clean water and proper drains, and streets had to be regularly cleaned. The councils also had to see that the food which was sold in the shops was clean and fit to eat and that the beer had not been watered down.

Another Act encouraged councils to pull down the worst slums in their districts. They could replace them by their own council-built houses which were cheap to rent and built to high standards of light and ventilation. Later, 20th-century councils followed up the Act on a large scale.

Although many people remained des-

Towards the end of the 19th century, private philanthropic bodies began to clear the slums and build carefully-planned estates for working people. The Shaftesbury Park Estate was at Lavender Hill in London.

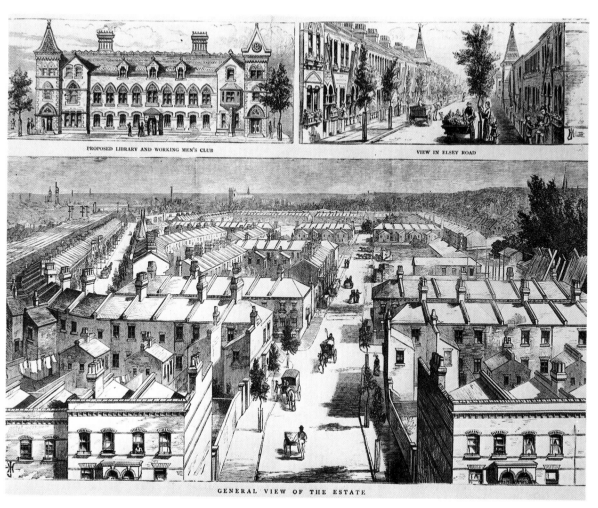

PROPOSED LIBRARY AND WORKING MEN'S CLUB

VIEW IN ELSEY ROAD

GENERAL VIEW OF THE ESTATE

perately poor, the conditions of other working-class families began steadily to improve at the end of the 19th century. Many a working family now rented a well-built, warm house in a terraced street. Better-paid working men – skilled craftsmen, for instance, such as engineers or shipwrights – joined trade unions. The unions were not only concerned with wages. In return for a weekly payment, the union would help a working man pay for a doctor when he or his family were ill. It would organize sick pay for him and provide him with a decent funeral. Or it would keep the family going during unemployment. The success of the London dock strike of 1889, when the dockers closed down the greatest port in the world for six weeks and won their demand for a basic wage of sixpence (2½p) an hour, led many unskilled labourers to join unions.

Wages were slowly improving and working people at last had some leisure. Early-closing days became compulsory for shopkeepers. Fewer and fewer people worked on Saturday afternoons. Men went regularly to football matches, standing in their thousands on draughty terraces to cheer their local club.

Parliament ordered regular bank holidays to be observed. If the banks were shut, businesses were shut too. This meant that everybody had at least a few days off – such as Christmas Day, Easter and August Bank Holiday. The family week at the seaside – if you could afford it – had been popular since 1850 or before. Now the day at Blackpool, Margate or a multitude of other seaside resorts was added to it. The steamers that sailed from Westminster steps to Margate Pier started the "special offer" weekend excursion ticket. The railways replied with the cheap day return ticket.

By 1900, townspeople – particularly young people – were bicycling from the town into the countryside at weekends. The new bicycles were particularly popular with clerks and office workers. During the 19th century, growing numbers of men and women worked in commerce – in banks, insurance offices and on the Stock Exchange.

Also by 1900, Londoners could travel cheaply all over the capital by underground – or tube-train. As they did so, they took to reading popular newspapers and magazines. The *Daily Mail*, which was the first daily paper written for ordinary people and not the well-educated, appeared in 1896. *Tit Bits*, the first popular magazine, had come out earlier. The most popular Saturday night entertainment of the time was the music hall.

The habit of regular church going, which had been part of country life, did not continue in the towns. Hundreds of thousands of people lost touch with Christianity. But the Methodist Church was well attended in the industrial towns and had a considerable influence on the lives of working people. Many of the first Labour leaders were Methodists. The Salvation Army did particularly devoted work among the poor. They would be found at work in the poorest areas of big towns – especially London – and provided shelters for the thousands of homeless men and women who would otherwise sleep rough on the city streets. The National Society for the Prevention of Cruelty to Children and the Church of England's Children Society helped thousands of orphan children who would otherwise have been homeless.

Christian missionaries took their faith to Africa, India and many other areas of the British Empire. They suffered hardships for their beliefs as they travelled in areas where Christianity was unknown. Some of them were killed.

In 1905 a new Liberal government won a large majority in the general election. They promised more reforms, supported by members of the new Labour Party, who were elected to bring about improvements in working people's ways of life. The first thing they did was to change the law so that employers could not sue trades unions for profits lost during strikes.

After that they passed a number of Acts which helped the poorest people in Britain. They started the school meals service, and gave free meals to pupils whose parents could not afford to pay for them. Hundreds of thousands of children now ate a good meal each day for the first time in their lives. A free school medical service was started. Many children now saw a doctor and a dentist for the first time in their lives.

The Liberals, with Herbert Asquith as their Prime Minister and David Lloyd George as their strongest personality, introduced old-age pensions for the first time in Britain. They were only paid to the poorest men and women, but they were a welcome start.

So, too, was the National Insurance Act of 1911. Workers earning less than £3 a week could now be treated free by a doctor. They could also draw 35p a week for up to fifteen weeks (and no more) if they were unemployed. This was paid for by small payments each week from the worker, his employer and the government. Later improvements have made Lloyd George's Act seem very inadequate, but it started the move towards providing help for people in times of trouble, so that they no longer had to starve – or steal.

All these reforms had to be paid for and this led to serious trouble between the House of Commons and the House of Lords. There had long been a contradiction between the idea of democracy and the existence of the House of Lords. For the peers in the House of Lords were not elected. They could sit, debate and vote simply because they were the sons of dukes, earls or barons. When Lloyd George, in his "People's" Budget of 1909, proposed to increase taxes on those who could most easily afford them – the rich – the Lords refused to pass the budget.

Two years of argument, and two general elections followed. By what right, asked the Liberals, have the Lords rejected our budget? For centuries – ever since the Civil Wars – the House of Commons has decided the taxes which the country pays. Now unelected people have changed that arrangement. Why, in a democracy, should the House of Lords be allowed to have any power at all?

In the end the Liberal government proposed a compromise. The Parliament Act of 1911 said that in future the House of Lords could never debate taxation. And they also proposed that in future any Act which was passed by the House of Commons three times during two years would become law, even if the Lords rejected it. Reluctantly, when the King, as over the 1832 Reform Bill, threatened to appoint numbers of new peers who would support the Parliament Act, the House of Lords gave in. They passed the Act. From that time onwards the House of Lords has had only a minor say in governing Britain. The Act also said that MPs should be paid.

If the existence of the House of Lords seemed to contradict the very idea of democracy, the fact that women could not vote in Parliamentary elections seemed even more unfair. How could you talk about the rule of the country by those whom the people had elected if half the people could not vote? Step by step during the 19th century more and more men had been given the vote. Now a campaign began to give votes to women.

In 1903 Mrs Emmeline Pankhurst formed the Women's Social and Political Union. She and her three daughters began to try to bring about the introduction of votes for women by writing articles and holding public meetings and marches. They succeeded in persuading numbers of men that their cause was just. But when it became clear that the government would not help them, they turned to other methods.

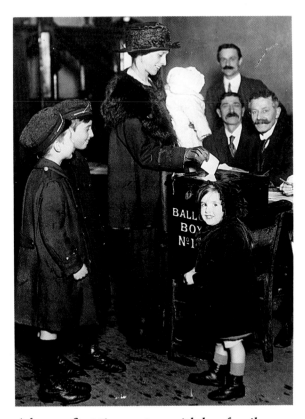

A happy first time voter, with her family, dropping her vote into the ballot box (1918). Votes for women – at last!

From 1908 they called attention to their cause – the cause of the "Suffragettes" ("suffrage" means vote) – by every method which did not include personal violence. They interrupted Liberal or Conservative Party public meetings with cries of "Votes for Women!" They chained themselves to the railings of 10 Downing Street. They ran down Oxford Street smashing shop windows. They put up with rough and cruel treatment from the police. They got themselves imprisoned and went on hunger strike in prison. One of their leaders, Emily Davison, threw herself under the hooves of the King's horse as it rode in the Derby – and killed herself. Six thousand women marched in her funeral procession. Some wore black and carried purple irises. Others were dressed in white. It was an impressive occasion.

Yet by the outbreak of the First World War in 1914 the Suffragettes had still not achieved their aim. No woman could vote for Parliament or become an MP.

The war saw a quiet change in men's attitudes. Women worked in munitions (weapons) factories. They saved thousands of lives as nurses and ambulance drivers. When at the end of the war, in 1918, a bill proposing votes for women came up again before Parliament, it was passed. It was as if Parliament wanted to thank women for the work they had done. Soon the first woman MP – Lady Astor – was elected. People, at long last, could honestly say that Britain was a democracy. The people – not just the men – had the vote.

The World at War (1914–1918)

The First World War was one of the greatest disasters which Britain has experienced in its history. In four years nearly one million young British men were killed. Over two million were wounded, many of them for life. It was like a modern Black Death.

Yet the British entered the First World War in the most cheerful of moods. The cry was that "the boys would be home for Christmas". Only a few generals and leading politicians realized just how many people were likely to be killed in a modern war. They thought it wisest to keep their knowledge to themselves.

The majority of British people supported the war. Ever since the 1880s, the Germans and the British had been competing for colonies in Africa. From the battle of Trafalgar (1805) onwards, the British had dominated the world's seas. They resented the growing power of the German navy, which openly challenged that domination. Both countries competed hectically with each other in building bigger and better battle ships.

After the Germans had defeated the French in the Franco-Prussian War of 1870, they had become the strongest military power in Europe. To the east, Russia feared the power of Germany and its ally, Austria-Hungary. In the west, France was itching for revenge.

Britain had become more friendly with France in the years before 1914, but it was by no means certain that it would join in if another war broke out between France and Germany.

It was the German attack on Belgium in August 1914, which made up the minds of the British Liberal Government. Britain had signed a treaty promising to

help if Belgium was attacked. The Germans, hoping to knock out the French army before the French attacked them, decided to do so by a surprise route. On 3rd August they attacked Belgium. Their plan was to march through Belgium, cross the undefended frontier into France, and capture Paris in forty days.

The British government and people now became convinced that the Germans had to be stopped. As in the Hundred Years War and the French wars of 1793–1815, Britain feared that the greatest power in Europe – which had been France and was now Germany – would control the whole coastline of northern Europe. Such control would threaten British interests, and particularly British trade. War was declared.

Two Liberal MPs in the Cabinet felt unable to support the war and resigned. A few well-known men – Ramsay Mac-

Donald, for instance, who later became the first British Labour Prime Minister, and Bertrand Russell, the philosopher – also opposed the war. Some people, the Quakers, for instance, refused to take part in any war. Known as conscientious objectors (their consciences would not allow them to fight), they were jeered at and scorned in the most cruel way. Women came up to them in the street and gave them white feathers – symbols of cowardice. In fact they showed very great courage to face such unpopularity.

The German generals had assumed that their men would be in Paris before the British armies had time to go into action. But the British Expeditionary Force arrived in France much sooner than the Germans expected. A hundred thousand British soldiers fought at Mons in Belgium on 23rd August 1914. They showed tremendous courage, though they were outnumbered and without machine-guns.

The German army was stopped outside Paris in the first battle of the Marne in September 1914. From then on millions of soldiers faced each other in northern France across a few hundred metres of churned-up mud. French, Britons (including thousands of Canadians, South Africans, Australians and New Zealanders) and Germans dug deep trenches on either side of this No Man's Land and fought each other to a standstill. Millions of young men were killed. The Western Front – the line along which the troops fought – did not change by more than 15 kilometres in either direction in three and a half years.

The trenches were dug deep into the ground and connected with each other, so that men could pass along kilometres of trenches, taking messages or bringing help to comrades. Here they ate, slept, played cards, and hoped that a shell from an enemy gun would not explode on top of them. Unless this happened the trench was a safe hiding place – if you could stand the wet, the lice, and the continual noise of the guns.

It was when you put your head above the parapet that German machine-gunners would open fire from a few metres away. This you might do when you were on look-out duty. But most men were killed when they were on patrol or taking part in an offensive.

Both sides tried to test out the defences of the other by patrols. It was no good men going out of the trenches during the day. What chance would they have against the enemy big guns (artillery), with their sights set on No Man's Land ready to explode their shells? Or what chance would they have against the machine-gunners, who had only to keep their fingers steady on their triggers to kill them with ease?

For these reasons most patrols took place at night. Led by their platoon commanders, the men – given extra courage by a ration of rum – lurched across the potholes of No Man's Land, bayonets at the ready. They would keep as close to the ground as possible. Their target was the nearest enemy trench on the other side of the divide. Wire-cutting squads went in front of them. If they reached their destination, they would silently cut the line of enemy barbed wire which was razor sharp to the touch. Flares lit up the night. When they found the enemy trenches, the men lobbed bombs or grenades into them, then they went into them with their bayonets to kill the Germans and capture the trench.

This sort of patrol took place every night, all along the line. But the massive casualties occurred when the generals on one side or the other decided that the time had come for a breakthrough.

Then, for hour upon hour, shells whined over the heads of the tense, stooping troops waiting to go "over the top".

At last, when the commanders believed that no man could still be alive in the enemy trenches, the guns stopped firing. Then the infantrymen were ordered to advance. Now the faith which the generals placed in the power of their artillery was generally shown to be misguided. As the whistles blew and the men attacked, enemy machine-gunners, who had somehow survived the bombardment, opened fire. Enemy artillery, which had waited for just such a moment, shelled the advancing troops. Thousands upon thousands of young men fell dead before they even reached the enemy trenches.

The British lost 60,000 men in this way on the first day of the battle of the Somme in 1916. At the battle of Passchendaele in 1917, the preliminary bombardment was so fierce that it destroyed the drainage system of the German trenches. The British troops fought their way into great lakes of water and mud in which thousands drowned. They advanced eight kilometres, but then had to retreat. They lost 324,000 men, killed and wounded, in this one battle.

Commanders on both sides tried to think of other ways of achieving a breakthrough. In 1915 the Germans used poison gas; the British soon used it back. But gas provided neither side with a clear advantage. One of the worst of its horrors was that when the wind changed direction, the gas was blown back into the lungs of your own men.

The invention of tanks by the British and the development of military aircraft by both sides promised to bring about a breakthrough on the western front. But the promise was never fulfilled.

Hopes rested on defeating the Germans in other parts of the world. Then they would be forced to draw back in the west. At the start of the war, the Russian armies had taken the Germans by surprise. They advanced into eastern Germany and threatened the capital Berlin itself. At one time it seemed possible that Russian troops would spend Christmas 1914 in Berlin, while German troops ate their Christmas dinner in Paris.

But the Germans sent back some of their best troops and commanders from Belgium and France in early September 1914. In this way, they saved Berlin, but probably ended their chance of occupying Paris. They defeated the Russians at the battle of Tannenberg in August 1914. From then on the Russian troops retreated farther and farther into their own country. Finally, in 1917, hundreds of thousands of men deserted and Russia experienced two revolutions. The second was the Communist Revolution. The Communist government took the Russians out of the war at the end of 1917.

In 1915 Winston Churchill, who was First Lord of the Admiralty, decided to use the British Navy to land half a million men – including large numbers of Australian and New Zealand troops – on the Gallipoli Peninsula in Turkey. The Turks had entered the war on the German side. The British dreamed of capturing the Turkish capital Constantinople (Istanbul), and of joining up with the Russian armies to the north. The Russians would take new heart, and the two allies would march on Berlin. The Germans would have to withdraw thousands of soldiers from the western front, and Germany would fall apart under the strain of attacks from all sides.

The plan was a disaster. Turkish gun-

Over the top in the First World War.

ners lying on the hills overlooking the landing beaches mowed down the British troops. Their big guns trained their sights on British battleships when they came too close to the shore. Half the troops were killed or wounded and the Gallipoli campaign was abandoned.

The Germans were the only country in the world to see that U-boats (submarines) could win a war. They knew that the British relied on importing arms and, even more important, food, from the United States and Canada. Without that food the British would starve.

In February 1917, with the Russians virtually knocked out of the war, the Germans took their biggest gamble. They announced that their submarines would sink any ship they found in the seas around Britain even if it belonged to a neutral country which was trading with Britain — in other words any American grain ship. The Germans knew that once they carried out their threat, the United States would probably declare war against them — which is what happened in April 1917. But they thought Britain would be starved into surrender before that could make much difference.

The German U-boats were so successful at sinking British and American merchant ships that Britain soon had only six weeks' supply of wheat left. At this point, Lloyd George, who had now become Prime Minister, ordered the commanders of the British Navy to adopt a convoy system — merchant ships would be escorted across the Atlantic by Navy warships in a group, or convoy. By New Year 1918, few merchant ships were being sunk and the threat was over. No American troop-ship was ever sunk on its way across the Atlantic.

The Germans' last chance of victory came in 1918. Now that their armies no longer had to fight the Russians, the Germans had more than three and a half million men on the western front. In March they at last broke the deadlock of the trenches and advanced to within 60 kilometres of Paris. If they could occupy the capital before huge numbers of American soldiers joined the British and French, they would win.

Once again Paris was saved — at the second battle of the Marne in the spring of 1918. On 18th July 1918, the French counter-attacked, and advanced eight kilometres. On 8th August, British tanks broke through the German line at Amiens. The Germans began to retreat. By early September 1918, the Americans were sending more than 250,000 troops a month into France and it was known that they could raise an army of four million if necessary. On 11th November 1918, the Germans surrendered before fighting reached German soil.

At least eight million young men were killed in the war and twenty million were seriously injured. Perhaps only a poet can express feelings worthy of such a calamity. Wilfred Owen, a young British officer who was killed right at the end of the war, wrote "Futility" about the body of a young soldier killed at the front:

Move him into the sun —
Gently its touch awoke him once,
At home, whispering of fields unsown.
Always it woke him, even in France,
Until this morning and this snow.
If anything might rouse him now
The kind old sun will know.

Think how it wakes the seeds —
Woke, once, the clays of a cold star.
Are limbs, so dear-achieved, are sides,
Full-nerved — still warm — too hard to stir?
Was it for this the clay grew tall?
O what made fatuous sunbeams toil
To break earth's sleep at all?

Ireland and Home Rule

The First World War had united the British people. Rich and poor, landowners and businessmen, men and women, Scots, Welsh and Irish – all worked together to defeat Germany. Half-way through the war, the main political parties dropped their disagreements. Under the new Prime Minister, David Lloyd George – a man of driving energy – a coalition (combined) government was formed. Liberals, Conservatives and Labour leaders joined it. They put aside their differences until the war was ended.

After the war was over, Lloyd George called a general election. His coalition government won a huge majority. Now the government was expected to satisfy the hopes of the British people and, above all, of the soldiers returning from the trenches. They had survived experiences they could never forget, and felt they deserved a better country than Britain had been before 1914. Lloyd George himself raised their hopes when, during the election campaign, he promised that his government would build "homes fit for heroes to live in".

Britain before 1914 had been torn apart by three groups who felt that their needs were unrecognized – women, working-class men, and the Irish.

We have already seen that women gained the vote in 1918. During the next twenty years, they lost many of the gains which they had made during the war. Many of the jobs which they had been doing during the war – in factories, in business and on the land – were once more done by men. Women were not paid as well as men who did the same work. But they had achieved their main aim – the vote. For the time being, the passions aroused among both men and women by the suffragettes' campaigns subsided.

During the war the trade unions had been treated, for the first time in their history, with the respect they deserved. In the munitions factories, managers and workers worked together. Their only aim was to produce as many guns or shells as they could for the men who were fighting and dying in the trenches. Workers were consulted about the best methods of production. Lloyd George himself, first when he was Minister for Munitions and later as Prime Minister during the war years, always consulted the trade union leaders. He regarded them as important men and women without whose co-operation the war could not be won.

All this changed after the war. Bitter strikes broke out all over the country. There was even a police strike. But the struggles between employers and workers were most bitter in the areas where the Industrial Revolution had first started. Here – in the coal and iron mining districts of south Wales, in the north-east of England and Scotland, and among the cotton workers of Lancashire and the woollen workers of Yorkshire – there were strikes about wages and working conditions.

After the war, British goods faced competition from Polish, American and Japanese manufacturers. The employers were determined to cut wages, not raise them. But the workers were equally determined not to slip back to conditions before the war. Lloyd George used troops to break strikes by miners and railway workers, and lost the support of most working people by doing so.

In Ireland, centuries of bitter divisions and outright warfare now reached their climax. Slowly English governments had righted the worst of Irish wrongs. In 1793 Irish Roman Catholics won the right to vote; in 1828 they could stand for Parliament and for their local town councils. The Roman Catholic faith could now be openly practised. Gladstone had set up courts to fix fair rents and protect Irish tenant farmers from being exploited by their landlords. (Many of the landlords lived in Britain and never even visited Ireland.) Successful schemes had been introduced to let Irish tenant farmers borrow money at cheap rates from the British government. With it they bought their own land. They need no longer be dependent on British landlords. By 1914, 250,000 Irish farmers had joined the scheme.

Gladstone had tried twice to give Ireland its own parliament – or Home Rule. In 1886 and again in 1893 his Liberal government had proposed a plan to set up an Irish parliament in Dublin which would be in charge of Irish affairs. Matters of general United Kingdom concern, such as foreign policy, defence, and taxes necessary to support the UK government, would still be decided in the House of Commons. Gladstone's party split over the proposals, and a group of Liberal MPs, led by Joseph Chamberlain and calling themselves Unionists (because they supported a United Britain, including Ireland), joined the Conservatives. The Conservatives had never agreed with Home Rule. Between them, Unionists and Conservatives defeated the first Home Rule Bill. The House of Lords turned down the second.

The few reforms passed by the British Parliament failed to impress those Irish who believed that their country would never be at peace until the British left the whole island. After the Irish potato famine in 1845–1846, such feelings gained strength.

As we saw in Chapter 38, the British population had increased enormously during the first half of the 19th century. The same had happened in Ireland. In 1800 the Irish population was four and a half million. In 1845 it stood at eight and a half million. Millions emigrated to England or the United States. Of those who stayed, many were very poor. The main crop grown by Irish farmers was potatoes, and about half the population ate potatoes as their main food.

In 1845–1846, blight killed three-quarters of the potato crop in Ireland. Thousands starved. Thousands more just survived on famine relief, much of it from Britain. Within ten years one and a half million people left Ireland, most of them bound for the United States. The exodus continued. By 1926 the population had dropped to four and a half million again – a staggering fall. No other country in the modern world has halved its population in the same way.

The famine and the exodus convinced many Irishmen that Home Rule, land reforms and religious freedoms were not enough. An independent Ireland would never have allowed its people to suffer such calamities. The Irish, they believed, must now be fully independent.

Some Irish believed independence could only be achieved by force. From the 1850s onwards violence occurred all over Ireland. Bombs were exploded, cattle belonging to British landlords were maimed and hayricks were burnt. Landlords and their agents were murdered.

Irish Americans formed the Fenian Brotherhood, which swore never to cease its fight until independence was won. At the turn of the century, the Sinn Fein party was formed – Sinn Fein means "ourselves alone".

The last opportunity for achieving Home Rule – rather than total independence – occurred just before the First World War. By this time there was a group of Irish Nationalist MPs in the House of Commons, who, led first by Charles Stewart Parnell and later by John Redmond, had campaigned for Home Rule with increasing success. The Liberal government, as we have seen, was determined to reduce the power of the House of Lords after the Lords had rejected Lloyd George's budget. It could only do so with the support of the eighty-two Irish Nationalist MPs.

A deal was made. The Irish Nationalist MPs agreed to vote with the Liberals to pass the Parliament Act, which reduced the power of the Lords, in 1911. In return, in 1912, Asquith's Liberal government introduced its Irish Home Rule Bill. Now the House of Lords would not be able to stop it after it was passed by the Liberals and Irish Nationalists in the House of Commons.

But the bill caused an outcry among the people living in the six counties in the north of Ireland known as Ulster. Here the descendants of the English and Scottish "planters" made it clear that they wanted no part in an all-Irish parliament in Dublin. These Ulstermen were strongly Protestant. They distrusted the Catholic south and wanted to go on being governed by Britain. An English Conservative politician, Lord Randolph Churchill, had already warned that if Home Rule was threatened, "Ulster will fight and Ulster will be right".

The Ulster Unionists, under their leader, Sir Edward Carson, were supported by the British Conservative Party then in opposition. The Conservatives encouraged the Ulstermen to stand firm, and seemed to turn a blind eye to the way that Carson was secretly arming his Ulster Volunteer Force of 100,000 men, partly with German weapons. Carson's Catholic opponents, the Irish Volunteers, were also arming themselves. Ireland was on the point of civil war, when the First World War broke out.

Eamonn de Valera in October 1917, campaigning in southern Ireland for Sinn Fein. He told his supporters to fight in trenches in Ireland, not trenches in France. Notice the priests in the audience.

The war brought an end to the divisions for the time being. Irishmen fought alongside Scotsmen, Welshmen and Englishmen with great courage. Then in 1916 the Irish Easter Rising occurred.

In 1916 Sir Roger Casement, an Irishman who worked in the British foreign service, set to work on an ambitious plan. He went to Germany and toured the prisoner of war camps persuading Irish prisoners to join an Irish revolution, helped by the Germans. He planned to land in southern Ireland from a German submarine. Casement, who was in touch with Sinn Fein supporters in Ireland, planned the landing to coincide with a Sinn Fein rising in Dublin at Easter.

But Casement failed to recruit enough Irishmen in Germany, and on Good Friday he landed from a German submarine to tell the Sinn Feiners that the plan was cancelled. British intelligence officers were waiting for him on the beach. On Easter Monday 1916 a group of Sinn Feiners, led by P. H. Pearse and James Connolly, seized the Dublin General Post Office and proclaimed an independent Irish republic. Fighting continued for four days, before they finally surrendered.

The treatment of the Sinn Fein leaders turned Irish opinion against the British once and for all. Casement was hanged. Fifteen Sinn Feiners were shot. One other Irish leader, Eamonn de Valera, was given life imprisonment only because he was born in the United States.

At the 1918 election the Irish people showed their support for Sinn Fein by electing Sinn Fein MPs in every constituency in Ireland outside Ulster. The new MPs set up their own parliament, the Dail, in Dublin. The Dail established its own courts and taxes, even its own postal services. All Irish men and women were expected to deal with these new authorities rather than the British government. De Valera escaped from gaol and was declared president of the new republic.

Three years of war followed. The Irish Republican Army (the IRA), under its leader Michael Collins, received plenty of money from supporters in the United States. They were determined to shoot the British out of Ireland. Barracks were bombed, railway lines blown up, lorries hijacked. The British recruited special regiments of soldiers – known from their uniforms as "Black and Tans". The IRA and the Black and Tans fought until December 1921. Each side committed terrible atrocities.

Finally Lloyd George signed a treaty with a group of Irish leaders by which eighty per cent of Ireland became an Irish Free State. British troops withdrew, though Ireland remained in the British Commonwealth. Ulster continued to be part of the United Kingdom, as it is to this day.

Many leading Irishmen, including de Valera, opposed the treaty because the Irish Free State did not include Ulster. It was only passed in the Dail by sixty-four votes to fifty-seven. But those who supported it included Arthur Griffith, the founder of Sinn Fein, and Michael Collins, though Collins was soon to be shot by his own men.

Civil war now broke out between those Irish who supported the treaty and those who opposed it. The war lasted two bitter years, before de Valera changed his mind. He reluctantly accepted the separation of Ulster, at least for the time being. When he became Prime Minister of Ireland in 1937, the Irish Free State became the republic of Eire and broke all ties with Britain.

Between the Wars

Four years after the end of the First World War, Lloyd George's coalition government broke up. Britain returned to party politics. Now, though, there were three main parties instead of two.

The Labour Party had won fifty-three seats in the election of 1906, at which the Liberals gained a large majority. The new party, which worked closely with the trade unions, aimed to improve the conditions of the poorest class in Britain – the working class. They backed Liberal reforms, such as the introduction of the school meals service, old-age pensions, and the start of health and insurance schemes for working people. Now they wanted to go further and form a government of their own. They were supported by many of those who returned from their wartime experiences determined to reduce the great differences between the country's rich and poor.

Labour's opportunity came when the Liberal Party split into two groups, one following Lloyd George, the other Asquith. For a while, the Conservatives, under their popular new leader Stanley Baldwin, formed a government. Then,

The "No More War" demonstration in Hyde Park in July 1923 summed up the between-wars feelings, particularly of young people.

297

after the general election of 1923, the first Labour government in Britain's history took office. Its Prime Minister was Ramsay MacDonald.

There was little the Labour government could do to carry out its policies, as it did not have a real majority (the Liberals held the balance of power.) But MacDonald's Minister of Health, J. Wheatley, was determined to build large numbers of council houses. His policy was accepted, in fits and starts, by later governments. By the outbreak of the Second World War, one million council houses had been built all over Britain. Often for the first time in their lives, working people moved into well-built, three-bedroomed houses, with a separate kitchen, indoor toilet and bathroom, mains drainage and electricity. They rented them at cheap rents from their local council.

At the end of 1924 another general election was held. The Conservatives won with a large majority. From now on – except for a short period in which Labour held power from 1929 to 1931 – the Conservatives governed Britain until the start of the Second World War in September 1939. The most important event in Britain during these fifteen years was the General Strike of 1926.

Ever since 1918 miners and their employers had been bitterly divided. The miners had gone on strike and had improved their wages. But in 1925 the employers announced a cut in miners' wages of twenty-five per cent. They said that British coal exports were falling because of Polish and German competition. For months the two sides argued but could reach no agreement. Finally on 1st May 1926, the employers shut the

Between the wars there was terrible unemployment in north-east England. From Jarrow the unemployed marched to London in 1936 to draw the nation's attention to their plight.

mines. They would not reopen them, they said, until the miners accepted lower wages and longer hours. The miners' leader, A. J. Cook, replied: "Not a penny off the pay, not a minute on the day." The general council of the Trades Union Congress (the TUC), which represented the country's main unions, called on its members to support the miners by going on strike. They responded on such a wide scale that their response was called a General Strike.

All the steelworks now shut. There were no trains, buses or trams. Building work stopped, and only emergency supplies of gas and electricity were provided. There were no national newspapers. A week later the shipyard workers and engineers joined the strike. The country faced the closest thing to a national shutdown it has ever experienced.

But the government stood firm. Unlike the TUC, it had been planning for months what it would do if a General Strike occurred. It divided the country up into regions, with a commissioner in charge of each. Volunteers drove buses and trams. Troops escorted food lorries from the docks through jeering crowds. The government even published a special daily newspaper, and skilfully used the BBC to present its case to the nation.

The TUC seems to have had little contact with the miners. Deep in their hearts the leaders of the other unions did not believe in the General Strike. They feared their members would drift back to work, and they would lose authority. On 12th May the TUC called the strike off. In December 1926 the miners went back to work. They accepted lower wages and longer hours – many pennies were taken off the pay and minutes added to the day.

The unions were weak throughout the 1920s and 1930s because there was so much unemployment. Employers knew

A wealthy suburban couple during the 1930s. A growing number of more prosperous families moved out of towns into the suburbs during these years.

that if people would not accept the pay and conditions they offered, they could replace them with others who would. There were between one and three million men and women who were unemployed during those years, the worst time being during the worldwide Depression of 1929–1933. The worst unemployment was in the old industrial areas – South Wales, Lancashire, Yorkshire, Clydeside and the north-east of England – where industries had begun to do badly because of foreign competition.

In these areas life for hundreds of thousands of workers became a monotonous daily round. Once a week they would join the queue to draw unemployment benefit (or "dole"). The money was barely enough to live on, and in 1931 it was cut further. They would pass the day standing on the street corner, doing little jobs at home, reading the newspapers in the public library, and walking to the Labour Exchange to see if any new vacancy had been posted on the notice-board. Their wives struggled to bring up their families as best they could.

Only the coming of the Second World War brought jobs once more. The cotton workers spun shirts for the Army, while the woollen workers wove uniforms. The shipyards of Jarrow and Glasgow built destroyers and frigates for the British Navy. As large supplies of coal were needed again to run the arms factories even the miners had jobs.

However, outside the areas of high unemployment life improved for most people. Baldwin's government introduced small pensions for widows and for orphaned children. During the 1930s, councils carried out huge slum-clearance schemes, particularly the energetic London County Council. More and more families could now afford a week's holiday by the seaside every year. Almost every home had a radio and most people read a daily newspaper. By 1939 there were two million cars on the road.

Right through the 1930s the outbreak of a Second World War seemed more and more likely. The Germans were thirsting for revenge after their defeat in 1918 and the peace treaty of Versailles which followed it. Germany was a democracy, but in 1933 Adolf Hitler, the leader of the German National Socialist Party – the Nazis – took over the government as a dictator. Hitler made no attempt to disguise his determination to conquer the whole of Europe.

The Conservative governments of the 1930s, under their Prime Ministers Baldwin and Neville Chamberlain, followed a policy of "appeasing" Hitler and his ally, the Italian dictator Mussolini. They thought that if they let the dictators have their way, instead of opposing them, it would prevent a war. Neville Chamberlain, in particular, believed he could persuade Adolf Hitler to drop his warlike plans. At the Munich Conference in September 1938, Chamberlain and Daladier (the French Prime Minister) agreed to let the Germans take over large parts of Czechoslovakia even though Czechoslovakia was Britain's and France's ally.

Chamberlain believed that the Munich Conference marked the end of Hitler's ambitions. He called it "peace in our time". Huge crowds cheered him from the airport to 10 Downing Street when he returned from seeing Hitler. When he entered the House of Commons, MPs of all parties rose to their feet and cheered wildly. People remembered the terrible suffering in the trenches of the First World War and cried with relief in the streets when they were told that there was not going to be another war.

Such dreams were soon ended. In March 1939 Hitler took over the rest of Czechoslovakia by force. In September 1939 Germany attacked Poland, for whom Britain and France had promised to fight. They kept their promise.

For years Winston Churchill, a rebel Conservative MP, along with a small group of MPs of all parties who agreed with him, had been urging the government to build up Britain's Army and Navy ready for war. Churchill and his supporters had had some effect, though not much. The Royal Air Force had been provided with a few fine new fighter aircraft – Hurricanes and Spitfires. But it was a poorly armed Britain which went to war again with Germany on 3rd September 1939.

The Second World War (1939–1945)

Six months passed before Britain felt the full effects of the Second World War. At first the atmosphere of calm was eerie. Everybody had been led to expect that modern war would start with devastating bombing of cities and towns. People said that London would be flattened in the first twenty-four hours of war. Then nothing happened.

The evacuation of mothers and children from London and other big cities began the moment war broke out. Mothers with children under five were the first to go. Primary schoolchildren soon followed with their teachers. They were taken in special trains to the country areas, where they would be safer. Here they were sent to live with local families, who were paid (though not very much) to take them in. One and a half million people went on such government schemes. Two million people moved out under private arrangements.

Evacuation had been carefully planned, and it worked amazingly smoothly. But when the bombing failed to come, millions of evacuees went home – only to return to the country again later.

Many of the evacuees who arrived in the country from the big cities were poor and underfed, with ragged clothes and shoes which leaked. This shocked the people who saw them. Most people had no idea such poverty existed in Britain.

Other precautions against bombing were also taken when war broke out. All the street lights went out. They stayed out until Germany was defeated. No light could be shown in any house. Every person in Britain was given a gas mask, which he or she was supposed to carry at

A soldier saying goodbye to his son (1939). The child is being evacuated to the country complete with his gas mask in a cardboard box and a label to tie around his neck.

all times. Hospitals were told to leave large numbers of their beds empty, ready for air-raid casualties.

In Europe the German armies soon overran Poland. French, British and German troops faced each other along the borders of France with Germany. Neither made a move. Then in April 1940 Hitler occupied Denmark and Norway. In May the Germans attacked France, again through Belgium. They quickly occupied Holland.

Winston Churchill took over from Neville Chamberlain as Prime Minister. The Labour and Liberal leaders joined him in a coalition government.

This time France could not stand up to

the ferocity of the German attack. The Germans had learned the lessons of the First World War. They used regiments of tanks. Low-flying aircraft went in front of their advancing armies, machine-gunning soldiers and civilians alike, and creating chaos on the roads. On 22nd June 1940 the French surrendered. The Germans had even brought forward their First World War timetable: they had reached Paris in under six weeks.

Hitler did not believe that Britain would continue fighting once France had surrendered. But the British were determined to do so. They were in a stronger position than the Germans realized.

At the end of May the British Expeditionary Force had retreated to the French Channel port of Dunkirk. From here the troops were rescued by British ships and taken back to Britain.

A total of 338,000 men were taken off the Dunkirk beaches, 200,000 of them British, the rest French. The evacuation took a week. The sea was utterly calm. The Navy asked the captains and crews of every sort of boat available to help in the evacuation. Fishing boats, pleasure steamers, river ferries, yachts and sailing dinghies – most of them from the Channel ports and the mouth of the Thames – responded.

The beaches were shelled by German guns, and bombed by the German air force. German fighter aircraft flew low, machine-gunning ships and men. The civilian boats could sail close to the beaches, where the Navy's destroyers could not. They ferried the men out to the waiting destroyers through continual gunfire. Though they lost almost all their guns and tanks, the British and French troops reached Britain, where they could prepare to defend the country against an invasion.

The British people were united in their determination to resist a German invasion. Their new Prime Minister, Churchill, spoke repeatedly on the radio, encouraging them. Those who heard his words will never forget them:

"We shall fight on the beaches, we shall fight on the landing grounds, we shall fight in the fields and in the streets, we shall fight in the hills; we shall never surrender."

The German plan was to land an army on the flat coast between Hythe in Kent and Hastings in Sussex. Parachute troops would be dropped round Ashford in Kent shortly before the men went ashore. But the German navy was not strong enough to convoy an invasion army across the Channel unless the German air force ruled the skies above. What if the landing ships and all the soldiers they were carrying were sunk by British aircraft as they crossed the Channel?

The German high command therefore insisted that before any invasion could occur the German air force must control the skies over the Channel and the landing places. Their decision led to the Battle of Britain. On 13th August 1940 German bombing and fighting aircraft thundered over south-east England. For a month they bombed British radar stations and airfields. Above all, they tried to lure the British fighter pilots, flying their new Hurricanes and Spitfires, up into the sky. If they could shoot down enough British aircraft, the Germans would control the skies and their invasion could go ahead.

Many of the young British fighter pilots had only just completed their hurried training. Nevertheless they fought back fiercely and skilfully. They shot

down 1733 German planes in a month. They lost 915 planes themselves. On 17th September Hitler called the invasion off. It was certainly not worth such losses. He turned instead to plans of bombing London into surrender, while preparing to attack Russia the following summer.

Once again Churchill movingly put into words what everyone in Britain was feeling about the fighter pilots:

"Never in the field of human conflict was so much owed by so many to so few."

People in London now settled down to night after night of bombing. From 7th September to 2nd November 1940 the Germans bombed London every night.

Firemen at work during the "Blitz". German planes began by bombing London and then bombed other towns. London was attacked again just before the end of the war, this time by German flying bombs ("doodle bugs") and rockets.

Many of the areas around the docks were devastated. Much of the old City of London was burned in one terrible air raid. The House of Commons was destroyed and Buckingham Palace damaged. Whole families took their bedding down to the underground stations and slept there each night; some for weeks on end. Nearly 200,000 people slept nightly in the London underground system. Londoners talked of this time as the months of "the Blitz" (from the German word

"Blitzkrieg" or "lightning war").

From November 1940 the Germans concentrated on other targets, though London was still attacked. Britain's main industrial cities were badly bombed. The centre of Coventry, for instance, was destroyed. Bombardment from the air went on until May 1941, then it began to tail off. In all, over three and a half million British houses were damaged or destroyed. Thirty thousand people were killed, over half of them in London.

Since the surrender of France, Britain had been fighting Germany alone. But in June 1941 Hitler attacked Russia, and the Russians came into the war. Then in December 1941 Germany's ally Japan attacked the United States' naval base in Hawaii, Pearl Harbor. The war became world wide – Britain, Russia and the United States fought Germany, Italy and Japan.

Throughout the war, the lives of people in Britain were dominated by the war effort. If they were not in the armed forces or doing some other essential job, men and women worked in factories to make guns, tanks, aircraft and ammunition. In the evenings the men trained in the Home Guard, the civilian army which was expected to fight with the Army if invasion came. Women worked on the land in the "land army". Conscientious objectors were sent to do work which helped the country. They were much less roughly treated than in the First World War.

Food was short, so it was rationed. So were clothes, shoes, soap and sweets. No petrol was available for private motoring. Prices were strictly controlled so that goods which were available were cheap. Orange juice and milk were available cheaply for those who really needed them – for example, pregnant women

and young children. The result was to make people in Britain healthier than ever before. Now everybody was eating much the same food. Now everybody had a job.

The country was united – more so even than in the First World War. People were all in it together. The rich were very heavily taxed. Few of them made big profits, as many had during the First World War. The Army authorities had learned from the mistakes of the First World War. The soldiers knew that their lives would not be thrown away so needlessly this time.

From 1943 onwards, men and women began to look forward to the years after the war was over. They were determined that this time things really would be better. Sir William Beveridge announced a plan for Britain after the war. The three main parties said they agreed with the Beveridge Plan.

Beveridge wanted a Britain in which all men and women had jobs, where people were insured against injuries at work and where mothers did not have to work immediately before and after they had babies. His plan promised proper medical attention for all whether they were poor or rich. The Minister for Education, R. A. Butler, wanted to raise the school leaving age to fifteen. He said that after the war all children would be able to attend free secondary schools. There was a general feeling of hope.

As the German bombers were heard less and less over Britain, the British air force – the RAF – began to bomb more and more German cities, chiefly at night. One night in 1942 the RAF used a thousand bombers to bomb Cologne. Later the Americans joined in the bombing, flying chiefly by day. Many of Germany's great industrial towns, as well as

During the Second World War people were encouraged to "dig for victory". Here, in June 1942, a family is starting to turn a bomb-site into an allotment.

the port of Hamburg and the capital, Berlin, were left in ruins. In February 1945 the RAF destroyed the German city of Dresden. Nobody knows how many men, women and children were killed that night – some say 60,000, some a quarter of a million.

The idea behind such bombing was to reduce the amount of goods which German factories were producing for their fighting men. But though it caused great devastation, it did not achieve its aim. Such devastation made the German people bitter, and they fought much harder because of it.

As in the First World War, the British Navy convoyed ships from the United States and Canada bringing food, soldiers, oil and tanks across the Atlantic. They also convoyed ships to Russia, sailing north of Norway, often in very

dangerous conditions. Once again many ships were sunk by German U-boats. But the U-boats were not as successful as they had been towards the end of the First World War.

The first important battles which the British Army fought were in Egypt. Here General Montgomery's Eighth Army defeated the German General Rommel's troops at the battle of El Alamein in October 1942. The Eighth Army went on to join up with the Americans, who were landing in north Africa. Between them they killed or captured all the German and Italian soldiers in north Africa, and went on to invade Italy in the summer of 1943.

During these years most of the German armies were fighting a grim campaign in Russia. At the battle of Stalingrad, towards the end of 1942, the Germans were utterly defeated. Their long retreat from Russia now began.

In June 1944 the British and American armies, led by the American General Eisenhower, who had become Supreme Allied Commander, were carried across the Channel. They landed on the beaches of Normandy in northern France. The invasion had been planned in the greatest detail for two years. The British Navy controlled the seas in the area of the Normandy landings. In the skies above the beaches the British and American planes kept out German aircraft. The men fought their way ashore and dug in.

For the next year British, American and Russian armies advanced first towards and then into Germany. The Germans fought bitterly all the way. But finally, in May 1945, they surrendered. Hitler shot himself in his underground bunker under the ruins of Berlin.

Since the end of 1941, the British and Americans had been fighting not only the Germans and Italians but the Japanese. The Japanese started with a number of remarkably quick victories. They occupied Malaysia and captured the great British naval base at Singapore. They advanced to within a few kilometres of Australia.

During 1942 huge American armies and navies began to drive back the Japanese. British troops stopped Japanese armies from invading India, and forced them to retreat through the jungles in Burma. It was here that British troops suffered some of the grimmest experiences of the war.

Finally, in August 1945, American aircraft dropped atomic bombs on Hiroshima and Nagasaki. More than 110,000 people died immediately. Thousands more died later from the after-effects of radiation. Five days after the bombing of Nagasaki the Japanese surrendered. If two bombs could cause such devastation, the Japanese leaders asked themselves, what other terrible suffering would befall their people if they went on fighting?

So the greatest war ever fought faced people with a new and simple question: "With weapons like these, is war ever worth fighting again?"

The atomic bomb dropped by the Americans on Nagasaki in Japan, ended the Second World War. It caused terrible destruction, both at the time and for years afterwards through radiation. The fear of nuclear war has dominated people's minds ever since.

The ever-changing present

After the Second World War it seemed that the British people were about to enter a new period in their history. For the first time everybody could expect a job, a house, good medical care and a decent school for their children. No longer, people hoped, would hundreds of thousands of people emigrate because there was no chance of a decent life for them in their own country. No longer would millions be without work.

Towards the end of the war, in July 1945, a general election was held. To people's surprise, the Labour Party won a large majority. Under Clement Attlee as Prime Minister, the new government set out to satisfy the wishes of the voters. It tried to make Britain, in the words of their party's slogan, a place where there were "Fair shares for all".

The government's first and most important aim was to give everybody the opportunity of a job. After the high hopes of the First World War, thousands of soldiers had returned to live "on the dole". After the Second World War, by careful planning, there were jobs available for all who wanted to work.

The health and insurance schemes which Lloyd George had introduced before the First World War were now extended to everybody. The wartime Beveridge Plan had been popular. Now the National Insurance Act of 1946 fulfilled the hopes which Beveridge had raised, and went further.

Every man and woman in the country who was at work had to pay national insurance money each week. So did their employers. Out of the fund which was created, everyone who contributed could claim benefits if they became unable to earn a regular wage. When a baby was born, the mother could claim money to help her pay the new bills. The unemployed or ill were entitled to claim weekly benefits. Old-age pensions were available for everybody. When you died your relatives could claim money to help pay for your funeral. The national insurance scheme helped you, as the government said, from "your cradle to your grave".

The government's boldest scheme was the National Health Service. The Labour Minister for Health, Aneurin Bevan, established a free service for everybody — not just for those on the lowest wages, as in Lloyd George's scheme. It was paid for out of taxes. Now everyone in the country was able to go to a doctor or into hospital without having to pay for treatment. Nor did you have to pay if you went to the dentist or needed spectacles.

Millions of people now received proper medical and dental treatment for the first time in their lives. For years many people's greatest worry had been: "How can I pay for the doctor when I or one of my family is ill?" That worry was now removed.

Aneurin Bevan was also responsible for the organization of house-building after the war. The shortage of houses and flats, particularly in the big cities, was almost as big a problem for ordinary people as medical care. Millions of houses had been destroyed or damaged by bombing. Millions more needed repair, for no repair work had been done during the war. Hundreds of thousands of slum houses were still standing.

Bevan believed that local councils were the people to solve the problem. They alone let well-built homes at cheap rents to those who needed them. He helped council tenants with grants, and helped councils to obtain building materials which were in short supply after the war. Out of 850,000 houses built in the five years after the war, 650,000 were built by local councils.

Many new schools were built during these years. Primary schools were particularly attractive and well designed. Like the National Health Service, the new schools were admired all over the world. In 1947 the school leaving age was raised to fifteen.

All these improvements were brought about at a particularly difficult time. During the war, everyone had concentrated on the war effort. But after the war was over, it became obvious that Britain was no longer the leading industrial nation that it had been. The industries which had been so successful in the 19th century – coal, iron and steel, shipbuilding, wool and cotton – were now operating with worn-out equipment. Foreigners who had not been able to buy British goods because of the war decided that they no longer needed them – they could buy them from other countries or produce their own.

The Labour government believed that the main industries of the country should not be owned by private companies.

Planners planning better housing at the end of the Second World War in Stepney in London's East End. The bomb-damaged houses will soon be pulled down and new ones built. The worst bombed parts of London were the poorest, like Stepney.

They should be owned by the government, and run in the interests of the British people, not for private profit. So coal, steel, railways, airlines, gas and electricity were nationalized. In this way, the government hoped the profits from these industries could be spent on the new machinery and equipment needed to run them properly, instead of going into the owner's pockets.

Everyone in the country felt the effects of Britain's economic troubles. Food rationing continued for years after 1945. The rations themselves were sometimes even smaller than in wartime. There was still hardly any petrol available for private cars. During the very hard winter of 1946–1947 stocks of fuel ran very low. Factories were forced to close. Families huddled round gas fires on the lowest of pressures or electric fires that gave out little heat.

These shortages, to which people gave the general name "austerity", made the government unpopular. In the 1950 election, a Labour government was re-elected but with only a very small majority. In 1951 Winston Churchill led the Conservative Party to victory. He remained Prime Minister until 1955. The Conservatives remained in office, first under Sir Anthony Eden, then under Harold Macmillan, and finally under Sir Alec Douglas-Home, until 1964.

During the 1950s and 1960s standards of living improved considerably. The Conservatives accepted the main Labour reforms, and set out to make them work. Schemes such as national insurance and the National Health Service had created what became known as the Welfare State. British governments were now responsible for the welfare of all the people, not just the rich.

The Conservatives believed that by encouraging people – especially businessmen – to use their initiative they would make Britain much more prosperous. They were proved right. People

During the 1950s more and more families owned cars. A picnic in the country was a popular way of spending Sunday afternoon.

began to live much more comfortably than they had ever lived before. Hundreds of thousands of people bought their own homes through mortgage payments. Almost everyone had a television set; TV became a great influence on people's lives. Millions of people went abroad for their holidays. More and more people had cars. Refrigerators became as common as gas cookers. What were thought of as luxuries before the war were now regarded as necessities by millions of people.

These improvements continued during the next Labour government, from 1964 to 1970, when Harold Wilson was Prime Minister. The government once again encouraged councils to build many more council houses, and to put more energy into clearing slums. It continued the Welfare State policies of the earlier Labour government. Hanging was abolished and has never been restored. Men and women could vote at eighteen.

During the 1960s teenagers had more money in their pockets than ever before. They spent it on clothes specially designed for their age group and on their own style of music – "pop" music. One group, the Beatles, became famous all over the world. At school and at university young people refused to accept strict discipline. They demanded changes in the subjects they studied and in the ways they were taught.

Towards the end of the 1960s it became clear that people's wages were rising faster than the prices of goods in the shops. Soon the price of goods began to rise as well. This meant that money was losing its value – one way of describing inflation.

Both the Labour government under Harold Wilson and the Conservative government under Edward Heath (1970–1974) tried to persuade people to be satisfied with small but steady rises in wages – no more than the rise in the cost of the goods in the shops. These efforts, known as wages policies, were very unpopular with working people and the trade unions who represented them.

The miners turned down the wage rises offered them in 1972 and 1974 as being too low. The strikes which followed affected most people. As during the winter of 1946–1947, stocks of coal went rapidly down. The power stations were forced to stop the supply of electricity to whole areas for hours on end. Factories closed. The only light which people had in their homes for much of each evening was candlelight.

Finally Labour governments with small majorities were elected at the two general elections of 1974. At first Harold Wilson continued as Prime Minister. In 1976 he was succeeded by James Callaghan.

The Labour governments of 1974–1979 continued Welfare State policies. Inflation remained a serious problem. For a while the trade unions agreed to accept wages policies, but at the end of the 1970s there were serious and unpopular strikes in the local government and hospital services. The effects were felt by everybody.

The government gave millions of pounds to industries such as the motor industry to prevent them from going bankrupt. For Britain was no longer one of the main exporting nations in the world. Everywhere, German, Japanese and American firms were producing cheaper, more popular goods and putting British firms out of business. In industry after industry – and above all on the land – machines were taking over the work of men and women. People began to fear a return to the mass unemployment of the 1920s and 1930s.

With the return of a Conservative government under Margaret Thatcher in 1979, and again in 1983, the fears became reality. For the first time since the 1930s there were over three million people unemployed. Out of every hundred workers, eighty-five had jobs, fifteen did not.

Once again, unemployment was worst in the areas of the 19th-century Industrial Revolution – south Wales, Liverpool, Clydeside and the north-east of England. But now it was also found in the Midlands, in towns such as Birmingham and Coventry, for instance, which had been so prosperous in the 1950s and 1960s. Yet the south-east was still prosperous and wages there were high.

The Conservatives believed in encouraging enterprising businessmen, particularly those starting small businesses. They cut income tax. They returned some nationalised industries to private ownership. At the same time they cut government help to many industries, and cut the money spent on schools and hospitals. They succeeded in lowering the rate of inflation, and encouraged the National Coal Board to withstand another miners' strike. This one lasted a year (1984–1985) and ended, unlike those of 1972 and 1974, in a defeat for the miners.

Not only were the days of Britain as a great industrial power ended. By 1964 the British Empire was also gone. Cle-

Pickets massed outside Kellingley Colliery in Yorkshire during the miners' strike of 1984–85. They faced riot police with shields and vizors. Fighting between police and pickets made the strike the bitterest for fifty years.

ment Attlee and Lord Louis Mountbatten – the last British Viceroy of India – had brought about the independence of India and Pakistan in 1947. Later, other governments followed Attlee's example. Harold Macmillan's government, in particular, arranged the independence of Britain's African colonies. Everywhere British colonies became self-governing. No other example can be found in history of a great empire ending so peacefully and so quickly. The Roman Empire ended in a century of bloodshed. Within fifteen years, from 1947, Britain withdrew from a quarter of the world and lost very few lives in doing so. By the 1970s, all that Britain owned overseas were her bases – Hong Kong, Gibraltar and the Falkland Islands.

Britain now turned more and more to neighbouring countries in western Europe for support. After the Second World War, the Labour Foreign Minister Ernest Bevin had helped to form NATO (the North Atlantic Treaty Organization). This alliance of western European countries was caused by their fear that the Russians, who took over eastern Europe at the end of the war, would go on to threaten the rest of the continent. The United States and Canada also joined NATO. From now on the British Army was based mainly in Europe, as in the days of Wellington, Marlborough and Edward III. British troops were combined with those of its allies more closely than ever before.

Closer economic links with Europe followed. More and more British firms did business in Europe. More and more imports came from there. The countries of western Europe had joined together in the 1950s to form the European Economic Community (EEC). They traded freely with each other. Edward Heath's Conservative government brought Britain into the EEC in 1973. In 1975 there was a special vote – a referendum. Two out of three British voters voted to stay in the EEC. From that time onwards, British life has been increasingly linked with Europe's.

Britain has enjoyed forty years of peace since 1945, broken only on two occasions. In 1956 British and French troops attacked Egypt and occupied the Suez Canal. They claimed that they wanted to make Canal traffic secure during the war between Egypt and Israel which had just started. They withdrew when an international force from the United Nations took over. And in 1982 a British force reoccupied the Falkland Islands, when the Argentinians invaded, claiming they belonged to Argentina.

After the war Britain developed her own atomic and hydrogen bombs. Many people joined the Campaign for Nuclear Disarmament (CND), started at the end of the 1950s to protest against the country's possession of these terrible nuclear weapons. In the 1980s huge crowds have marched and demonstrated their support for CND, sometimes sitting down in non-violent protest, like the Suffragettes before them. But they have not yet succeeded in persuading British governments to change their minds and abandon nuclear weapons.

In Northern Ireland, the IRA has remained determined to make Ulster part of a united Ireland. It has organized a campaign of bomb explosions, kidnapping and assassinations like those carried out just after the First World War in southern Ireland. Some Roman Catholic Ulstermen want a united Ireland. But most people in Ulster, who are Protestants, want to stay in the United Kingdom. For the past eighteen years

A British soldier patrolling a Belfast street (1986). The cities and countryside of Ulster have been torn apart by the "troubles" for the past 18 years and no solution seems in sight.

British troops have been engaged in street warfare with the IRA in Ulster. Many young soldiers and many Ulster policemen have been killed.

As we have seen, once women had gained the vote, their position did not improve greatly between the wars. But from the 1960s onwards more and more women gained important positions in their professions. The election of a woman as Prime Minister in 1979 was a sign of the respect which women could now command in Britain. Nevertheless it is still unusual in Britain during the 1980s to find women in important positions. For example, only twenty-five women MPs were elected at the 1983 general election.

During the 1970s laws were passed designed to give women equal opportunities with men. More and more mar-ried women have gone out to work. Children, as a result, have sometimes been neglected but husbands have become more helpful in the home. Divorces have become easier, and one out of three modern marriages now ends in divorce – a fact which worries many people who fear for the effect of divorce upon children.

Throughout the 20th century, fewer and fewer people have been attending church regularly. As in the 19th century, however, the different Churches in Britain today have a far greater influence than the number of churchgoers would lead one to expect. They are responsible for many excellent Church schools. They are active wherever people are in need – in the poorest parts of big cities, for instance, or in organizing help for poorer countries overseas. Christians no longer attend church because it is respectable. They go because they believe in Jesus' teaching. In time Christianity may gain from its more humble position.

In the 1950s and early 1960s, after Britain's colonies in west Africa, India, the West Indies and Pakistan became self-governing, thousands of people from those countries came to settle in Britain. They looked forward to a higher standard of living and jobs at wages much higher than those being paid in their own countries. They settled in the cities, often in the poorest areas.

White people in Britain are often prejudiced against these and other immigrants and their families because of their colour. Race Relations Acts have been

313

passed to try to prevent people being treated unfairly because of their race.

As unemployment has increased in the 1980s, more and more young people are unemployed. In recent years this has led to rioting in areas of London, such as Brixton and Tottenham, in Toxteth in Liverpool, and in Handsworth in Birmingham, with police and young people fighting on the streets.

At the end of our story, we see problems crowding in upon Britain. At some future point the people of Scotland and Wales may well follow those of Ireland and wish for some form of self-government. Women are not yet equal with

A multi-racial classroom in today's Britain.

An old factory being demolished in the industrial Midlands. In 1986 Britain has 3½ million unemployed, many of them young people, and her old industries – coal, steel, textiles and ship-building – are no longer in world demand.

men in many ways. They want to become so. The divisions between rich and poor are getting worse. The north is much poorer than the south of England. Blacks and other coloured minorities deserve much better treatment. Ulster's problems are unsolved. There are enormous difficulties to overcome before everyone in the country can be provided with work.

Britain, which started the Industrial Revolution, is no longer a leading industrial nation. Its position in world manufacturing trade is growing worse. Over everything hangs the fear of a third world war, far more devastating than any which has been fought before.

Yet despite all this, the lives of most people in Britain in the 1980s are much more comfortable and healthy than ever before. Tremendous improvements have been made since the end of the Second World War. History is made up of problems and is the story of continual change. Before we grow too depressed by our problems, we should remember that those which faced our ancestors were very great too.

NOTES

1. Strabo, *Geography*, translated by Horace Jones (Loeb Classical Library)

2. Caesar, *The Conquest of Gaul*, translated by S.A. Handford (Penguin Classics) 1951. Copyright © S.A. Handford 1951. Reprinted by permission of Penguin Books Ltd.

3. Grant. M, *Tacitus: The Annals of Imperial Rome* (London University Press) 1977

4. Bede, *Ecclesiastical History*, ed. Colgrave, Bertram and Mynors (Oxford University Press) 1969

5. *Anglo-Saxon Poetry*, translated and edited by Robert Kay Gordon (Dent/Everyman) 1927

6. *The Anglo-Saxon Chronicle* ed. Dorothy Whitlock (Eyre and Spottiswoode) 1962

7. *St Patrick – His Writings and Muirchu's Life* ed. A.B.E. Hood (Phillimore) 1978

8. Page, R.I., *Anglo-Saxon Life* (Batsford) 1970

9. quoted in Douglas Woodruff's *Alfred* (Weidenfeld and Nicolson) 1974

10. *The Ely Book* ed. F.O. Blake (Camden Society) 1962

11. Kightly, Charles *Folk Heroes of Britain* (Thames & Hudson) 1982

12. quoted by Snellgrove in *The Early Modern Age* (Longman)

13. quoted by C.V. Wedgwood in *The Trial of Charles I* (Collins) 1964

14. from *The Diary of Samuel Pepys*. Quoted by permission of The Master, Fellows and Scholars of Magdalene College, Cambridge, Robert Latham and the Executors of William Matthews 1985, published by Bell & Hyman, London

15. quoted by A.J. Patrick in *History of Britain* (Penguin)

16. Dickens, Charles *A Tale of Two Cities*

17. Royston Pike, E. *Human Documents of the Industrial Revolution in Britain* (Allen and Unwin)

18. from Wilfred Owen *Collected Poems* (Chatto and Windus) 1967

BIBLIOGRAPHY

A good way to find out how people lived in different periods in history is to read stories about them. Here are some you might try:

Chapters 1 & 2
King, Clive *Stig of the Dump* (Kestrel) 1980
Kipling, Rudyard *Just So Stories* (Macmillan) 1965
Sutcliff, Rosemary *Sun Horse, Moon Horse* (Bodley Head) 1977
Sutcliff, Rosemary *Warrior Scarlet* (Penguin) 1976
Treece, Henry *The Dream Time* (Heinemann) 1974
Wibberley, Leonard *Altar of the Ice Valley* (Macdonald)

Chapters 3 & 4
Sutcliff, Rosemary *Song for a Dark Queen* (Knight Books)
Sutcliff, Rosemary *Eagle of the Ninth* (Oxford University Press)
Sutcliff, Rosemary *Frontier Wolf* (Oxford University Press)
Trease, Geoffrey *Word to Caesar*
Trease, Geoffrey *Ship to Rome* (Heinemann) 1972
Treece, Henry *Legions of the Eagle* (Penguin) 1970
Treece, Henry *Bronze Sword* (Pan Books) 1978

Chapters 6–9
Atterton, Julian *The Last Harper*
Atterton, Julian *The Fire of the Kings*
Beowulf translated by M. Alexander (Penguin) 1973
Crossley-Holland, Kevin *Earth-father* (Heinemann)
King, Clive *Ninny's Boat* (Kestrel) 1980
Nye, Robert *Beowulf the Bee Hunter* (Faber)

Sutcliff, Rosemary *Dragon Slayer* (Puffin Books) 1970
Sutcliff, Rosemary *The Lantern Bearers* (Oxford University Press)
White, T.H. *The Sword in the Stone* (Collins) 1977
Willard, Barbara *Augustine Came to Kent*

Chapter 10
Hunter, Mollie *The Stronghold* (Hamish Hamilton) 1974
Mackie, J.D. *A History of Scotland* (Pelican) 1970
Manning-Sanders, Ruth *Scottish Folk Tales* (Methuen)
Morris, Jan (Ed.) *My Favourite Stories of Wales* (Lutterworth) 1980
Picard, Barbara Leonie *Celtic Tales*
Picard, Barbara Leonie *Tales of the British People*
Sutcliff, Rosemary *The High Deeds of Finn MacCool* (Puffin Books)
Sutcliff, Rosemary *Hound of Ulster* (Heinemann)
Thomas, Frances *Blindfold Track* (Macmillan) 1980
Williams, Gwyn A *When Was Wales?* (Penguin)

Chapter 11
The Burning of Njal (Icelandic saga)
Treece, Henry *Road to Miklagard* (Puffin Books) 1967
Treece, Henry *Viking's Dawn* (Heinemann) 1971
Treece, Henry *Viking's Sunset* (Puffin Books) 1967
Treece, Henry *Vinland the Good* (Puffin Books) 1971

Chapter 12
Hodges, C. Walter *The Namesake* (Penguin) 1967
Hodges, C. Walter *The Marsh King* (Penguin) 1970
Trease, Geoffrey *Mist Over Athelney* (Macmillan)

Chapter 14
Kingsley, Charles *Heroes* (Macmillan) 1980
Kingsley, Charles *Hereward the Wake* (Macmillan) 1980
Sutcliff, Rosemary *Knight's Fee* (Oxford University Press) 1974
Treece, Henry *Man With a Sword* (Oxford University Press) 1974

Chapter 21
Paton Walsh, Jill *Parcel of Patterns*
Stephens, Peter J. *Shot from a Sling* (Andre Deutsch Ltd) 1975
Trease, Geoffrey *Baron's Hostage* (Heinemann) 1975
Welch, Ronald *Bowman of Crecy* (Oxford University Press) 1966

Chapters 22–25
Harnett, Cynthia *Ring Out Bow Bells!* (Methuen)
Harnett, Cynthia *Stars of Fortune* (Methuen) 1956
Harnett, Cynthia *The Wool-pack* (Methuen) 1951
Harnett, Cynthia *The Writing on the Hearth* (Penguin)
Welch, Ronald *Sun of York* (Oxford University Press)
Willard, Barbara *Cold Wind Blowing* (Kestrel) 1975
Willard, Barbara *Harrow and Harvest* (Kestrel) 1974
Willard, Barbara *The Iron Lily* (Kestrel) 1975
Willard, Barbara *The Lark and the Laurel* (Kestrel)
Willard, Barbara *The Sprig of Broom* (Kestrel) 1976

Chapters 28–30
Burton, Hester *When the Beacons Blazed* (Hamish Hamilton) 1978
Sutcliff, Rosemary *Brother Dusty-feet* (Oxford University Press) 1979
Hodges, C. Walter *Playhouse Tales* (G. Bell) 1974

Chapter 31
Burton, Hester *Thomas*
Burton, Hester *Kate Rider* (Oxford University Press)
Harnett, Cynthia *The Great House* (Penguin) 1968
Marryat, Frederick (Captain) *The Children of the New Forest* (Armada) 1977
Trease, Geoffrey *Mandeville*
Trease, Geoffrey *Saraband for Shadows* (Macmillan)
Sutcliff, Rosemary *Bonnie Dundee*
Welch, Ronald *For the King* (Oxford University Press)

Chapters 32–35
Hunter, Mollie *Ghosts of Glencoe* (Hamish Hamilton)
Trease, Geoffrey *The Field of the Forty Footsteps*
Trease, Geoffrey *Popinjay Stairs*

Chapter 36
Aiken, Joan *The Wolves of Willoughby Chase* (Penguin) 1971
Garfield, Leon *The Apprentices*
Garfield, Leon *John Diamond* (Puffin Books) 1981
Garfield, Leon *Smith* (Kestrel) 1977
Peyton, K.M. *Right-hand Man* (Oxford University Press) 1977
Stevenson, R.L. *Kidnapped* (Arrow Books) 1979
Stevenson, R.L. *Treasure Island* (Collins) 1976
Welch, Ronald *Captain of Dragons* (Oxford University Press) 1974

Chapters 37 & 38
Carter, Peter *The Sentinels* (Oxford University Press)

Cross, Gillian *The Iron Way* (Oxford University Press)
Darke, Marjorie *Ride the Iron Horse* (Kestrel) 1975
Leeson, Robert *Bess*
Leeson, Robert *Maroon Boy*
Orczy, Baroness *The Scarlet Pimpernel* (Hodder and Stoughton) 1968
Stowe, Harriet Beecher *Uncle Tom's Cabin* (Penguin)

Chapter 39
Carter, Peter *The Black Lamp* (Oxford University Press) 1973
Trease, Geoffrey *Comrades for the Charter*

Chapters 40 & 41
Avery, Gillian *The Call of the Valley*
Burnett, Frances Hodgson *The Little Princess* (Penguin) 1970
Burton, Hester *No Beat of the Drum*
Burton, Hester *Time of Trial* (Oxford University Press)
Price, Susan *Twopence a Tub* (Faber) 1975
Tate, Joan *Out of the Sun* (Heinemann) 1968

Chapters 42 & 43
Darke, Marjorie *A Long Way to Go* (Kestrel) 1978
Graves, Robert *Goodbye to All That* (Penguin) 1969
Owen, Wilfred *Collected Poems* (Chatto and Windus)
Peyton, K.M. *Flambards* (Penguin) 1980
Remarque, E.M. *All Quiet on the Western Front* (Mayflower) 1968
Sassoon, Siegfried *Selected Poems* (Faber) 1968
Welch, Ronald *Tank Commander* (Penguin) 1980

Chapters 44–46
Ballard, Martin *Dockie* (Longman) 1972
Bawden, Nina *Carrie's War* (Gollancz) 1973
Burton, Hester *In Spite of All Terror* (Oxford University Press)
Cross, Gillian *Revolt at Ratcliffe's Rags* (Oxford University Press)
Donaldson, Margaret *Journey into War* (Andre Deutsch Ltd) 1979
Donaldson, Margaret *The Moon's On Fire* (Andre Deutsch Ltd) 1980
Kilner, Geoffrey *Joe Burkinshaw's Progress* (Methuen)
Walsh, Jill Paton *Fireweed* (Puffin Books) 1972
Carter, Peter *Under Goliath* (Penguin) 1980

INDEX

Page numbers in italics refer to illustrations

Act of Settlement (1701) 244
Act of Union (1707) 245
Africa 255–6, 280–1
Agriculture *see* Farming;
    Tools, agricultural
Aidan, St 71, 74, 80, 107
Alexander III, King of
    Scotland 152
Alfred the Great, King of
    Wessex 86, 109, 109–10,
    111–15,
    royal 'tun' 96–7
Almshouses 194
America
    colonies 254–9
    discovery of 190
    emigration to 250
    Spanish empire in 203
    see also United States
American War of
    Independence 258–9, *259*
Amphitheatres, Roman *43*, 44
Angles 61–6, 104
Anglo-Saxon Britain 66, 86–
    99
Anglo-Saxon Chronicle, The
    65, 90, 106, 106–7, 110,
    111, 115, 122
Ann of Cleves 186
Anne, Queen 245, 246
Antonine Wall 53
Ardagh Chalice *80*
Armada *see* Spanish Armada
Army
    and the Napoleonic wars
        264–6
    New Model Army 223,
        224, 225, 227–8, *228*,
        230, 231, 232, 238
    private armies
        banning of 178, *179*
    19th-century reforms 283
    Norman 125–6
    Roman *33*, 33–5, 59
    in Wessex 111–12
Arthur, King, legend of 66
Athelstan, King 118–19
Attlee, Clement 307, 311–12
Australia *276*, 277, 280
Avebury stone circles 23, *25*

Bakewell, Robert 247
Baldwin, Stanley 297, 300
Ball, John 168, *169*, 170
Bank of England 249
Bannockburn, Battle of 153
Barons
    Anglo-Saxon lords 94
    and Henry VII 178, *179*
    in Ireland 153
    and King John 144–6
    medieval 134, 146–7, 166,
        175
    Norman 130, 131, 132
Basilica, Roman 43
Bates' Case 213
Baths, Roman *42*, 43–4
Bayeux Tapestry *121*, *122–3*,
    124
'Beaker' people 22
Bede, the Venerable, 61, 62,
    64–5, 74, 75, 76–7, 78–9,
    84, 99, 106

Beggars, 16th-century *194*,
    194
Beowulf 63, 93
Bertha, Queen of Kent 75, *77*
Bevan, Aneurin 307–8
Beveridge Plan 304, 307
Bevin, Ernest 312
Bill of Rights (1689) 244
Billingsgate in Roman times
    46–7
Black and Tans 296
Black Death *164–5*, 164–5,
    174
Black Prince, the *166*, 167,
    168
Blenheim, battle of 245
Boats
    of ancient Britons *28*
    in Celtic Ireland *103*
    emigrant ships 278–9
    17th-century London *233*,
        233
    slave ships *256*, 256
    Viking *93*, *108*, *109*
Boer War 281
Boleyn, Anne 183, 184, 186
Book of Common Prayer
    139, 195–6, 197, 198, 231
Book of Kells 70–1, *72*
Boroughs in Wessex *112*, 112
Boston Tea Party 258
Boudicca (Boadicea) 26, 36–7
Boulton, Matthew 264
Bow Street Runners 251
Boyne, battle of the 245
Breda, Treaty of 239
Brian Boru of Munster 102,
    103
Bridgewater Canal 260–1,
    261
Britain, Battle of 302–3
British Commonwealth 280
British Empire 276–81, 311–
    12
    Christian missionaries in
        285–6
Britons, ancient 25–8
    and Anglo-Saxons 65, 66
Bronze Age 22–5
Brown, Lancelot
    ('Capability') 249
Brunel, Isambard Kingdom
    267
Bubonic plagues *see* Plague
Buckingham, Duke of 213,
    214, 215–16
Burford Church, Oxfordshire
    177, 228
Burial mounds 18, *19*
    Sutton Hoo *93*, *94*
Butler, R.A. 304

Cabot, John 191
Cabot, Sebastian 192
Cade, John 172
Caesar, Julias 8, 30–2
Caledonian Canal 263
Callaghan, James 310
Canada 256–7, 277, 278–9,
    280
Canals 260–2, *261*
    Suez Canal 277, 312
Canterbury Tales 156, 176
Caractacus, King of the
    Catuvellauni 35
Carson, Sir Edward 295
Cartimandua, Queen of the
    Brigantes 35, 40
Cartwright, Edmund 264
Casement, Sir Roger 296
Castles
    Norman *126–7*, 126–8,
        131

in Scotland *152*
in Wales *150*, 150
Cathedrals, medieval 155–6
Catherine of Aragon 180,
    183–4
Catholic Church
    and the Bill of Rights 244
    and Elizabeth I 198, 200,
        202–3
    and the Gunpowder Plot
        211
    in Ireland 245, 294
    in medieval times 154–7
    in Norman times 132–3
    and the Popish Plot 240–1
    under Charles II 238, 240
    under Henry VIII 184–5
    under King John 144–5
    under Mary I 198–9
Cato Street Conspiracy 270
Cavaliers 221
Cave paintings 13
Caxton, William 176
Cecil, Robert 211
Cecil, William 201
Celtic Church 74, 80
Celts 25–8, *26–7*
    in Ireland 102–3
    in Scotland 104–5
    in Wales *100*, 100–1
Chadwick, Edwin 274
Chamberlain, Joseph 294
Chamberlain, Neville 300,
    301
Chancellor, Richard 192
Charlemagne, Emperor *106*,
    106
Charles, Prince (later Charles
    II) 229, 231–2
Charles I, King 214–26, *215*
    and the Civil War 221–5
    execution of 226, *227*
Charles II, King 233–41
Chartists 272–3
Chaucer, Geoffrey 156, 176
Children
    in 19th-century factories
        268–9
Chloroform, discovery of 275
Christianity
    and Alfred the Great 115
    and the Celtic Church 74,
        80
    conversion to
        in England 74–85
        in Ireland 67–71
        in Wales 67
    and the Methodist Church
        253, 285
    19th-century 285–6
    in Roman Britain 56
    in the 20th century 313
    see also Catholic Church;
        Church of England;
        Protestant Church;
        Puritans
Church of England
    in the 18th century 253
    and the Parliamentarians
        225
    and the poor 194
    under Charles II 238
    under Edward VI 195–7
    under Henry VIII 184, 185,
        195
    under James II 242–3
Church of Scotland 245
Churchill, John (later Duke of
    Marlborough) 243
Churchill, Lord Randolph 295
Churchill, Winston 290, 300,
    301, 302, 303, 309
Civil War 221–6

Clarendon, Earl of 239
Clothing
    in early Ireland 102–3, *103*
    Stone Age 12
    Vikings *116*
CND (Campaign for Nuclear
    Disarmament) 312
Cnut, King 86, 119–20
Coal mines
    children employed in *269*
    strikes in 310, *311*, 311
Cogidubnus, King (Roman
    times) 49
Coins
    Anglo-Saxon 99
    Celtic 28
    of King Cunobelinus *32*
    Roman 59
Coke, Thomas 248
Colchester
    in Roman times 32, 35, 36,
        37
Collins, Michael 296
Colston, Edward 249
Columba of Iona, St 71, 74
Columbus, Christopher 189–
    90
Common land 140, 192
Commonwealth
    (Protectorate) 227–32
Commonwealth, British 280
Congress of Vienna 276–7
Conscientious objectors 289,
    304
Constantine, Roman
    Emperor 53, 54, 56, 57
Cook, John 226
Corn Laws 282
Covenanters 217
Craftsmen
    Anglo-Saxon 98
    Bronze Age 22–3, *24*
    medieval 135, 159–62
    Neolithic period 17
    Roman 45, *48*
    Viking *117*, 118
Cranmer, Thomas,
    Archbishop of Canterbury
    184, 195, 199
Crimean War 274, 281
Cromwell, Oliver 218, 238
    and the Civil War 222–3,
        225
    death mask *232*
    Irish policy 217
    Protectorate 227–32
Cromwell, Richard 232
Cromwell, Thomas 185, 186
Crusades 142–4, 188
Culloden, Battle of 245, 278
Cunobelinus, King 32, 35
Cuthbert, St 89–90, 97

Danby, Earl of 241
Danelaw *110*, 110
Danes 103, 107–10, 111,
    116
Darnley, Earl of 202
Davison, Emily 287
De Montfort, Simon 146–7
De Valera, Eammon *295*, 296
Death penalty
    Anglo-Saxon 87–8
    in the 19th century 271
Declaration of Indulgence
    240, 242, 243
Defoe, Daniel 237
Depression (1929–33) 299–
    300
Despenser, Hugh 166
Dickens, Charles 262

Diggers 225, 227
Disraeli, Benjamin 284
Divine Right of Kings 210, 214
Domesday Book 121, 128, 129
Donne, John 216, 234
Drake, Francis 176, 203, 206–7

East India Company 257, 280
Edgehill, Battle of 221–2
Edmund the Martyr, St 109
Education Act (1870) 283
Edward I, King of England 148, *149*, 152, 153
Edward II, King of England 153, 166–7
Edward III, King of England 153, 167–8, *175*, 176
Edward IV, King of England 172–3, *174*
Edward V, King of England 173
Edward VI, King of England 186, 192, 195, 195–8
coronation procession *196–7*
Edward the Confessor 86, 120
Edward the Elder, King of Wessex 116
Edwin, King of Northumberland 78, 79
EEC (European Economic Community) 312
Eleanor of Aquitaine 131
Elizabeth I, Queen of England 176, 200–8, *201*
birth of *184*
financial policies 212
funeral procession *208*
Irish policy 228–9
and Parliament 209–10
Poor Law 194
religious policies 200–1, 202–3
and Roman Catholics 198, 200, 202–3
Ely rebellion
and the Norman conquest 124–5
Enclosures 192, *248*, 248
in medieval times 175
English Church *see* Church of England
English language
growth of 176
laws written in 114
Entertainments
19th-century 285
Ethelbald, King of Mercia 106
Ethelbert, King of Kent 75, 76, 77
Ethelburgh, Queen of Northumberland 78
Ethelred, King of Wessex 109, 119
Explorers 188–92

Factories
cotton industry 263–4, *264*, 268, 268–9
Factory Acts 273
Fairfax, Sir Thomas 222, 223, 227
Fairs, medieval *160–1*, 163

Falkland Islands 312
Farming
ancient Britons 27–8
in Anglo-Saxon times *64–5*, 66, 87, 94–6
in the 18th century 246–8, *247*, *248*
in Ireland 102–3
in medieval times *136–7*, *138–41*, *139*, 157, *174*, 174, *175*
Neolithic period 16–17
in the 19th century 282
in Norman times 128
in Roman times 38, 48, 54, 56
in the 16th century 192
Farmworkers
18th-century 249–50
Fates of Men, The 87, 88
Fawkes, Guy 211, *211*
Fens, East Anglia 88–9
rebellion in 124–5
Feudal system 166, 174
in England 143–41
in Wales 148
Field of the Cloth of Gold *182*, 182–3
Fire fighting
in medieval towns 159
17th-century London 235
Fire of London (1666) 235–7, *237*
First World War *see* World War I
Fishbourne Palace *49*, 49–51
Fisher, John, Bishop of Rochester 185
Flint mines, Neolithic 17
Flodden, Battle of 180
Food
in medieval times 138
in Roman times 48
Forests
in Anglo-Saxon times 88
Stone Age 13–14
Forts
Celtic 26–7
Roman 40, *52*, 60
Saxon Shore *58*, 58
Forum, Roman 42–3
Fountains Abbey *156*
Fox, George 231
France
and Charles II 239–40, 241
English territory in *146*
and Henry VII 178–9
and Henry VIII 182–3
and Mary, Queen of Scots 200, *201*
wars with
in Canada 256–7
18th century 245
Hundred Years War 167, *172*, 172
Napoleonic 264–6
Free trade 282
Fry, Elizabeth 271, 275

Gallipoli Campaign 290–2
Gama, Vasco da *188–9*, 189, *191*
Gaveston, Peter 166
Geddes, Jenny 217
General Strike (1926) 298–9
George I, King 246
George III, King 246, 248
Germany

and World War I 288–92
and World War II 300, 301–6
Gilbert, Sir Humphrey 254
Gin Lane (Hogarth) *251*
Gladiators 44
Gladstone, William 282–4, 294
Glyndŵr, Owain 150–1, *151*, 171
Gordon Riots 251–2
Grand Trunk Canal 261
Great Eastern (ship) 267
Great Fire of London 235–7, *237*
Great Interglacial 10–12
Great Plague of London 233–5
Grey, Lady Jane 198
Griffith, Arthur 296
Gruffyd ap Llywelyn of Dyfed 100–1
Guilds, medieval 162
Gunpowder Plot *211*, 211
Guthlac, St 88, 90
Guthrum (Danish king) 109–10

Habeas Corpus Act (1679) 243–4
Hadrian's Wall *52*, 52–3, *53*, 60
Halls, Anglo-Saxon *95*, 96
Hampton, John 218
Hardwick, Bess of *204*
Hardwick Hall 204–5
Hargreaves, James 263
Harold, King of England 86, 121–3, *124*
Harvey, William 220
Hastings, Battle of *123*, 123
Hawkins, Sir John 203, 207, 256
Heath, Edward 310, 312
Heaveningham Hall, Suffolk *246*
Henrietta Maria, Queen 214, 219, 238
Henry I, King of England *129*, 129, 130
Henry II, King of England 131–3, *133*, 153
Henry III, King of England 146–7, 148
Henry IV, King of England 150, 151, 170, 171, 176
Henry V, King of England 171
Henry VI, King of England 171–2, *173*
Henry VII, King of England 173, *178*, 178–9
Henry VIII, King of England 180–6, *181*, *182*
and Parliament 209
religious policies 184–6, 195
Scottish policies 197–8
Herbert, George 216
Hereward (leader of Ely rebellion) 124, 125
Highland 'clearances' 278–9
Highlands of Scotland
in Celtic times 104
Hill, Rowland 267
Hitler, Adolf 300, 304, 306
Holbein, Hans 186
Holland
and Charles II 239

and William III 245
House of Commons 147
in Tudor times 209–10
House of Lords 147, 227, 238, 286, 295
Houses
Anglo-Saxon *95*, 96–7, *96–8*
council house building 298, 308
18th-century country houses *246*, 246, 248–9
Elizabethan 204–5
medieval farmhouses *175*
in medieval towns 159, 162, 175
19th-century towns *284*, 284–5
post-war building of 307–8
Roman 44, 45, 48; *see also* Villas
in the 17th century 212
17th-century London 233
of villeins *138*, 138
see also Manor houses
Howard, Katherine 186
Howard of Effingham, Lord 207
Hudson, William 191–2
Hundred Years War 167, *172*, 172, 178
Hunt, William 271
Hunter-gatherers
Old Stone Age *11*, 11
Hywel Dda (the Good) 100

Ice Age 10, 12–13
Immigrants to Britain 313–14
India 257, 280, 312
Indian Mutiny (1857) 280
Industrial Revolution 260
Industries, nationalization of 308–9
Inflation 310
IRA (Irish Republican Army) 296, 312–13
Ireland
Celtic Britain 102–3
and the Civil War 224
Cromwell's policies in 228–9
early Christians 67–71
Easter Rising (1916) 296
French invasion from 265
and Home Rule 294–6
in medieval times 153
19th century
eviction of farmers *279*
potato famine 294
Northern Ireland
present-day troubles 312–13, *313*
in Tudor times 217
under William III 245
Iron Age 25–8

Jacobite risings 245
James, Duke of York (later James II) 240, 241
James I, King 208, 209, *210*, 210–13
James II, King 242–3, 245
James IV, King of Scotland 179, 180
Japan
atomic bombs dropped on *306*, 306

Jenner, Edward 274
Jewellery, Roman 48
Jews in Britain 162, 231
Joan of Arc 171, *171*
John, King 142, 144–6
John Balliol, King of Scotland 152
Jones, Inigo 213
Jonson, Ben 213
Julius Caesar 8, 30–2
Jutes 61

Kay, John 263
Ket, Robert 192, 197
Knox, John 201, 217

Lancaster, Thomas, Earl of 166
Lancastrian kings 173
Landowners
    and the Corn Laws 282
    18th-century 246, 248–9
    in Tudor times 209
Laud, William, Archbishop of Canterbury 216, 218, 219
Laws
    Anglo-Saxon 87–8
    Norman 132
    under Cromwell 231
    in Scotland 245
    in Wessex 112–14
Levellers 225, 227, 229, 269
Lindisfarne monastery 71, 80, 107
Lister, Joseph 275, *275*
Lloyd George, David 286, 292, 295, 296, 297, 307
Llywelyn ap Gruffydd 148
London
    Anglo-Saxon 119
    in the Blitz *303*, 303–4
    18th-century *251*, 251–2
    in medieval times 158, 162
    in Roman times *36*, 45–8, *46–7*
    17th-century *233*, 233–7
    16th-century *196–7*
Long Parliament 219
Longboats, 108, *109*
Lords
    Anglo-Saxon *94*
    see also Barons
Luddites 270–1
Lullingstone
    Roman villa at 55–6
Luther, Martin 184, 195

Macadam, John 262–3
MacDonald, Ramsay 289, 298
Macmillan, Harold 309, 312
Magellan, Ferdinand 190
Magna Carta 145–6, *147*
Make-up in Roman times 48
Malcolm II, King of Scotland 105
Manor houses
    Anglo-Saxon *94*, 96–7
    medieval 135–8, *136–7*
Marco Polo 188
Margaret of Anjou, Queen *173*
Markets, medieval *160–1*, 163
Marlborough, John Churchill, Duke of 245, 246
Marne, Battle of the 289, 292

Marston Moor, Battle of 222
Mary, Queen of Scots 198, 200, 201–2, 202, 206
Mary I, Queen of England 198–9, 200
Mary II, Queen 243
Mary Rose (ship)
    equipment found on *187*
Masques, 17th-century 213
Mayflower (ship) 216, 254
Medieval period see Middle Ages
Merchant Adventurers 175, 209
Merchants
    Anglo-Saxon 98, *98–9*, *99*
    18th-century 249
    in medieval towns 162–3, 175
    Venetian *188–9*
Metcalfe, John 262
Methodist Church 253, 285
Middle Ages
    the Church 154–7
    feudal system 134–41, *166*, 174
    Ireland 153
    Scotland 152–3
    towns 158–65
    Wales 148–51
Mines Act (1842) 273
Mining
    Neolithic period 17, *18*
    in Roman times 38, 40
    see also Coal mines
Minsters 80–4
Missionaries 285–6
Monasteries
    Anglo-Saxon 119
    dissolution of 185–6, 209
    of early Christians 80–4
    in Ireland 70–1, *73*
    medieval 155, 156
    minsters 80–4
    in Wales 67
Monk, General 232
Monks see Monasteries
Monmouth, Duke of 241, 242
More, Sir Thomas *183*, 185
Moulsford Torque *23*
Munich Conference (1938) 300
Mutiny Act (1689) 244

Napoleonic Wars 264–5
Naseby, Battle of 223, *224*
Nash, Richard 252
National Health Service 307
National Insurance Acts 286, 307
NATO (North Atlantic Treaty Organization) 312
Navarino Bay, Battle of 281
Navvies *267*, 267
Navy, British 265, 276
Nelson, Horatio, Admiral 265
Neolithic period 16–21
New England *255*, 255
New Model Army 223, *224*, 225, 227–8, 230, 231, 232, 238
New Stone Age 16–21, *18–21*
New Zealand 277, 280
Newark Castle *179*
Newcomen, Thomas 264

Newspapers, 19th-century 285
Niall of the Nine Hostages 102
Nightingale, Florence 274–5
Norman Conquest 124–8
Norman kings 129–33, 173
Norman England 129–33
Northern Ireland
    present-day troubles 312–13, *313*
    see also Ireland
Northmen see Vikings
Northumberland, Duke of (Protector) 192, 195, 196, 198
Norwegians 116
    invasion of Ireland 103
    and the Norman Conquest 124
    in Scotland *104–5*, 104–5
    in York 118
    see also Vikings
Nunneries 155, 156, 185–6

Oastler, Richard 273
Oates, Titus 240, 241
Offa, King of Mercia 99, 101, 106, 111
Offa's Dyke *101*
Old Stone Age 10–12
Orangemen 245
Orkneys
    Norwegian settlers 105
    Skara Brae 18–19, *20–1*
Oswald, King of Northumberland 79–80
Oswy, King of Northumbria 71, 74
Owen, Wilfred 292

Paintings in caves 13
Palaeolithic period 10–12
Pankhurst, Mrs Emmeline 287
Parliament
    beginnings of 147
    and the Civil War 221–6
    in the 18th century 246
    in the 19th century 269
    and the Popish Plot 240–1
    and the railways 267
    reform of 272
    in Tudor times 179, 209–10
    under Charles I 214–16, 218–20
    under Charles II 238, 240, 241
    under James I 212, 213
    under James II 242
Parliament Act (1911) 295
Parliamentarians 221
Parnell, Charles Stewart 295
Parr, Catherine 186
Pasteur, Louis 275
Patrick, St 68–71, *70*
Paulinus 78
Peasants' Revolt *167*, 168, 168–70, *169*
Pedlars 98
Peel, Sir Robert 271, 282
Penny post 267
People's Crusade 143
Pepys, Samuel 234–5, *235–6*
Peterloo Massacre 271
Petition of Right 215, 218
Philip II, King of Spain 198, 199, 200, 206

Picts 65, 71, 104
Pilgrim Fathers *216*, 254
Pilgrimage of Grace 186
Pilgrims 156
Plague
    Black Death 164–5, *164–5*
    Great Plague (1665) 233–5
Plantagenet kings 173
Plays, 17th-century 213
Police force, establishment of 271
Polo, Marco 188
Poor Law
    Elizabethan 194
    19th-century 268, 273
Popish Plot 240–1
Population
    in Ireland 294
    in the 19th century 260
    of Roman Britain 38
    of 17th-century London 233
    in the 16th century 192
Portugal, explorers from 189
Post, penny 267
Priests
    in medieval times 154
    under Alfred the Great 114–15
Printing, invention of *176*, 176
Prisons, reform of 271
Private armies, banning of 178, 179
Protectorate (Commonwealth) 227–32
Protestant Church
    Methodist 253
    in Scotland 201, 217, 245
    in 16th-century Europe 184, 185
    see also Church of England; Puritans
Public Health Acts 274, 284
Puritans *221*
    in the American colonies 254, 255
    Parliament chosen by 230
    Pilgrim Fathers 216, 254
    and the Toleration Act 244
    under Charles I 216, 216–17
    under Charles II 238
    under Elizabeth I 200
    under James II 242, 243
Pym, John 219, 222

Quakers see Society of Friends

Radicals 270, 271
Raedwald, King of East Anglia 92, 93
Railways *266*, 266–7
Raleigh, Sir Walter 254
Rayleigh Manor *136–7*
Reculver Church *84*
Redmond, John 295
Redwald, King of the East Angles 77
Reform Act (1832) 272, 282, 286
Retainers, banning of 178, 179
Revolution Settlement 243–5
Richard, Duke of York (Protector) 172
Richard I, King of England 142, *143*, 143–4

Richard II, King of England
168–70, *169*
Richard III, King of England
173
Richborough *58, 58*
Ridolfi Plot 202
Rillaton Cup 22–3, *23*
Rising of the North 202
Roads
in Anglo-Saxon times 89
18th-century
improvements 262–3
Roman 41, 51
see also Streets
Robert Bruce, King of
Scotland 153
Roman Britain 29–56
Roman Catholic Church *see*
Catholic Church
Roundheads 221
Royal Charles (ship) 239
Royalists 221
Rump Parliament 224, 225,
226, 227, *230*, 232
Rupert, Prince 222, 227
Russell, Bertrand 289
Russian Revolution 290
Ruthwell Cross 79

Salvation Army 285
Savoy House 233
Saxon Shore forts *58, 58*
Saxons 57, 59, 61–6, 85
Schools *283*, 283, 286, 308
Scotland
in Anglo-Saxon times 65
battles with England
under Edward VI 197–8
under Henry VIII 180
Celtic Britain 104–5
and the Civil War 222, 225
and the Commonwealth
227
Cromwell's policies in 228,
229
and Elizabeth I 200, 201
and Henry VII 179
Highland 'clearances' 278–9
Jacobite risings 245
in medieval times 152–3
Protestant Church in 245
Roman invasion of 40
in Roman times 52, 53
under Charles I 217, 218
and the Union of the
Parliaments 245
Scots 65, 104
Second World War *see* World
War II
Serfs 94, 134, 135; *see also*
Slaves
Seymour, Jane 186
Shaftesbury, Earl of
and the Factory Acts 273
Shakespeare, William 213
Sheep farming 175, 192, 278
Ships *see* Boats
Shops, Roman *41, 43, 45*
Sidney, Sir Philip 206
Simon, John 274
Simpson, James 275
Sinn Fein party 295, 296
Skara Brae 18–19, *20–1*
Skellig monastery *71*
Slave trade 249, 255–6, *256*
abolition of 273
Slaves
Anglo-Saxon 94
in Celtic Britain 28

and the cotton industry
263
Roman 44
Smallpox vaccination 274
Social reforms
19th century 268–75
20th century 286
Society of Friends (Quakers)
231, 238
and World War I 289
Solemn League and Covenant
(1643) 222
Somerset, Duke of (Protector)
192, 195, 197
Somerset House 233
Somme, Battle of the 290
South Africa 280–1
South African War 281
South Sea Bubble 249
Spain
and Elizabeth I 200, 203,
206–8
explorers 190–1
and the Napoleonic Wars
265
Spanish Armada *206*, 206–8,
207
Squires, 18th-century 249
St Paul's Cathedral
and the Great Fire of
London 236–7
Stage coaches, journeys by
262
Stamp Act 258
Star Carr
Stone Age settlement *15*,
15
Steam power, use of 264
in railways 266
Stephen, King of England
129, 130, 131
Stephenson, George 266
Stone Age people 8–15
Stonehenge 23–5
Strafford, Thomas
Wentworth, Earl of 217,
218, 219, 228
Straw, Jack 170
Streets
medieval 159
Roman *41*
17th-century London 233
see also Roads
Strikes
between the wars 293–4
General Strike (1926) 298–9
of miners 310, *311*, 311
Suez Canal 277, 312
Suffragettes 286–7
Superstitions, Anglo-Saxon
90–1
Sutton Hoo burial mound 93, 94

Tarmac roads 263
Taxes
and the American colonies
257–8
in medieval times 168
under Charles I 214, 218
under Charles II 238
Telford, Thomas 261, 263,
267
Test Act (1673) 240, 242,
243
repeal of 272
Thanksgiving Day 254–5
Thatcher, Margaret 311
Theatres

Roman amphitheatres *43*,
44
17th-century 213·
Thistlewood, Arthur 270
Thomas Beckett, St 132–3,
133, 133
Tintagel monastery 67
Tissot, J.J. 278
Toleration Act (1689) 244
Tolls
on 18th-century roads 262,
263
Tolpuddle martyrs 271–2
Tongue, Israel 240
Tools
agricultural
of Celtic Britons 27–8
New Stone Age 17
in Roman times 48, 54
Bronze Age 23
mining
Neolithic period 18
Stone Age 8, 9, 11, 12, *14*,
15
Tower of London 127, *127*
Towns
Anglo-Saxon 119
and the Industrial
Revolution 260
medieval 158–65, 175
19th-century 274
Norman 130
Roman 41–8, 60
in Wessex *112*, 112
Townshend, Lord ('Turnip
Townshend') 247
Trade
Anglo-Saxon 98–9
Bronze Age 22
Celtic Britons 28
free trade 282
and the Industrial
Revolution 260
in medieval times 162–3,
174–5
in Norman times 130
slave trade 255–6
and Venetian merchants
188–9
with Russia 192
with Vikings 118
Trade unions 271–2, 283–4,
285, 293
Trading companies 249
Trafalgar, Battle of 265
Trevithick, Richard 266
Trial by jury 132
Trial by ordeal 113, 132
TUC (Trades Union
Congress) 299
Tull, Jethro 247
Turnpike trusts 262
Tyler, Walter (Wat) 168, *169*,
170

Unemployment
in the 1930s 298, 299–300
in the 1980s 311, 314
Unionists 294
United States 292, 294; *see
also* America

Vaccination 274
Vaughan, Henry 216
Vienna, Congress of 276–7
Vikings 106–10
boats *93, 108, 109*
Villages, medieval 135–41

Villas, Roman 40, 45, *54–5*,
55, *60*, 60
Villeins 134, 135, 138, 140–
1, 174
Vortigern (Welsh king) 63–4
Vote, Parliamentary
for women 286–7, *287*
and Irish Catholics 294
in the 19th century 269,
270, 272, 282–3

Wages policies 310
Wales
Celtic Britain *100*, 100–1
early Christians 67
in medieval times 148–51
Norman castles in 127
Roman forts in 40
Wallace, Sir William 152–3
Walpole, Sir Robert 246
Wars of the Roses 170, 172–
3, 174, 178
Waterloo, Battle of 265
Watt, James 264
Weapons, Roman *37*
Weaver, Thomas 247
Wedgwood, Josiah 261–2
Welfare State 307, 309, 310
Wellington, Duke of 265
Wesley, Charles 253
Wesley, John 253
Wessex 111–15
Weston, Sir Richard 216
White, John 191
White Tower 127
Whitney, Elias 263
Wilberforce, William 273,
275
Wilkes, John 269–70
William, Duke of Normandy
(William I, King of
England) 121, 122–33
125, 126, 128, *129*, 129,
152
William II, King of England
129, 129
William III, King 243, 245
William of Orange (later
William III) 217, 240, 243
William of Sens *129*, 156
Wilson, Harold 310
Windmill Hill settlement 16
Witchcraft 113
Wolsey, Cardinal Thomas
182, 184, 185
Women
in Celtic Britain 28
18th-century *250*, 250
equal opportunities for
313, 314
in medieval times 141
Roman 48
votes for 286–7, *287*
and World War I 293
Workhouses 273
World War I 287, 288–92,
291, 293
World War II *301*, 301–6,
303, 305
Wren, Sir Christopher 236,
237
Writing tablet, Roman *45*, 45
Wyatt, Sir Thomas 198
Wycliffe, John 185

Yeomen 134–5, *174*, 174
York, Norwegians in 118
Yorkist kings 173